The Problem
of Consciousness

To M B

The Problem of Consciousness
Essays Towards a Resolution

Colin McGinn

BLACKWELL
Oxford UK & Cambridge USA

Copyright © Colin McGinn 1991

First published 1991

First published in paperback 1993
Reprinted 1994

Blackwell Publishers
108 Cowley Road, Oxford, OX4 1JF, UK

238 Main Street
Cambridge, Massachusetts 02142, USA

British Library Cataloguing in Publication Data

A CIP catalogue record for this book is available from the British Library.

Library of Congress Cataloging-in-Publication Data

McGinn, Colin, 1950–
The problem of consciousness: essays towards a resolution/Colin McGinn.
p. cm.
Includes bibliographical references and index.
ISBN 0–631–17698–5   0–631–18803–7 (pbk)
1. Mind and body.   2. Consciousness.   3. Philosophy of mind.
Title.
BF161.M45   1991
128'.2—dc20

Typeset in 11 on 13 pt Sabon
by Graphicraft Typesetters Ltd., Hong Kong
Printed and Bound in Great Britain by
Athenaeum Press Ltd, Newcastle upon Tyne.

This book is printed on acid-free paper

Contents

Preface

The chapters herein assembled represent the course of my thinking about the mind–body problem over a number of years – more than ten, I discover to my surprise. They fall into two groups. The first four chapters were written over the last two or three years, and contain ideas that had not occurred to me before that time. The first two of these have already been printed elsewhere, while the (much longer) second two appear here for the first time. They are presented in the order in which they were written, the later ones not having been planned at the time the earlier ones came into existence. Inevitably, there is some repetition in this material: but I hope clarity and cogency will be aided thereby – the basic ideas revealing themselves afresh from a variety of angles. The second group, consisting of the remaining four chapters, date from an earlier period, when I was thinking along somewhat different lines. I include them here because friends have suggested that it would be useful to bring them more accessibly together, and because they serve to throw the newer chapters into sharper relief. I am grateful to the relevant publishers for permissions to reprint.

The new perspective on the problem of consciousness that I advocate in what follows struck me with some force when it first occurred to me. (I even went so far as to get out of bed in the dead of night to write down some notes!) It had the welcome effect of dissolving the nagging intellectual discomfort that I had long associated with the problem. For the first time I felt able to *relax* in the face of the mind–body problem – as if an incessant torment had been finally laid to rest. In composing the chapters, I have tried, philanthropically, to induce the same sense of relief in my audience: I want the reader first to feel the problem aching in his or her bones, and then (to switch metaphors) watch it lift like an oppressive mist at dawn. (No doubt I have failed in this aspiration.) But I am also anxious to bring out the full repercussions, disturbing as they are, of the view I am proposing: first comes the bad news; then the good news; but then more bad news to follow. The upshot is a kind of dystopian utopia, intellectually speaking.

I have also made an effort to write in a way that will be accessible to interested parties outside the narrow ranks of professional philosophers (particularly in chapters 3 and 4). The problem of consciousness concerns not just philosophers but scientists, artists, and even regular folk: it is the question of what it is to be a conscious organism. You do not need special philosophical training to feel the pull of the problem, and I would like to think that what I have written might administer relief to members of all three cultures, not only the professionally philosophical.

In addition to those thanked in individual chapters, I should like to express my gratitude particularly to the following people for their comments and encouragement: Malcolm Budd, Stephan Chambers, Consuelo Preti, Galen Strawson. I owe a special debt to Thomas Nagel, whose work on the mind-body problem pointed me in the direction I ended up pursuing. I doubt if I would have arrived at the present view had I not first been steeped in his ideas (which is not to say that he agrees with me).

On the negative side, I should like to record my contempt for the educational policies of the present British government, which have done so much harm to philosophy in Britain – as to much else. I must also express my regret at the treatment accorded me by the General Board of Oxford University (1989), which greatly impeded the completion of the present work.

Colin McGinn
New York

1

Can We Solve the Mind–Body Problem?*

How it is that anything so remarkable as a state of consciousness comes about as a result of initiating nerve tissue, is just as unaccountable as the appearance of the Djin, where Aladdin rubbed his lamp in the story ... (Julian Huxley)

We have been trying for a long time to solve the mind–body problem. It has stubbornly resisted our best efforts. The mystery persists. I think the time has come to admit candidly that we cannot resolve the mystery. But I also think that this very insolubility – or the reason for it – removes the philosophical problem. In this chapter I explain why I say these outrageous things.

The specific problem I want to discuss concerns consciousness, the hard nut of the mind–body problem. How is it possible for conscious states to depend upon brain states? How can technicolour phenomenology arise from soggy grey matter? What makes the bodily organ we call the brain so radically different from other bodily organs, say the kidneys – the body parts without a trace of consciousness? How could the aggregation of millions of individually insentient neurons generate subjective awareness? We know that brains are the *de facto* causal basis of consciousness, but we have, it seems, no understanding whatever of how this can be so. It strikes us as miraculous, eerie, even faintly comic. Somehow, we feel, the water of the physical brain is turned into the wine of consciousness, but we draw a total blank on the nature of this conversion. Neural transmissions just seem like the wrong kind of materials with which to bring consciousness into the world, but it appears that in some

* Previously published in *Mind*, Vol. xcviii, no. 891, July 1989, this article appears by permission of the publishers, Oxford University Press.

way they perform this mysterious feat. The mind–body problem is the problem of understanding how the miracle is wrought, thus removing the sense of deep mystery. We want to take the magic out of the link between consciousness and the brain.[1]

Purported solutions to the problem have tended to assume one of two forms. One form, which we may call constructive, attempts to specify some natural property of the brain (or body) which explains how consciousness can be elicited from it. Thus functionalism, for example, suggests a property – namely, causal role – which is held to be satisfied by both brain states and mental states; this property is supposed to explain how conscious states can come from brain states.[2] The other form, which has been historically dominant, frankly admits that nothing merely natural could do the job, and suggests instead that we invoke supernatural entities or divine interventions. Thus we have Cartesian dualism and Leibnizian pre-established harmony. These 'solutions' at least recognize that something pretty remarkable is needed if the mind–body relation is to be made sense of; they are as extreme as the problem. The approach I favour is naturalistic but not constructive: I do not believe we can ever specify what it is about the brain that is responsible for consciousness, but I am sure that whatever it is it is not inherently miraculous. The problem arises, I want to suggest, because we are cut off by our very cognitive constitution from achieving a conception of that natural property of the brain (or of

---

[1] One of the peculiarities of the mind–body problem is the difficulty of formulating it in a rigorous way. We have a sense of the problem that outruns our capacity to articulate it clearly. Thus we quickly find ourselves resorting to invitations to look inward, instead of specifying precisely *what* it is about consciousness that makes it inexplicable in terms of ordinary physical properties. And this can make it seem that the problem is spurious. A creature without consciousness would not properly appreciate the problem (assuming such a creature could appreciate other problems). I think an adequate treatment of the mind–body problem should explain why it is so hard to state the problem explicitly. My treatment locates our difficulty in our inadequate conceptions of the nature of the brain and consciousness. In fact, if we knew their natures fully we would already have solved the problem. This should become clear later.
[2] I would also classify panpsychism as a constructive solution, since it attempts to explain consciousness in terms of properties of the brain that are as natural as consciousness itself. Attributing specks of proto-consciousness to the constituents of matter is not supernatural in the way postulating immaterial substances or divine interventions is; it is merely extravagant. I shall here be assuming that panpsychism, like all other extant constructive solutions, is inadequate as an answer to the mind–body problem – as (of course) are the supernatural 'solutions'. I am speaking to those who still feel perplexed (almost everyone, I would think, at least in their heart).

consciousness) that accounts for the psychophysical link. This is a kind of causal nexus that we are precluded from ever understanding, given the way we have to form our concepts and develop our theories. No wonder we find the problem so difficult!

Before I can hope to make this view plausible, I need to sketch the general conception of cognitive competence that underlies my position. Let me introduce the idea of *cognitive closure*. A type of mind M is cognitively closed with respect to a property P (or theory T) if and only if the concept-forming procedures at M's disposal cannot extend to a grasp of P (or an understanding of T). Conceiving minds come in different kinds, equipped with varying powers and limitations, biases and blindspots, so that properties (or theories) may be accessible to some minds but not to others. What is closed to the mind of a rat may be open to the mind of a monkey, and what is open to us may be closed to the monkey. Representational power is not all or nothing. Minds are biological products like bodies, and like bodies they come in different shapes and sizes, more or less capacious, more or less suited to certain cognitive tasks.[3] This is particularly clear for perceptual faculties, of course: perceptual closure is hardly to be denied. Different species are capable of perceiving different properties of the world, and no species can perceive every property things may instantiate (without artificial instrumentation anyway). But such closure does not reflect adversely on the reality of the properties that lie outside the representational capacities in question; a property is no less real for not being reachable from a certain kind of perceiving and conceiving mind. The invisible parts of the electromagnetic spectrum are just as real as the visible parts, and whether a specific kind of creature can form conceptual representations of these imperceptible parts does not determine whether they exist. Thus cognitive closure with respect to P does not imply irrealism about P. That P is (as we might say) *noumenal* for M does not show that P does not occur in some

---

[3] This kind of view of cognitive capacity is forcefully advocated by Noam Chomsky in *Reflections* on *Language*, Pantheon Books, 1975, and by Jerry Fodor in *The Modularity of Mind*, (The MIT Press: Cambridge, Mass., 1983.) Chomsky distinguishes between 'problems', which human minds are in principle equipped to solve, and 'mysteries', which systematically elude our understanding; and he envisages a study of our cognitive systems that would chart these powers and limitations. I am here engaged in such a study, citing the mind–body problem as falling on the side of the mysteries.

naturalistic scientific theory T – it shows only that T is not cognitively accessible to M. Presumably monkey minds and the property
of being an electron illustrate this possibility. And the question must
arise as to whether human minds are closed with respect to certain
true explanatory theories. Nothing, at least, in the concept of reality
shows that everything real is open to the human concept-forming
faculty – if, that is, we are realists about reality.[4]

Consider a mind constructed according to the principles of classical empiricism, a Humean mind. Hume mistakenly thought that
human minds were Humean, but we can at least conceive of such a
mind (perhaps dogs and monkeys have Humean minds). A Humean
mind is such that perceptual closure determines cognitive closure,
since 'ideas' must always be copies of 'impressions'; therefore the
concept-forming system cannot transcend what can be perceptually
presented to the subject. Such a mind will be closed with respect to
unobservables; the properties of atoms, say, will not be represent-
able by a mind constructed in this way. This implies that explanatory theories in which these properties are essentially mentioned
will not be accessible to a Humean mind.[5] And hence the observable phenomena that are explained by allusion to unobservables
will be inexplicable by a mind thus limited. But notice: the incapacity to explain certain phenomena does not carry with it a lack of
recognition of the theoretical problems the phenomena pose. You
might be able to appreciate a problem without being able to formulate (even in principle) the solution to that problem (I suppose
human children are often in this position, at least for a while). A
Humean mind cannot solve the problems that our physics solves,
yet it might be able to have an inkling of what needs to be explained. We would expect, then, that a moderately intelligent en-

---

[4]   See Thomas Nagel's discussion of realism in *The View From Nowhere* (Oxford University
Press: Oxford, 1986), ch. 6. He argues there for the possibility of properties we can never
grasp. Combining Nagel's realism with Chomsky–Fodor cognitive closure gives a position
looking very much like Locke's in the *Essay Concerning Human Understanding*: the idea that
our God-given faculties do not equip us to fathom the deep truth about reality. In fact, Locke
held precisely this about the relation between mind and brain: only divine revelation could
enable us to understand how 'perceptions' are produced in our minds by material objects.
[5]   Hume, of course, argued, in effect, that no theory essentially employing a notion of
objective causal necessitation could be grasped by our minds – and likewise for the notion of
objective persistence. We might compare the frustrations of the Humean mind to the
conceptual travails of the pure sound beings discussed in ch. 2 of P. F. Strawson's *Individuals*,
(Methuen: London, 1959); both are types of mind whose constitution puts various concepts
beyond them. We can do a lot better than these truncated minds, but we also have our
constitutional limitations.

quiring Humean mind will feel permanently perplexed and mystified by the physical world, since the correct science is forever beyond its cognitive reach. Indeed, something like this was precisely the view of Locke. He thought that our ideas of matter are quite sharply constrained by our perceptions and so concluded that the true science of matter is eternally beyond us – that we could never remove our perplexities about (say) what solidity ultimately is.[6] But it does not follow for Locke that nature is itself inherently mysterious; the felt mystery comes from our own cognitive limitations, not from any objective eeriness in the world. It looks today as if Locke was wrong about our capacity to fathom the nature of the physical world, but we can still learn from his fundamental thought – the insistence that our cognitive faculties may not be up to solving every problem that confronts us. To put the point more generally: the human mind may not conform to empiricist principles, but it must conform to *some* principles – and it is a substantive claim that these principles permit the solution of every problem we can formulate or sense. Total cognitive openness is not guaranteed for human beings and it should not be expected. Yet what is noumenal for us may not be miraculous in itself. We should therefore be alert to the possibility that a problem that strikes us as deeply intractable, as utterly baffling, may arise from an area of cognitive closure in our ways of representing the world.[7] That is what I now want to argue is the case with our sense of the mysterious nature of the connection between consciousness and the brain. We are biased away from arriving at the correct explanatory theory of the psychophysical nexus. And this makes us prone to an illusion of objective mystery. Appreciating this should remove the philosophical problem: consciousness does not, in reality, arise from the brain in the miraculous way in which the Djin arises from the lamp.

I now need to establish three things: (i) there exists some property of the brain that accounts naturalistically for consciousness; (ii) we are cognitively closed with respect to that property; but (iii) there is

[6] See the *Essay*, Book II, ch. 4. Locke compares the project of saying what solidity ultimately is to trying to clear up a blind man's vision by talking to him.

[7] Some of the more arcane aspects of cosmology and quantum theory might be thought to lie just within the bounds of human intelligibility. Chomsky suggests that the causation of behaviour might be necessarily mysterious to human investigators: see *Reflections on Language*, p. 156. I myself believe that the mind–body problem exhibits a qualitatively different, and higher, level of mystery from this case (unless it is taken as an aspect of that problem).

no philosophical (as opposed to scientific) mind–body problem. Most of the work will go into establishing (ii).

Resolutely shunning the supernatural, I think it is undeniable that it must be in virtue of *some* natural property of the brain that organisms are conscious. There just *has* to be some explanation for how brains subserve minds. If we are not to be eliminativists about consciousness, then some theory must exist which accounts for the psychophysical correlations we observe. It is implausible to take these correlations as ultimate and inexplicable facts, as simply brute. And we do not want to acknowledge radical emergence of the conscious with respect to the cerebral: that is too much like accepting miracles *de re*. Brain states cause conscious states, we know, and this causal nexus must proceed through necessary connections of some kind – the kind that would make the nexus intelligible *if* they were understood.[8] Consciousness is like life in this respect. We know that life evolved from inorganic matter, so we expect there to be some explanation of this process. We cannot plausibly take the arrival of life as a primitive brute fact, nor can we accept that life arose by some form of miraculous emergence. Rather, there must be some natural account of how life comes from matter, whether or not we can know it. Eschewing vitalism and the magic touch of God's finger, we rightly insist that it must be in virtue of some natural property of (organized) matter that parcels of it get to be alive. But consciousness itself is just a further biological development, and so it too must be susceptible of some natural explanation – whether or not human beings are capable of arriving at this explanation. Presumably there exist objective natural laws that somehow account for the upsurge of consciousness. Consciousness, in short, must be a natural phenomenon, naturally arising from certain organizations of matter. Let us then say that there exists some property P, instantiated by the brain, in virtue of which the brain is the basis of consciousness. Equivalently, there exists some theory T, referring to P, which fully explains the dependence of conscious states on brain states. If we knew T, then we would have a constructive solution to the mind–body problem. The ques-

---

[8] Cf. Nagel's discussion of emergence in 'Panpsychism', in *Mortal Questions* (Cambridge University Press: Cambridge, 1979). I agree with him that the apparent radical emergence of mind from matter has to be epistemic only, on pain of accepting inexplicable miracles in the world.

tion then is whether we can ever come to know T and grasp the nature of P.

Let me first observe that it is surely *possible* that we could never arrive at a grasp of P; there is, as I said, no guarantee that our cognitive powers permit the solution of every problem we can recognize. Only a misplaced idealism about the natural world could warrant the dogmatic claim that everything is knowable by the human species at this stage of its evolutionary development (consider the same claim made on behalf of the intellect of cro-Magnon man). It *may* be that every property for which we can form a concept is such that *it* could never solve the mind–body problem. We *could* be like five-year-old children trying to understand Relativity Theory. Still, so far this is just a possibility claim: what reason do we have for asserting, positively, that our minds are closed with respect to P?

Longstanding historical failure is suggestive, but scarcely conclusive. Maybe, it will be said, the solution is just around the corner, or it has to wait upon the completion of the physical sciences. Perhaps we simply have yet to produce the Einstein-like genius who will restructure the problem in some clever way and then present an astonished world with the solution.[9] However, I think that our deep bafflement about the problem, amounting to a vertiginous sense of ultimate mystery, which resists even articulate formulation, should at least encourage us to explore the idea that there is something terminal about our perplexity. Rather as traditional theologians found themselves conceding cognitive closure with respect to certain of the properties of God, so we should look seriously at the idea that the mind–body problem brings us bang up against the limits of our capacity to understand the world. That is what I shall do now.

There seem to be two possible avenues open to us in our aspiration to identify P: we could try to get to P by investigating consciousness directly; or we could look to the study of the brain for P. Let us consider these in turn, starting with consciousness. Our

[9] Despite his reputation for pessimism over the mind–body problem, a careful reading of Nagel reveals an optimistic strain in his thought (by the standards of the present chapter): see, in particular, the closing remarks of 'What is it Like to be a Bat?', in *Mortal Questions*. Nagel speculates that we might be able to devise an 'objective phenomenology' that made conscious states more amenable to physical analysis. Unlike me, he does not regard the problem as inherently beyond us.

acquaintance with consciousness could hardly be more direct; phenomenological description thus comes (relatively) easily. 'Introspection' is the name of the faculty through which we catch consciousness in all its vivid nakedness. By virtue of possessing this cognitive faculty we ascribe concepts of consciousness to ourselves; we thus have 'immediate access' to the properties of consciousness. But does the introspective faculty reveal property P? Can we tell just by introspecting what the solution to the mind–body problem is? Clearly not. We have direct cognitive access to one term of the mind–brain relation, but we do not have such access to the nature of the link. Introspection does not present conscious states *as* depending upon the brain in some intelligible way. We cannot therefore introspect P. Moreover, it seems impossible that we should ever augment our stock of introspectively ascribed concepts with the concept P – that is, we could not acquire this concept simply on the basis of sustained and careful introspection. Pure phenomenology will never provide the solution to the mind–body problem. Neither does it seem feasible to try to extract P from the concepts of consciousness we now have by some procedure of conceptual analysis – any more than we could solve the life-matter problem simply by reflecting on the concept *life*.[10] P has to lie outside the field of the introspectable, and it is not implicitly contained in the concepts we bring to bear in our first-person ascriptions. Thus the faculty of introspection, as a concept-forming capacity, is cognitively closed with respect to P; which is not surprising in view of its highly limited domain of operation (*most* properties of the world are closed to introspection).

But there is a further point to be made about P and consciousness, which concerns our restricted access to the concepts of consciousness themselves. It is a familiar point that the range of concepts of consciousness attainable by a mind M is constrained by the specific forms of consciousness possessed by M. Crudely, you cannot form concepts of conscious properties unless you yourself instantiate those properties. The man born blind cannot grasp the

---

[10] This is perhaps the most remarkably optimistic view of all – the expectation that reflecting on the ordinary concept of pain (say) will reveal the manner of pain's dependence on the brain. If I am not mistaken, this is in effect the view of common-sense functionalists: they think that P consists in causal role, and that this can be inferred analytically from the concept of conscious states. This would make it truly amazing that we should ever have felt there to a mind–body problem at all, since the solution is already contained in our mental concepts. What optimism!

concept of a visual experience of red, and human beings cannot conceive of the echolocatory experiences of bats.[11] These are cases of cognitive closure within the class of conscious properties. But now this kind of closure will, it seems, affect our hopes of access to P. For suppose that we were cognitively open with respect to P; suppose, that is, that we had the solution to the problem of how specific forms of consciousness depend upon different kinds of physiological structure. Then, of course, we would understand how the brain of a bat subserves the subjective experiences of bats. Call this type of experience B, and call the explanatory property that links B to the bat's brain P_1. By grasping P_1 it would be perfectly intelligible to us how the bat's brain generates B-experiences; we would have an explanatory theory of the causal nexus in question. We would be in possession of the same kind of understanding we would have of our own experiences if we had the correct psychophysical theory of them. But then it seems to follow that grasp of the theory that explains B-experiences would *confer* a grasp of the nature of those experiences: for how could we understand that theory without understanding the concept B that occurs in it? How could we grasp the *nature* of B-experiences without grasping the *character* of those experiences? The true psychophysical theory would seem to provide a route to a grasp of the subjective form of the bat's experiences. But now we face a dilemma, a dilemma which threatens to become a reductio: either we *can* grasp this theory, in which case the property B becomes open to us; or we *cannot* grasp the theory, simply because property B is *not* open to us. It seems to me that the looming reductio here is compelling: our concepts of consciousness just *are* inherently constrained by our own form of consciousness, so that any theory the understanding of which required us to transcend these constraints would *ipso facto* be inaccessible to us. Similarly, I think, any theory that required us to transcend the finiteness of our cognitive capacities would *ipso facto* be a theory we could not grasp – and this despite the fact that it might be needed to explain something we can see needs explaining.

[11]　See Nagel, 'What is it Like to be a Bat?' Notice that the fugitive character of such properties with respect to our concepts has nothing to do with their 'complexity'; like fugitive colour properties, such experiential properties are 'simple'. Note too that such properties provide counter-examples to the claim that (somehow) rationality is a faculty that, once possessed, can be extended to encompass all concepts, so that if *any* concept can be possessed then *every* concept can.

We cannot simply stipulate that our concept-forming abilities are indefinitely plastic and unlimited just because they would have to be to enable us to grasp the truth about the world. We constitutionally lack the concept-forming capacity to encompass all possible types of conscious state, and this obstructs our path to a general solution to the mind–body problem. Even if we could solve it for our own case, we could not solve it for bats and Martians. P is, as it were, too close to the different forms of subjectivity for it to be accessible to all such forms, given that one's form of subjectivity restricts one's concepts of subjectivity.[12]

I suspect that most optimists about constructively solving the mind–body problem will prefer to place their bets on the brain side of the relation. Neuroscience is the place to look for property P, they will say. My question then is whether there is any conceivable way in which we might come to introduce P in the course of our empirical investigations of the brain. New concepts have been introduced in the effort to understand the workings of the brain, certainly: could not P then occur in conceivable extensions of this manner of introduction? So far, indeed, the theoretical concepts we ascribe to the brain seem as remote from consciousness as any ordinary physical properties are, but perhaps we might reach P by diligent application of essentially the same procedures: so it is tempting to think. I want to suggest, to the contrary, that such procedures are inherently closed with respect to P. The fundamental reason for this, I think, is the role of *perception* in shaping our understanding of the brain – the way that our perception of the brain constrains the concepts we can apply to it. A point whose significance it would be hard to overstress here is this: the property of consciousness itself (or specific conscious states) is not an observable or perceptible property of the brain. You can stare into a living

[12] It might be suggested that we borrow Nagel's idea of 'objective phenomenology' in order to get around this problem. Instead of representing experiences under subjective descriptions, we should describe them in entirely objective terms, thus bringing them within our conceptual ken. My problem with this is that, even allowing that there could be such a form of description, it would not permit us to understand how the subjective aspects of experience depend upon the brain – which is really the problem we are trying to solve. In fact, I doubt that the notion of objective phenomenology is any more coherent than the notion of subjective physiology. Both involve trying to bridge the psychophysical gap by a sort of stipulation. The lesson here is that the gap cannot be bridged just by applying concepts drawn from one side to items that belong on the other side; and this is because neither sort of concept could ever do what is needed.

conscious brain, your own or someone else's, and see there a wide variety of instantiated properties – its shape, colour, texture, etc. – but you will not thereby *see* what the subject is experiencing, the conscious state itself. Conscious states are simply not, *qua* conscious states, potential objects of perception: they depend upon the brain but they cannot be observed by directing the senses onto the brain. You cannot see a brain state *as* a conscious state. In other words, consciousness is noumenal with respect to perception of the brain.[13] I take it this is obvious. So we know there *are* properties of the brain that are necessarily closed to perception of the brain; the question now is whether P is likewise closed to perception.

My argument will proceed as follows. I shall first argue that P is indeed perceptually closed; then I shall complete the argument to full cognitive closure by insisting that no form of *inference* from what is perceived can lead us to P. The argument for perceptual closure starts from the thought that nothing we can imagine perceiving in the brain would ever convince us that we have located the intelligible nexus we seek. No matter what recondite property we could see to be instantiated in the brain we should always be baffled about how it could give rise to consciousness. I hereby invite you to try to conceive of a perceptible property of the brain that might allay the feeling of mystery that attends our contemplation of the brain–mind link: I do not think you will be able to do it. It is like trying to conceive of a perceptible property of a rock that would render it perspicuous that the rock was conscious. In fact, I think it is the very impossibility of this that lies at the root of the felt mind–body problem. But why is this? Basically, I think, it is because the senses are geared to representing a spatial world; they essentially present things in space with spatially defined properties. But it is precisely *such* properties that seem inherently incapable of resolving the mind–body problem: we cannot link consciousness to the brain in virtue of spatial properties of the brain. There the brain is, an object of perception, laid out in space, containing spatially

---

[13] We should distinguish two claims about the imperceptibility of consciousness: (i) consciousness is not perceivable by directing the senses onto the brain; (ii) consciousness is not perceivable by directing the senses anywhere, even towards the behaviour that 'expresses' conscious states. I believe both theses, but my present point requires only (i). I am assuming, of course, that perception cannot be unrestrictedly theory-laden; or that if it can, the infusions of theory cannot have been originally derived simply by looking at things or tasting them or touching them or ...

distributed processes; but consciousness defies explanation in such terms. Consciousness does not seem made up out of smaller spatial processes; yet perception of the brain seems limited to revealing such processes.[14] The senses are responsive to certain *kinds* of properties – those that are essentially bound up with space – but these properties are of the wrong sort (the wrong *category*) to constitute *P*. Kant was right, the form of outer sensibility is spatial; but if so, then *P* will be noumenal with respect to the senses, since no spatial property will ever deliver a satisfying answer to the mind –body problem. We simply do not understand the idea that conscious states might intelligibly arise from spatial configurations of the kind disclosed by perception of the world.

I take it this claim will not seem terribly controversial. After all, we do not generally expect that every property referred to in our theories should be a potential object of human perception: consider quantum theory and cosmology. Unrestricted perceptual openness is a dogma of empiricism if ever there was one. And there is no compelling reason to suppose that the property needed to explain the mind–brain relation should be in principle perceptible; it might be essentially 'theoretical', an object of thought not sensory experience. Looking harder at nature is not the only (or the best) way of discovering its theoretically significant properties. Perceptual closure does not entail cognitive closure, since we have available the procedure of hypothesis formation, in which *un*observables come to be conceptualized.

I readily agree with these sentiments, but I think there are reasons for believing that no coherent method of concept introduction will ever lead us to *P*. This is because a certain principle of *homogeneity* operates in our introduction of theoretical concepts on the basis of observation. Let me first note that consciousness itself could not be introduced simply on the basis of what we observe about the brain and its physical effects. If our data, arrived at by perception of the brain, do not include anything that brings in conscious states, then the theoretical properties we need to explain these data will not

---

[14]   Nagel discusses the difficulty of thinking of conscious processes in the spatial terms that apply to the brain in *The View From Nowhere*, pp. 50–1, but he does not draw my despairing conclusion. The case is exactly *un*like (say) the dependence of liquidity on the properties of molecules, since here we do think of both terms of the relation as spatial in character; so we can simply employ the idea of spatial composition.

include conscious states either. Inference to the best explanation of purely physical data will never take us outside the realm of the physical, forcing us to introduce concepts of consciousness.[15] Everything physical has a purely physical explanation. So the property of consciousness is cognitively closed with respect to the introduction of concepts by means of inference to the best explanation of perceptual data about the brain.

Now the question is whether P could ever be arrived at by this kind of inference. Here we must be careful to guard against a form of magical emergentism with respect to concept formation. Suppose we try out a relatively clear theory of how theoretical concepts are formed: we get them by a sort of analogical extension of what we observe. Thus, for example, we arrive at the concept of a molecule by taking our perceptual representations of macroscopic objects and conceiving of smaller scale objects of the same general kind. This method seems to work well enough for unobservable material objects, but it will not help in arriving at P, since analogical extensions of the entities we observe in the brain are precisely as hopeless as the original entities were as solutions to the mind–body problem. We would need a method that left the base of observational properties behind in a much more radical way. But it seems to me that even a more unconstrained conception of inference to the best explanation would still not do what is required: it would no more serve to introduce P than it serves to introduce the property of consciousness itself. To explain the observed physical data we need only such theoretical properties as bear upon those data, not the property that explains consciousness, which does not occur in the data. Since we do not need consciousness to explain those data, we do not need the property that explains consciousness. We shall never get as far away from the perceptual data in our explanations of those data as we need to get in order to connect up explanatorily with consciousness. This is, indeed, why it seems that consciousness is theoretically epiphenomenal in the task of accounting for physical events. No concept needed to explain the workings of the physical world will suffice to explain how the physical world produces consciousness. So if P is perceptually noumenal, then it will be

[15] Cf. Nagel: 'it will never be legitimate to infer, as a theoretical explanation of physical phenomena alone, a property that includes or implies the consciousness of its subject', 'Panpsychism', p. 183.

noumenal with respect to perception-based explanatory inferences. Accordingly, I do not think that P could be arrived at by empirical studies of the brain alone. Nevertheless, the brain *has* this property, as it has the property of consciousness. Only a magical idea of how we come by concepts could lead one to think that we can reach P by first perceiving the brain and then asking what is needed to explain what we perceive.[16] (The mind–body problem tempts us to magic in more ways than one.)

It will help elucidate the position I am driving towards if I contrast it with another view of the source of the perplexity we feel about the mind–brain nexus. I have argued that we cannot know which property of the brain accounts for consciousness, and so we find the mind–brain link unintelligible. But, it may be said, there is another account of our sense of irremediable mystery, which does not require positing properties our minds cannot represent. This alternative view claims that, even if we *now* had a grasp of P, we would *still* feel that there is something mysterious about the link, because of a special epistemological feature of the situation. Namely this: our acquaintance with the brain and our acquaintance with consciousness are necessarily mediated by distinct cognitive faculties, namely perception and introspection. Thus the faculty through which we apprehend one term of the relation is necessarily distinct from the faculty through which we apprehend the other. In consequence, it is not possible for us to use one of these faculties to apprehend the nature of the psychophysical nexus. No single faculty will enable us ever to apprehend the fact that consciousness depends upon the brain in virtue of property P. Neither perception alone nor introspection alone will ever enable us to witness the dependence. And this, my objector insists, is the real reason we find the link baffling: we cannot make sense of it in terms of the deliverances of a single cognitive faculty. So, even if we now had concepts for the properties of the brain that explain consciousness, we would still feel a residual sense of unintelligibility; we should still take there to

[16] It is surely a striking fact that the microprocesses that have been discovered in the brain by the usual methods seem no nearer to consciousness than the gross properties of the brain open to casual inspection. Neither do more abstract 'holistic' features of brain function seem to be on the right lines to tell us the nature of consciousness. The deeper science probes into the brain the more remote it seems to get from consciousness. Greater knowledge of the brain thus destroys our illusions about the kinds of properties that might be discovered by travelling along this path. Advanced neurophysiological theory seems only to deepen the miracle.

be something mysterious going on. The necessity to shift from one faculty to the other produces in us an illusion of inexplicability. We might in fact have the explanation right now but be under the illusion that we do not. The right diagnosis, then, is that we should recognize the peculiarity of the epistemological situation and stop trying to make sense of the psychophysical nexus in the way we make sense of other sorts of nexus. It only *seems* to us that we can never discover a property that will render the nexus intelligible.

I think this line of thought deserves to be taken seriously, but I doubt that it correctly diagnoses our predicament. It is true enough that the problematic nexus is essentially apprehended by distinct faculties, so that it will never reveal its secrets to a single faculty; but I doubt that our intuitive sense of intelligibility is so rigidly governed by the 'single-faculty condition'. Why *should* facts only seem intelligible to us if we can conceive of apprehending them by one (sort of) cognitive faculty? Why not allow that we can recognize intelligible connections between concepts (or properties) even when those concepts (or properties) are necessarily ascribed using different faculties? Is it not suspiciously empiricist to insist that a causal nexus can only be made sense of by us if we can conceive of its being an object of a single faculty of apprehension? Would we think this of a nexus that called for touch and sight to apprehend each term of the relation? Suppose (*per impossible*) that we were offered *P* on a plate, as a gift from God: would we still shake our heads and wonder how that could resolve the mystery, being still the victims of the illusion of mystery generated by the epistemological duality in question? No, I think this suggestion is not enough to account for the miraculous appearance of the link: it is better to suppose that we are permanently blocked from forming a concept of what accounts for that link.

How strong is the thesis I am urging? Let me distinguish *absolute* from *relative* claims of cognitive closure. A problem is absolutely cognitively closed if no possible mind could resolve it; a problem is relatively closed if minds of some sorts can in principle solve it while minds of other sorts cannot. Most problems, we may safely suppose, are only relatively closed: armadillo minds cannot solve problems of elementary arithmetic but human minds can. Should we say that the mind–body problem is only relatively closed or is the closure absolute? This depends on what we allow as a possible concept-forming mind, which is not an easy question. If we allow for minds that form their concepts of the brain and consciousness in ways that are quite independent of perception and introspection, then there may be room for the idea that there are possible minds for which the mind–body problem is soluble, and easily so. But if we suppose that *all* concept formation is tied to perception and introspection, however loosely, then no mind will be capable of understanding how it relates to its own body – the insolubility will be absolute. I think we can just about make sense of the former kind of mind, by exploiting our own faculty of a priori reasoning. Our mathematical concepts (say) do not seem tied either to perception or to introspection, so there does seem to be a mode of concept formation that operates without the constraints I identified earlier. The suggestion might then be that a mind that formed all of its concepts in this way – including its concepts of the brain and consciousness – would be free of the biases that prevent *us* from coming up with the right theory of how the two connect. Such a mind would have to be able to think of the brain and consciousness in ways that utterly prescind from the perceptual and the introspective – in somewhat the way we now (it seems) think about numbers. This mind would conceive of the psychophysical link in totally a priori terms. Perhaps this is how we should think of God's mind, and God's understanding of the mind–body relation. At any rate, something pretty radical is going to be needed if we are to devise a mind that can escape the kinds of closure that make the problem insoluble for us – if I am right in my diagnosis of our difficulty. *If* the problem is only relatively insoluble, then the type of mind that can solve it is going to be very different from ours and the kinds of mind we can readily make sense of (there may, of course, be cognitive closure here too). It certainly seems to me to be at least an open question whether the problem is absolutely insoluble; I would not be surprised if it were.[17]

My position is both pessimistic and optimistic at the same time. It is pessimistic about the prospects for arriving at a constructive solution to the mind–body problem, but it is optimistic about our hopes of removing the philosophical perplexity. The central point

[17] The kind of limitation I have identified is therefore not the kind that could be remedied simply by a large increase in general intelligence. No matter how large the frontal lobes of our biological descendants may become, they will still be stumped by the mind–body problem, so long as they form their (empirical) concepts on the basis of perception and introspection.

here is that I do not think we need to do the former in order to achieve the latter. This depends on a rather special understanding of what the philosophical problem consists in. What I want to suggest is that the nature of the psychophysical connection has a full and non-mysterious explanation in a certain science, but that this science is inaccessible to us as a matter of principle. Call this explanatory scientific theory T: T is as natural and prosaic and devoid of miracle as any theory of nature; it describes the link between consciousness and the brain in a way that is no more remarkable (or alarming) than the way we now describe the link between the liver and bile.[18] According to T, there is nothing eerie going on in the world when an event in my visual cortex causes me to have an experience of yellow – however much it seems to *us* that there is. In other words, there is no intrinsic conceptual or metaphysical difficulty about how consciousness depends on the brain. It is not that the correct science is compelled to postulate miracles *de re*; it is rather that the correct science lies in the dark part of the world for us. We confuse our own cognitive limitations with objective eeriness. We are like a Humean mind trying to understand the physical world, or a creature without spatial concepts trying to understand the possibility of motion. This removes the philosophical problem because it assures us that the entities *themselves* pose no inherent philosophical difficulty. The case is unlike, for example, the problem of how the abstract world of numbers might be intelligibly related to the world of concrete knowing subjects: here the mystery seems intrinsic to the entities, not a mere artefact of our cognitive limitations or biases in trying to understand the relation.[19]

[18] Or again, no more miraculous than the theory of evolution. Creationism is an understandable response to the theoretical problem posed by the existence of complex organisms; fortunately, we now have a theory that renders this response unnecessary, and so undermines the theism required by the creationist thesis. In the case of consciousness, the appearance of miracle might also tempt us in a 'creationist' direction, with God required to perform the alchemy necessary to transform matter into experience. Thus the mind–body problem might similarly be used to prove the existence of God (no miracle without a miracle-maker). We cannot, I think, refute this argument in the way we can the original creationist argument, namely by actually producing a non-miraculous explanatory theory, but we can refute it by arguing that such a naturalistic theory must *exist*. (It is a condition of adequacy upon any account of the mind–body relation that it avoid assuming theism.)

[19] See Paul Benacerraf, 'Mathematical Truth', *Journal of Philosophy*, 1973, for a statement of this problem about abstract entities. Another problem that seems to me to differ from the mind–body problem is the problem of free will. I do not believe that there is some unknowable property Q which reconciles free will with determinism (or indeterminism); rather, the concept of free will contains internal incoherencies – as the concept of consciousness does not. This is why it is much more reasonable to be an eliminativist about free will than about consciousness.

It would not be plausible to suggest that there exists a science, whose theoretical concepts we cannot grasp, which completely resolves any sense of mystery that surrounds the question how the abstract becomes an object of knowledge for us. In this case, then, eliminativism seems a live option. The *philosophical* problem about consciousness and the brain arises from a sense that we are compelled to accept that nature contains miracles – as if the merely metallic lamp (*lump*) of the brain could really spirit into existence the Djin of consciousness. But we do not need to accept this: we can rest secure in the knowledge that some (unknowable) property of the brain makes everything fall into place. What creates the philosophical puzzlement is the assumption that the problem must somehow be scientific but that any science *we* can come up with will represent things as utterly miraculous. And the solution is to recognize that the sense of miracle comes from us and not from the world. There is, in reality, nothing mysterious about how the brain generates consciousness. There is no *metaphysical* problem.[20]

So far that deflationary claim has been justified by a general naturalism and certain considerations about cognitive closure and the illusions it can give rise to. Now I want to marshall some reasons for thinking that consciousness is actually a rather simple natural fact; objectively, consciousness is nothing very special. We should now be comfortable with the idea that our own sense of difficulty is a fallible guide to objective complexity: what is hard for us to grasp may not be very fancy in itself. The grain of our thinking is not a mirror held up to the facts of nature.[21] In particular, it may be that the extent of our understanding of facts about the mind is not commensurate with some objective estimate of their intrinsic complexity: we may be good at understanding the mind in

[20]   A test of whether a proposed solution to the mind–body problem is adequate is whether it relieves the pressure towards eliminativism. If the data can only be explained by postulating a miracle (i.e. not explained), then we must repudiate the data – this is the principle behind the impulse to deny that conscious states exist. My proposal passes this test because it allows us to resist the postulation of miracles; it interprets the eeriness as merely epistemic, though deeply so. Constructive solutions are not the only way to relieve the pressure.
[21]   Chomsky suggests that the very faculties of mind that make us good at some cognitive tasks may make us poor at others; see *Reflections on Language*, pp. 155–6. It seems to me possible that what makes us good at the science of the purely physical world is what skews us away from developing a science of consciousness. Our faculties bias us towards understanding matter in motion, but it is precisely this kind of understanding that is inapplicable to the mind–body problem. Perhaps, then, the price of being good at understanding matter is that we cannot understand mind. Certainly our notorious tendency to think of everything in spatial terms does not help us in understanding the mind.

some of its aspects but hopeless with respect to others, in a way that cuts across objective differences in what the aspects involve. Thus we are adept at understanding action in terms of the folk psychology of belief and desire, and we seem not entirely out of our depth when it comes to devising theories of language. But our understanding of how consciousness develops from the organization of matter is non-existent. But now, think of these various aspects of mind from the point of view of evolutionary biology. Surely language and the propositional attitudes are more complex and advanced evolutionary achievements than the mere possession of consciousness by a physical organism. Thus it seems that we are better at understanding some of the more complex aspects of mind than the simpler ones. Consciousness arises early in evolutionary history and is found right across the animal kingdom. In some respects it seems that the biological engineering required for consciousness is less fancy than that needed for certain kinds of complex motor behaviour. Yet we can come to understand the latter while drawing a total blank with respect to the former. Conscious states seem biologically quite primitive, comparatively speaking. So the theory T that explains the occurrence of consciousness in a physical world is very probably less objectively complex (by some standard) than a range of other theories that do not defy our intellects. If only we could know the psychophysical mechanism it might surprise us with its simplicity, its utter naturalness. In the manual that God consulted when he made the earth and all the beasts that dwell thereon the chapter about how to engineer consciousness from matter occurs fairly early on, well before the really difficult later chapters on mammalian reproduction and speech. It is not the *size* of the problem but its *type* that makes the mind–body problem so hard for us. This reflection should make us receptive to the idea that it is something about the tracks of our thought that prevents us from achieving a science that relates consciousness to its physical basis: the enemy lies within the gates.[22]

The position I have reached has implications for a tangle of intuitions it is natural to have regarding the mind–body relation. On the one hand, there are intuitions, pressed from Descartes to

[22] I get this phrase from Fodor, *The Modularity of Mind*, p. 121. The intended contrast is with kinds of cognitive closure that stem from exogenous factors – as, say, in astronomy. Our problem with P is not that it is too distant or too small or too large or too complex; rather, the very structure of our concept-forming apparatus points us away from P.

Kripke, to the effect that the relation between conscious states and bodily states is fundamentally contingent.[23] It can easily seem to us that there is no necessitation involved in the dependence of the mind on the brain. But, on the other hand, it looks absurd to try to dissociate the two entirely, to let the mind float completely free of the body. Disembodiment is a dubious possibility at best, and some kind of necessary supervenience of the mental on the physical has seemed undeniable to many. It is not my aim here to adjudicate this longstanding dispute; I want simply to offer a diagnosis of what is going on when one finds oneself assailed with this flurry of conflicting intuitions. The reason we feel the tug of contingency, pulling consciousness loose from its physical moorings, may be that we do not and cannot grasp the nature of the property that intelligibly links them. The brain has physical properties we can grasp, and variations in these correlate with changes in consciousness, but we cannot draw the veil that conceals the manner of their connection. Not grasping the nature of the connection, it strikes us as deeply contingent; we cannot make the assertion of a necessary connection intelligible to ourselves. There *may* then be a real necessary connection; it is just that it will always strike us as curiously brute and unperspicuous. We may thus, as upholders of intrinsic contingency, be the dupes of our own cognitive blindness. On the other hand, we are scarcely in a position to assert that there *is* a necessary connection between the properties of the brain we can grasp and states of consciousness, since we are so ignorant (and irremediably so) about the character of the connection. For all we know, the connection may be contingent, as access to P would reveal if we could have such access. The link between consciousness and property P is not, to be sure, contingent – virtually by definition – but we are not in a position to say exactly how P is related to the 'ordinary' properties of the brain. It may be necessary or it may be contingent. Thus it is that we tend to vacillate between contingency and necessity; for we lack the conceptual resources to decide the question definitively – or to understand the answer we are inclined to give. The indicated conclusion appears to be that we can never really know whether disembodiment is metaphysically possible, or whether necessary

---

[23] Saul Kripke, *Naming and Necessity*, (Basil Blackwell: Oxford, 1980). Of course, Descartes explicitly argued from (what he took to be) the essential natures of the body and mind to the contingency of their connection. If we abandon the assumption that we know these natures, then agnosticism about the modality of the connection seems the indicated conclusion.

supervenience is the case, or whether spectrum inversion could occur. For these all involve claims about the modal connections between properties of consciousness and the ordinary properties of the body and brain that we can conceptualize; and the real nature of these connections is not accessible to us. Perhaps P makes the relation between C-fibre firing and pain necessary or perhaps it does not: we are simply not equipped to know. We are like a Humean mind wondering whether the observed link between the temperature of a gas and its pressure (at a constant volume) is necessary or contingent. To know the answer to that you need to grasp atomic (or molecular) theory, and a Humean mind just is not up to attaining the requisite theoretical understanding. Similarly, we are constitutionally ignorant at precisely the spot where the answer exists.

I predict that many readers of this chapter will find its main thesis utterly incredible, even ludicrous. Let me remark that I sympathize with such readers: the thesis is not easily digestible. But I would say this: if the thesis *is* actually true, it will still strike us as hard to believe. For the idea of an explanatory property (or set of properties) that is noumenal for us, yet is essential for the (constructive) solution of a problem we face, offends a kind of natural idealism that tends to dominate our thinking. We find it taxing to conceive of the existence of a real property, under our noses as it were, which we are built not to grasp – a property that is responsible for phenomena that we observe in the most direct way possible. This kind of realism, which brings cognitive closure so close to home, is apt to seem both an affront to our intellects and impossible to get our minds around. We try to think of this unthinkable property and understandably fail in the effort; so we rush to infer that the very supposition of such a property is nonsensical. Realism of the kind I am presupposing thus seems difficult to hold in focus, and any philosophical theory that depends upon it will also seem to rest on something systematically elusive.[24] My response to such misgivings,

[24] This is the kind of realism defended by Nagel in ch. 6 of *The View From Nowhere*: to be is not to be conceivable by us. I would say that the mind–body problem provides a demonstration that there *are* such concept-transcending properties – not merely that there *could* be. I should also say that realism of this kind should be accepted precisely because it helps solve the mind–body problem; it is a metaphysical thesis that pulls its weight in coping with a problem that looks hopeless otherwise. There is thus nothing 'epiphenomenal' about such radical realism: the existence of a reality we cannot know can yet have intellectual significance for us. Anti-realists are unable to solve the mind–body problem, in addition to their other troubles.

2

Consciousness and Content*

Naturalism in the philosophy of mind is the thesis that every property of mind can be explained in broadly physical terms.[1] Nothing mental is physically mysterious. There are two main problems confronting a naturalistically inclined philosopher of mind. There is, first, the problem of explaining consciousness in broadly physical terms: in virtue of what does a physical organism come to have conscious states? And, second, there is the problem of explaining representational content – intentionality – in broadly physical terms: in virtue of what does a physical organism come to be intentionally directed towards the world? We want to know how consciousness depends upon the physical world; and we want to know, in natural physical terms, how it is that thoughts and experiences get to be *about* states of affairs. We want a naturalistic account of subjectivity and mental representation.[2] Only then will the naturalist happily accept that there are such things as consciousness and content.

* This paper was read to the British Academy on 29 November 1988 and was published in the *Proceedings*, LXXIV, 1988, 219–39. Published with permission.
[1] This is the standard contemporary view of naturalism. See, e.g. Jerry Fodor, *Psychosemantics* (The MIT Press: Cambridge, Mass., 1987), ch. 4. I do not say that it is my view of what it takes to be a good naturalist. As will become clear, I think we can view the mind naturalistically without being able to offer broadly physical explanations of its powers. (I say 'broadly physical' in order to include biological properties and higher-order causal properties, as well as the properties directly treated in physics.) An alternative way of putting the naturalistic demand is this: explain why it is that the mental is supervenient on the physical, given that it is. The general motive behind such naturalism is the avoidance of some sort of radical 'emergence' of the mental with respect to the physical. See Thomas Nagel, 'Panpsychism', *Mortal Questions* (Cambridge University Press, 1979), on why emergence is to be avoided.
[2] A third, and connected, problem is explaining how a physical organism can be subject to the norms of rationality. How, for example, does *modus ponens* get its grip on the causal

Recent years have witnessed a curious asymmetry of attitude with respect to these two problems. While there has been much optimism about the prospects of success in accounting for intentionality, pessimism about explaining consciousness has deepened progressively. We can, it is felt, explain what makes a mental state have the content it has; at least there is no huge barrier of principle in the way of our doing so. But, it is commonly conceded, we have no remotely plausible account of what makes a mental state have the phenomenological character it has; we do not even know where to start. Books and articles appear apace offering to tell us exactly what mental aboutness consists in, while heads continue to be shaken over the nature of consciousness. Indeed, standard approaches to content tend simply to ignore the problem of consciousness, defeatedly postponing it till the next century. True, there are those rugged souls who purport to see no difficulty of principle about consciousness; but among those who do appreciate the difficulty there coexists much optimism about content. This is curious because of the apparently intimate connexion between consciousness and content: intentionality is a property precisely of conscious states, and arguably only of conscious states (at least originally). Moreover, the content of an experience (say) and its subjective features are, on the face of it, inseparable from each other. How then can we pretend that the two problems can be pursued quite independently? In particular, how can we prevent justified pessimism about consciousness spreading to the problem of content? If we cannot say, in physical terms, what makes it the case that an experience is *like* something for its possessor, then how can we hope to say, in such terms, what makes it the case that the experience is *of* something in the world – since what the experience is like and what it is of are not, prima facie, independent properties of the experience? That is the question I shall be addressing in this chapter.

I mean to be considering a broad family of naturalistic theories of

---

transitions between mental states? This question is clearly connected with the question about intentionality, since rationality (as we ordinarily understand it) requires intentionality (the converse thesis is less obvious). But it is not so clear how closely connected are the problems of rationality and consciousness: can the former exist without the latter? If we find consciousness theoretically daunting (as I argue we should), then we should hope that rationality can be separated from it. There is a general question here: how much of the mind can be explained without being able to explain consciousness? This, as I suggest later, is the same as the question how much of the mind can be explained.

intentionality here; the tension just mentioned does not arise from one sort of theory alone. There are currently a number of theories to choose from: causal theories, functionalist theories, computational theories, teleological theories.[3] Take any of these and ask yourself whether that theory accounts satisfactorily for consciousness: does it, specifically, provide sufficient conditions for being in a conscious state? If it does not, then the question must be faced how it can be an adequate explanation of content *for* conscious states. Consider, for instance, teleological theories (my own favourite). This type of theory identifies the content of a mental state with (roughly) its world-directed biological function. A desire state has a content involving *water*, say, just if that state has the function of getting the organism to obtain water. A perceptual experience represents squareness, say, just if its function is to indicate (covary with) the presence of square things in the environment. But now these contents serve to fix the phenomenological aspects of the states in question, what it is like subjectively to be in them; yet the theory itself seems neutral on the question of consciousness. Certainly the teleological descriptions of the states seem insufficient to confer conscious subjective features on them. *Any* naturalistic theory of the kinds currently available looks to be inadequate as an account of what makes a mental state have a particular *conscious* content, a specific phenomenology. Yet phenomenology seems configured by content.[4]

This question is especially pressing for me, since I have come to hold that it is literally impossible for us to explain how conscious-

[3] For discussions of these approaches see: Jerry Fodor, *Psychosemantics* (The MIT Press: Cambridge, Mass., 1987); Fred Dretske, *Knowledge and the Flow of Information* (The MIT Press: Cambridge, Mass., 1988); Hilary Rutnam, *Representation and Reality* (The MIT Press: Cambridge, Mass., 1988); Ruth Millikan, *Language, Thought and Other Biological Categories* (The MIT Press: Cambridge, Mass., 1984); Colin McGinn, *Mental Content* (Basil Blackwell: Oxford, 1989).

[4] My focus in this chapter is on the content of perceptual experiences, mental states for which the notion of a subjective phenomenology is best suited. But essentially the same questions arise for thoughts, mental states for which the notion of what it is like to have them seems strained at best (thoughts are not inherently 'qualia-laden'). Thoughts are conscious, of course, and the question, what confers this consciousness, is equally pressing for them as it is for experiences. Moreover, the content of thoughts looks even more closely tied to their conscious features than in the case of experiences; so it is even harder to see how we could pull apart the theory of content for thoughts and the theory of what gives thoughts their conscious aspect. What more is there to the specific way a thought is present in the stream of consciousness than its having the particular content it has?

ness depends upon the brain, even though it does so depend.[5] Yet I also believe (or would like to believe) that it is possible for us to give illuminating accounts of content.[6] Let me briefly explain my reasons for holding that consciousness systematically eludes our understanding. Noam Chomsky distinguishes between what he calls 'problems' and 'mysteries' that confront the student of mind.[7] Call that hopeful student S, and suppose S to be a normal intelligent human being. Chomsky argues that S' cognitive faculties may be apt for the solution of some kinds of problem but radically inadequate when it comes to others. The world need not in all of its aspects be susceptible of understanding by S, though another sort of mind might succeed where S constitutionally fails. S may exhibit, as I like to say, *cognitive closure* with respect to certain kinds of phenomena: her intellectual powers do not extend to comprehending these phenomena, and this as a matter of principle.[8] When that is so Chomsky says that the phenomena in question will be a perpetual mystery for S. He suspects that the nature of free choice is just such a mystery for us, given the way our intellects operate. That problem need not, however, be intrinsically harder or more complex than other problems we can solve; it is just that our cognitive faculties are skewed away from solving it. The structure of a knowing mind determines the scope *and limits* of its cognitive powers. Being adept at solving one kind of problem does not guarantee explanatory omniscience. Human beings seem remarkably good (surprisingly so) at understanding the workings or the physical world – matter in motion, causal agents in space – but they do far less well when it comes to fathoming their own minds. And why, in evolutionary terms, should they be intellectually equipped to grasp how their minds ultimately operate?

Now I have come to the view that the nature of the dependence of consciousness on the physical world, specifically on the brain, falls into the category of mysteries for us human beings, and possibly for all minds that form their concepts in ways constrained by perception and introspection. Let me just summarize why I think

---

[5]   See ch. 1, this volume.
[6]   See my, *Mental Content* (Basil Blackwell: Oxford, 1989). The present chapter is an attempt to reconcile the optimism of that book with the pessimism of the chapter cited above.
[7]   See his, *Reflections on Language* (Pantheon Books, 1975), ch. 4.
[8]   Cf. Fodor's notion of 'epistemic boundedness: *The Modularity of Mind* (The MIT Press: Cambridge, Mass., 1983), Part V.

this; a longer treatment would be needed to make the position plausible. Our concepts of the empirical world are fundamentally controlled by the character of our perceptual experience and by the introspective access we enjoy to our own minds. We can, it is true, extend our concepts some distance beyond these starting-points, but we cannot prescind from them entirely (this is the germ of truth Kant recognized in classical empiricism). Thus our concepts of consciousness are constrained by the specific form of our own consciousness, so that we cannot form concepts for quite alien forms of consciousness possessed by other actual and possible creatures.[9] Similarly, our concepts of the body, including the brain, are constrained by the way we perceive these physical objects; we have, in particular, to conceive of them as spatial entities essentially similar to other physical objects in space, however inappropriate this manner of conception may be for understanding how consciousness arises from the brain.[10] But now these two forms of conceptual closure operate to prevent us from arriving at concepts for the property or relation that intelligibly links consciousness to the brain. For, first, we cannot grasp other forms of consciousness, and so we cannot grasp the theory that explains these other forms: that theory must be general, but *we* must always be parochial in our conception of consciousness. It is as if we were trying for a general theory of light but could only grasp the visible part of the spectrum. And, second, it is precisely the perceptually controlled conception of the brain that we have which is so hopeless in making consciousness an intelligible result of brain activity. No property we can ascribe to the brain on the basis of how it strikes us perceptually, however inferential the ascription, seems capable of rendering perspicuous how it is that damp grey tissue can be the crucible from which subjective consciousness emerges fully formed. That is why the feeling is so strong in us that there has to be something *magical* about the mind–brain relation. There must *be* some property of the brain that accounts non-magically for consciousness, since no-

---

[9]   Nagel discusses this in *The View From Nowhere* (Oxford University Press, 1986), ch. 2.
[10]   That is, our natural perception-based sense of similarity underestimates the objective difference there must be between brains and other physical objects, if brains are to be (as they are) the basis of consciousness. To God, brains seem *sui generis*, startlingly different from other physical objects. His sense of similarity, unlike ours, does justice to the uniqueness we know the brain must possess. (Compare the fallibility of our natural sense of similarity with respect to natural kinds.)

thing in nature happens by magic, but no form of inference from what we perceive of the brain seems capable of leading us to the property in question. We must therefore be getting a partial view of things. It is as if we were trying to extract psychological properties themselves from our awareness of mere physical objects; or again, trying to get normative concepts from descriptive ones. The problem is not that the brain lacks the right explanatory property; the problem is that this property does not lie along any road we can travel in forming our concepts of the brain. Perception takes us in the wrong direction here. We feel the tug of the occult because our methods of empirical concept formation are geared towards properties of kinds that cannot in principle solve the problem of how consciousness depends upon the brain. The situation is analogous to the following possibility: that the ultimate nature of matter is so different from anything we can encounter by observing the material world that we simply cannot ever come to grasp it. Human sense organs are tuned to certain kinds of properties the world may instantiate, but it may be that the theoretically basic properties are not ones that can be reached by starting from perception and workings outwards; the startingpoint may point us in exactly the wrong direction. Human reason is not able to travel unaided in just any theoretical direction, irrespective of its basic input. I think that honest reflection strongly suggests that nothing *we* could ever empirically discover about the brain *could* provide a fully satisfying account of consciousness. We shall either find that the properties we encounter are altogether on the wrong track or we shall illicitly project traits of mind into the physical basis.[11] In particular, the essentially spatial conception we have, so suitable for making sense of the nonmental properties of the brain, is inherently incapable of removing the sense of magic we have about the fact that conscious-

---

[11]   This latter tendency gives rise to illusions of understanding. We think we are seeing how consciousness depends upon the brain when all we are doing is reading consciousness into the physical basis. This tendency is particularly compelling when the brain is conceived as a computer: thinking of neurons as performing computations, we are tempted to credit them with conscious states (or proto-conscious states). Then it seems easy enough to see how neurons could generate consciousness. But, of course, this just pushes the question back (as well as being false): for how do these conscious properties of neurons arise from their physical nature? (Panpsychism now threatens.) If we are to describe physical processes computationally, then we must be clear that this does not involve consciousness – and then it will also be clear that we can not get consciousness out of such descriptions. Either we presuppose what we should be explaining or we find ourselves as far away as ever from our explanandum.

ness depends upon the brain. We need something radically different from this but, given the way we form our concepts, we cannot free ourselves of the conceptions that make the problem look insoluble. Not only, then, is it *possible* that the question of how consciousness arises from the physical world cannot be answered by minds constructed as ours are, but there is also strong positive reason for supposing that this is actually the case. The centuries of failure and bafflement have a deep source: the very nature of our concept-forming capacities. The mind–body problem is a 'mystery' and not merely a 'problem'.

The foregoing is only intended to provide a flavor of the reasons I should give for abject pessimism over the problem of consciousness. My question in this chapter concerns the consequences of such pessimism for the problem of content. Must we suppose likewise that intentionality is closed to our theoretical understanding, that the correct naturalistic theory treats of properties that lie outside the area of reality we can comprehend? Or is there some way to stop the mystery of consciousness spreading to content? Before considering some possible suggestions on how to contain the mystery, let me focus the tension a bit more sharply.

Consider conscious perceptual experiences, such as my now seeing a scarlet sphere against a blue background. We can say, following Thomas Nagel and others, that there is something it is like to have such experiences; they have a subjective aspect.[12] That is to say, there is something it is like *for the subject* of such experiences: subjective aspects of experience involve a reference to the subject undergoing the experience – this is what their *subjectiv*ity consists in. But we can also say that perceptual experiences have a world-directed aspect: they present the world in a certain way, say as containing a scarlet sphere against a blue background. This is their representational content, what states of affairs they are *as of*. Thus perceptual experiences are Janus-faced: they point outward to the external world but they also present a subjective face to their subject; they are of something other than the subject and they are like something for the subject. But these two faces do not wear different expressions: for what the experience is like is a function of what it is of, and what it is of is a function of what it is like. Told

---

[12]   Thomas Nagel, 'What is it Like to be a Bat?', *Mortal Questions* (Cambridge University Press, 1979); Brian Farrell, 'Experience', *Mind* 1950.

that an experience is as of a scarlet sphere you know what it is like
to have it; and if you know what it is like to have it, then you know
how it represents things. The two faces are, as it were, locked
together. The subjective and the semantic are chained to each other.
But then it seems that any conditions necessary and sufficient for
the one aspect will have to be necessary and sufficient for the other.
If we discover what gives an experience the (full) content it has,
then we will have discovered what gives it its distinctive phenomenology; and the other way about. But now we are threatened
with the following contraposition: since we cannot give a theory of
consciousness we cannot give a theory of content, since to give the
latter would *be* to give the former (at least in the case of conscious
experiences). Accordingly, theories of content are cognitively closed
to us: we cannot say in virtue of what an experience has the content
it has. Suppose, for example, that we favoured some sort of causal
theory of perceptual content: content is fixed by regular causal
connexions between experiences and properties instantiated in the
surrounding world, say being scarlet or spherical.[13] Such causal
facts would be deemed sufficient for having the kind of content in
question. But if this content fixes the subjective side of the experience – what it is like for the subject – then we are committed, it
seems, to holding that such causal facts are sufficient for this subjective side also. For what fixes content fixes qualia. But these causal
conditions seem manifestly insufficient for subjectivity, intuitively,
and the claim contradicts the closure I said I concede. Intentionality
has a first-person aspect, and this seems impossible to capture in
the naturalistic terms favoured by causal theories and their ilk.[14]
If consciousness is a mystery, then so must its content be. So the
challenge runs.

How, if at all, can we escape this argument? One response would
be not to try: accept that intentionality is inexplicable by us but
insist that it is not inherently mysterious or inconsistent with what

---

[13] This kind of theory is defended by (among others) Tyler Burge, 'Individualism and
Psychology', *Philosophical Review*, January 1986. I criticize such views in *Mental Content*
(Basil Blackwell: Oxford, 1989).
[14] Such theories stress the third-person perspective: how we determine what someone else is
referring to or thinking about. But we must not forget the perspective of the subject: how he
experiences the intentional directedness of his mental states. It is the same stress on the
third-person perspective that makes the likes of functionalism about sensations seem more
adequate than it ought to seem.

we know of the physical world. This would be to extend to content the treatment I should propose for consciousness. About consciousness I should say that there is no objective miracle in how it arises from the brain; it only seems to us that there is because of the veil imposed by cognitive closure. We project our own limitations on to nature, thus making nature appear to contain supernatural facts. In reality, there is no metaphysical mind–body problem; there is no *ontological* anomaly, only an epistemic hiatus. The psychophysical nexus is no more intrinsically mysterious than any other causal nexus in the body, though it will always strike *us* as mysterious. This is what we can call a 'nonconstructive' solution to the problem of how consciousness is possible. But if that solution removes the basic philosophical problem, as I think it does, then we can say the same about intentionality. We do not need to be able to produce a constructive solution to 'Brentano's problem' in order to convince ourselves that there is no inherent mystery in the phenomenon of intentionality; we can rest secure in the knowledge that *some* property of the physical world explains that phenomenon in an entirely natural way – though we cannot ever discover what that property is.[15] To the omniscient intellect of God intentionality in a physical organism is no more remarkable than digestion is. Thus there is no pressure towards eliminativism about content arising from the fact that *we* can never make content (physically) comprehensible to ourselves; any more than a minded creature who is constitutionally unable to grasp the correct theory of digestion has to deny that anything ever gets digested. So we can, according to this response, solve the philosophical problem of intentionality without actually *specifying* the correct theory.

I do not think this nonconstructive response can be rejected on general grounds, since I believe it applies to the case of conscious-

[15] Here, then, is a possible response to Hartry Field's demand that truth and reference be reducible if they are to be respectable: see his 'Mental Representation', in Ned Block (ed.), *Readings in Philosophy of Psychology* (Harvard University Press: Cambridge, Mass., 1981). We need to distinguish being able to *give* a reduction from knowing that a reduction *exists* – in order not to rule out the possibility that the reduction can be specified only in a science that is cognitively inaccessible to us. We cannot infer elimination from irreducibility *by us*. Nor can we simply *assume* that the correct naturalistic account of intentionality employs 'broadly physical' notions, if this means that these notions do not extend our present physical concepts beyond what is intelligible to us. In a word, we must not be dogmatic conceptual conservatives. The correct reduction (if that is the right word) might not be recognizable by us as correct. (I take this to be an expression of realism.)

ness. But I think it is implausibly extreme in the case of content; for we can, I believe, produce naturalistic theories of content that provide substantial illumination as to its workings. It is not as if the theories now available strike us as just hopelessly misguided, as telling us nothing whatever about the nature of intentionality. Whereas I do think that the usual theories of consciousness (e.g. functionalism) do not even begin to make a dent in our incomprehension. Thus it seems to me that teleological theories, in particular, promise to shed a good deal of light on the roots of intentionality; they provide real insight. Who can deny that the vast amount of work devoted to the nature of reference and belief in the last twenty or so years has added significantly to our understanding of their nature? Something, I venture to suggest, has been learned. So it cannot be that the whole nature of intentionality is hidden from us, that we simply cannot form the kinds of concepts that would shed light on it. The question is how to square this apparent illumination with extreme pessimism about consciousness. How is such illumination *possible*, given that we are completely in the dark about consciousness?

At this point it is natural to pin one's hopes on what I shall call the 'insulation strategy'. The insulation strategy proposes radically to separate the two theories: in particular, it proposes to do the theory of content in complete isolation from the theory of consciousness. How might this insulation of theories be made plausible? The obvious first move is to switch theoretical attention to (so-called) subpersonal content, the kind that exists without benefit of consciousness. We attribute content of a sort to machines and to subconscious processes in the nervous system; and this kind of content might be thought to be explicable without bringing in consciousness. It is true that content is also possessed by conscious states, but this is only a contingent truth about content, a dispensable accretion. Then once we have a theory for subpersonal content we can extend it to conscious content, simply by adding in the fact that the content is conscious. In principle, this strategy insists, the conditions necessary and sufficient for content are *neutral* on the question whether the bearer of the content happens to be a conscious state. Indeed, the very same range of contents that are possessed by conscious creatures could be possessed by creatures without a trace of consciousness. Consciousness is simply a further fact, super-added; it is not itself in any way constitutive of content. This contingency claim might then be bolstered by the consideration that the outstanding problem in the naturalistic theory of content – namely, accounting for the possibility of error or misrepresentation – does not seem to require invoking consciousness: it is not the fact that a state is conscious that makes it susceptible to error and hence semantic evaluation. We do not ascend from mere natural indication or nomic dependence to full-blown truth and falsity by ensuring that there is something it is like to be in the state in question. Subjectivity is not what creates the possibility of error. Hence subjective features lie quite outside the proper domain of the theory of content.

There are two problems with this suggestion. The first is tactical: we do not want the possibility of a theory of content to depend upon the particular conception of the relation between content and consciousness that the suggestion assumes. One view, by no means absurd, is that *all* content is originally of conscious states. There is no (underivative) intentionality without consciousness. (Brentano's thesis was that all consciousness is intentional: this 'converse Brentano thesis' is that all intentionality is conscious – or somehow derivative from consciousness.) Our attributions of content to machines and cerebral processes is, on this view, dependent or metaphorical or instrumental; there would be no content in a world without consciousness. Accordingly, we labour under an illusion if we think we can *complete* the theory of content without even mentioning that contentful states are associated with consciousness. There is no ofness without likeness. When we think we are conceiving of content in the absence of consciousness we are really treating a system *as if* it were conscious, while simultaneously denying that this is what we are up to.

Now it is not that I myself agree with this extreme thesis of dependence; I have yet to see a convincing argument for the claim that any kind of representation worthy of the name requires consciousness. But I should agree that the possibility of subpersonal content of *some* kind does not serve to insulate the two theories when it comes to the kind of content distinctively possessed by conscious states. And this brings us to the second point. There may indeed be two species of content, personal and subpersonal, but this does not show that the personal kind lacks distinctive properties that tie it essentially to consciousness. I doubt that the self-same *kind* of content possessed by a conscious perceptual experience, say, could be possessed independently of consciousness; such content seems essentially conscious, shot through with subjectivity. This is because of the Janus-faced character of conscious content: it involves presence to the subject, and hence a subjective point of view. Remove the inward-looking face and you remove something integral – what the world *seems* like to the subject. Just as there are two types of 'meaning', natural and non-natural, so there seem to be two types of content, conscious and nonconscious; the subjective perspective creates, as it were, a new and special kind of content. This is why what an experience is as of already contains a phenomenological fact – how the subject is struck in having the experience. So we cannot hope to devise an exhaustive theory of the nature of conscious content while remaining neutral on whether such content is conscious. Content distinctions confer subjective distinctions. Experiential content is essentially phenomenological.

I suspect that the insulation strategy is fuelled by a conception of consciousness that we can call the 'medium conception': consciousness is to its content what a medium of representation is to the message it conveys. Compare sentences, spoken or written. On the one hand, there is their sound or shape (the medium); on the other, their meaning, the proposition they express. We can readily envisage separate studies of these two properties of a sentence, neither presupposing the other. In particular, we could have a theory of the content of sentences that was neutral as to their sound or shape. The meaning could vary while the sound or shape stayed constant, and there could be variations in sound or shape unaccompanied by variations in meaning. Message and medium can vary along independent dimensions. Suppose, then, that we try to think of perceptual experience in this way: subjective features are analogous to the sound or shape of the sentence, content to its meaning. The content is *expressed* in a particular conscious medium but we can in principle separate the properties of the medium from the message it carries. What it is like to have the experience is thus fixed by intrinsic features of the medium, whereas what the experience is about is fixed by certain extrinsic relations to the world. According to this conception, then, the absolute intractability of consciousness need not infect the theory of content in the slightest. Consciousness is to be conceived, in effect, as a mysterious medium in which something relatively mundane is (contingently) embedded.

I think the medium conception is the kind of view which, once clearly articulated, sheds whatever attractions it may have initially possessed. In effect, it tries to treat perceptual experience as if its phenomenology were analogous to that of (non-representational) bodily sensations: content comes from subtending this intrinsic phenomenology with causal or other relations to the world, these relations being strictly orthogonal to that intrinsic phenomenology. Or again, it tries to conceive of experiential content as if it operated like truth or veridicality: whether a belief is true or an experience veridical is not a phenomenological property of the state in question, so that any theory of what confers these properties need not encroach on consciousness itself. A causal account of veridicality, for example, is not, and is not intended as, an account of what gives an experience the representational content it has (what it is as of). *If* we could think of content itself as lying in this way 'outside' of phenomenology, then we could indeed insulate the two theories. But, as I have insisted, this attempted extrusion of the subjective from the semantic just does not work. The content of an experience simply does contribute to what it is like to have it, and indeed it is not at all clear that anything else does. A visual experience, for example, presents the world to the subject in specific ways, as containing spatially disposed objects of various shapes and colours, and this kind of 'presentation-to' is constitutive of what it is like to have visual experience. It is true, of course, that different sense-modalities may present the same kinds of environmental feature, e.g. shape or texture – as with sight and touch – but the subjectively distinct experiences that present these features also present *other* features. It is not that sight and touch present precisely the *same* range of features yet differ phenomenologically, so that we need something like a medium conception to capture the difference; it is rather that they overlap in the features they present at certain points but are disjoint at others – notably, in the secondary qualities they present. These differences in the range of contents available to different types of experience seem enough to capture the obvious phenomenological differences in the experiences associated with different senses. Bats perceive different secondary qualities from us when they employ their echolocation sense; it is not that they perceive precisely the same qualities and embed them in a different (non-representational) medium. But even if there were subjective distinctions that could not be captured in terms of distinctions of content, this would not help the insulation strategy, since there are too many subjective distinctions that *are* generated by distinctions of content. The difference between a visual experience of red and a visual experience of green just is a difference in what it is like to have these two types of experience. The case is quite unlike the difference between a veridical and an hallucinatory experience, or a true belief and a false one. Content, we might say, is *internal* to phenomenology; the link here is anything but contingent.

If this is right, then we cannot suppose that the theory of content simply has nothing to do with the nature or constitution of consciousness. Since distinctions of content can constitute (or contribute towards) distinctions of phenomenology, we cannot totally insulate the theory of the former from the theory of the latter; we must admit that a correct theory of content will deliver resources sufficient to capture subjective features of conscious states. But if we are convinced that no naturalistic theory of the kinds available to us can explain conscious features, then we are again in a state of tension. Either we can explain features of consciousness ('qualia') naturalistically or we can not explain content naturalistically. The fate of the one theory seems yoked to the fate of the other. Yet I, for one, should like to believe that we can make progress with content, while accepting that consciousness is beyond us. Where then can I turn to have this tension relieved?

Instead of attempting to insulate the two theories entirely, I want to suggest that we limit the scope of the theory of content. We should accept that there is a part or aspect of intentionality that our theories do not and probably cannot capture, but we should also hold that there is a part or aspect that they do have some prospect of illuminating. There is *partial* cognitive closure with respect to content: we can naturalize certain properties of the total phenomenon but we cannot naturalize all of its properties (though, as I said earlier, all the properties are in themselves entirely natural). And this will imply that there are *some* features of consciousness – subjective features – that we can treat naturalistically. There is a feasible branch of the theory of content that delivers an account of certain phenomenological facts: but this falls short of a full explanation of conscious intentionality.

Let me distinguish two questions. The first is the question what *individuates* contents: what accounts for identity and difference between contents; what makes a content of this rather than that? We classify experiences according to what they represent, and the question is what principles underlie these classifications. The second question concerns the *nature* of content: what does it consist in for a creature to have intentional states at all; what makes a creature enjoy mental 'directedness' on the world in the first place? Thus, we can ask what natural facts make a creature an intentional being, and then we can ask what natural facts *target* this intentionality in specific ways? The question of nature is the more fundamental question: it asks what this directedness, grasping, apprehension, encompassing, reaching out ultimately consists in. It wants to know by virtue of what natural facts the mind is endowed with the power to 'point' beyond itself. The question of individuation takes this for granted and enquires how the intentional capacity picks up the particular objects and properties it does. *Given* that consciousness has the power to 'lasso' things in the world, what determines the direction of its throw? Putting it in terms of linguistic intentionality or reference: we can ask what makes a physical organism capable of referring (the act itself), and we can ask how it is that this act is tied down to particular objects and properties. 'What is reference?' is one question; 'How does reference get targeted this way rather than that?' is another question.

Now, assuming this distinction is sufficiently clear, I can state my proposal: the *nature* of intentionality is cognitively closed to us but the *individuation* of intentional contents is in principle open. We can say what makes a content of this rather than that but we cannot say what the relation of intentionality itself consists in. We cannot specify, in naturalistic (i.e. broadly physical) terms, the essential nature of the conscious mental act of apprehending states of affairs, but we can say in such terms what distinguishes one such act from another. Let me now try to defend this proposal. First I shall explain why the proposal is consistent. Then I shall defend the pessimistic part of the proposal. Finally I shall urge a qualified optimism about the question of content individuation.

The proposal is consistent because we do not need to fathom the nature of the intentional *act* in order to provide constraints on the identity conditions of instances of the act. I can tell you what distinguishes referring to redness from referring to greenness without being able to tell you what referring is *au fond*. The direction of reference may be constrained by relations with which reference itself cannot literally be *identified*. An analogy from action theory may help here. We can ask what distinguishes different kinds of world-directed bodily action without asking what the nature of intentional action in general is. Thus I can tell you what distinguishes intentionally kicking a brick from intentionally kicking a cat – there are different objects on the end of my toe – without having to explain what intentional action is in general. Consider, then, causal theories of mental aboutness. I can tell you, in terms of causal history, what distinguishes thinking about London from thinking about New York – there are different cities at the causal origin of these thoughts – without having to venture on the question what mental aboutness is to start with. The causal relations in question make these thoughts home in on certain objects, but we do not need to infer that mental aboutness is reducible to these relations. I do not have to be able to explain or analyse the act of grasping itself in order to be able to lay down laws that fix what is grasped. I don't have to be able to provide a naturalistic account of the intentional *structure* of consciousness in order to be in a position to pin down what gives that structure the specific content it has. Specific content is, as it were, the 'logical product' of the intentional capacity and the natural relations that target that capacity in particular ways; the capacity is not reducible to the relations. In view of this distinction of questions, we have to be very careful when we offer what we are pleased to call a 'theory of intentionality/reference'. Suppose we favour causal theories of perceptual content: content is individuated by regular causal links between experiences and properties instantiated in the subject's environment. It is tempting to suggest that such links give us the very nature of perceptual representation, that the conscious act of enjoying an experience as of a scarlet sphere against a blue background is analysable as a special kind of causal relation. But if I am right this is not what we should say. Rather, we should say that causal relations tie the intentional structure of perceptual experience down to specific states of affairs but that such relations do not constitute the very nature of that structure. Intentional directedness is not exhaustively analysable as a causal relation, however complex. And similarly for teleological theories. Neither do we need to suppose this in order to find a point for naturalistic theories of content; we need rather to locate their legitimate area of application some way short of a full account of what it is stand in intentional relations to things.

The pessimism about the essential nature of intentionality can be motivated in two ways. First we can simply deduce it from pessimism about consciousness: if consciousness cannot be explained (by us) naturalistically, in broadly physical terms, then neither can the constitutive structures of consciousness. The intentionality of experiences and thoughts belongs with the subjective 'feel' of sensations: neither admits of objective physical explanation. But, second, we can also generate a mood of pessimism more directly: we can ask ourselves whether it really seems plausible that any of the standard theories capture the complete nature of conscious intentionality. In the case of sensations we have a strong sense that standard naturalistic theories, e.g. reductive functionalism, omit something essential – the 'feel' of the sensation. And I think our intuitions about intentionality parallel our intuitions about sensations: it really does seem that causal or teleological theories omit something essential in the intentional relation as it occurs in consciousness. They do not capture that phenomenological feature we describe (somewhat metaphorically) as grasping, apprehending, reaching out, taking in, and so forth. There is an *internality* about the relation between an experience and its object that seems hard to replicate in terms of 'external' causal or teleological relations. Presence *to* the subject of the object of his experience seems not exhaustively explicable in terms of such natural relations. These kinds of relations hold, after all, between all sorts of things, not just brains and items in their environment, and it seems unsatisfactory to try to assimilate conscious intentional directedness to these ordinary relations. Conscious intentionality is more special than this sort of account suggests. (This is, of course, why Brentano claimed that intentionality is what distinguishes minds from mere physical objects.) Naturalistic theories fail to do justice to the *uniqueness* of conscious intentionality. Nothing we know about the brain, including its relations to the world, seems capable of rendering unmysterious the capacity of conscious states to 'encompass' external states of affairs.[16] I think this is a very primitive intuition, by which I suspect many of us have been struck at some point in our philosophical lives. How *can* our minds reach out to the objects of experience? What is it about our brains, and their location in the world, that could possibly explain the way consciousness *arcs out* into the world? Consciousness seems to extend an invisible hand into the world it represents (If I may put it so): how on earth could my *brain* make that possible? No ethereal prehensile organ protrudes from my skull! Phenomenologically, we feel that the mind 'lays hold' of things out there, mentally 'grasps' them, but we have no physical model of what this might consist in. We flounder in similes. It is precisely our perplexity about this question that makes it seem to us that there could be a creature whose brain had all the same natural properties and relations as ours and yet enjoyed no such conscious arcing out. For none of the natural properties and relations we come across seems to add up to what we know from the first-person point of view of conscious aboutness. It is thus reasonable to suspect that cognitive closure is operative here. Somehow we are not keyed in to the kinds of natural fact that actually underlie intentionality – as we are not to consciousness in general. Something about our make-up explains how consciousness can reach out into the world in the way it does, but we seem constitutionally blind to what that something is.

Cautious optimism is possible, however, since we do not need to

[16] Two thinkers who have recognized the mysterious-seeming nature of meaning and reference are Thomas Nagel and Ludwig Wittgenstein. Nagel draws attention to the way meaning seems to be able to 'take in' much more of the world than its basis in the particular doings and undergoings of speakers could permit: it can reach across vast stretches of space and time; it has a universality or generality that transcends the particular actions and experiences of speakers; it determines indefinitely many uses of language, past and future, as correct or incorrect. See his, *What Does It All Mean?* (Oxford University Press, 1987), ch. 5. Wittgenstein, for his part, speaks of 'the mysterious relation of the object and its name', and he says of the 'mental activities' of wishing and believing that 'for the same reason [they] have something mysterious and inexplicable about them': *The Blue and Brown Books* (Basil Blackwell: Oxford, 1958), pp. 172–3. Wittgenstein's idea, though, is that this sense of mystery arises from a (correctable) mistake: 'A primitive philosophy condenses the whole usage of the name into the idea of a relation, which thereby becomes a mysterious relation' (p. 173). I am inclined to agree with him about the aura of mystery, but I doubt that it can be dispelled in the way he suggests, namely by reminding ourselves of how we actually use names or ascribe propositional attitudes. I do not think a deflationary response of this kind is adequate to the problem.

explain everything about intentionality in order to be able to say something illuminating about it. And I think it is undeniable that illuminating things have been said about content in recent years; all is not darkness. Teleological theories, in particular, seem to me to contain valuable insights. The question is *what* precisely has been illuminated. And my suggestion is that these naturalistic theories should be seen as contributions to the individuation conditions of mental states: they tell us what differentiates one kind of intentional state from another: they tell us how intentional states collect their specific content. They may also tell us something about the natural antecedents of conscious intentionality – what basic natural relations got transformed by consciousness into genuine content. First there were preconscious states with certain functions relating them to things in the world; then consciousness built upon this natural foundation to produce the intentional relation. The 'intentional arc' is not reducible to this foundation but it takes its rise from it. So there is room for naturalistic speculation about where intentionality came from, if not what it ultimately consists in. We can pursue these more modest questions without having to take on the full explanatory task of reducing intentionality to something we can understand, something broadly physical. In fact, something like this perspective is already implicit in much work on reference and content. It is not invariably assumed that causal theories (say) give us the real nature of the reference relation, that they successfully analyse the capacity to refer; rather, they tell us how that capacity gets targeted, what constrains the direction of acts of reference.[17] So we can be grateful for this kind of illumination without insisting that it be spread across the whole phenomenon.

[17] This seems the right way to interpret Saul Kripke's remarks about naming and reference in *Naming and Necessity* (Basil Blackwell: Oxford, 1980). Kripke disavows any intention of analysing or reducing the relation of reference, offering us only a 'picture' of how reference operates; but he does give us substantive constraints on *which* object is being referred to by the use of a name – the object which lies at the origin of the 'causal chain' of uses that historically lead up to the use in question. Nor is there anything in the kind of closure I acknowledge to preclude descriptive work in the theory of reference: distinguishing the different kinds of referential device, articulating the modes of identification that underlie uses of these different devices, showing how sense and reference are related in different cases, and so forth. Nothing I say undermines the viability and usefulness of, say, Gareth Evans's work in *The Varieties of Reference* (Oxford University Press, 1982). What I am doubting is the possibility of a certain kind of explanatory enterprise: giving a broadly physical account of the very nature of the reference relation. We can prune the pretensions of causal theories (say) without declaring them completely out of a job.

Yet there is a residual puzzle. We have resisted the insulation strategy, arguing that content colours consciousness. Differences of content do determine differences of subjectivity; 'ofness' fixes 'likeness'. But this staining of subjectivity by reference does imply that we can provide a naturalistic theory of subjective distinctions, since we can say in naturalistic terms what individuates the content of experience. Here we have an objective handle on to the constitution of the subjective. An experience as of a red square thing is subjectively distinct from an experience as of a green triangular thing, in virtue of the fact that different kinds of objects are represented; and this distinction can be captured, we have agreed, in terms of natural relations that these experiences stand in to the properties represented – say, teleological relations. So it looks as though we are committed to accounting for *some* features of consciousness naturalistically; not *all* phenomenological facts are closed to us. I think this does indeed follow: there are some features of consciousness whose natural explanation, in broadly physical terms, is in principle available to us. Our concept-forming capacities afford us partial access to the natural basis of these subjective features of consciousness. But this is puzzling because one would expect the closure to be total: how can it be impossible for us to explain how consciousness arises from the physical world and yet not so very difficult to account naturalistically for distinctions *within* consciousness? Why should the general phenomenon of consciousness be so recalcitrant to natural explanation while specific determinations of consciousness yield to naturalistic account? It's puzzling. Even where consciousness is not mysterious it is mysterious why it is not mysterious!

This puzzle should be set beside another. A moderate externalist about content will hold that objective properties, e.g. being square, enter into the identity of contentful states; they occur as 'constituents' of content.[18] Thus objective properties penetrate experiences

---

[18]   For a discussion of this see my *Mental Content* (Basil Blackwell: Oxford, 1989). I set aside here the question of how secondary qualities enter into the content of experience. If these are subjectively constituted, then there is a sense in which the subjective gets turned back on itself when colours (say) penetrate the content of colour experience. Still, colours are properties of external objects, so colour experience – like shape experience – does reach out to the world beyond the subject. (We may wonder whether the ultimate explanation of why we perceive secondary qualities at all is one of those questions about consciousness whose answer is forever closed to us. That would certainly account for my struggles to explain it in *The Subjective View* (Oxford University Press, 1983.)

in ways that fix their phenomenology. Again, the subjective is invaded by the objective. Combining this act of colonization with the previous one we get a double dependence of the subjective on the objective: objective items figure as 'constituents' of subjective states, so shaping their phenomenology, *and* these states collect those objective 'constituents' by way of objective natural relations – say, biological function. What now begins to look mysterious is the way consciousness is so resistant to objective physical reduction and yet is so permeated by the objective and physical. Consciousness, as it were, appropriates the objective while holding itself aloft from it; it takes the physical in but it refuses to be ruled by it. And, oddly enough, it is just this capacity to 'incorporate' the physically objective, to bring it within consciousness, that the physical brain seems so inadequate to.[19] The puzzles multiply. But then the more you think about consciousness the more puzzling it comes to seem. It is comforting to reflect that from God's point of view, i.e. the point of view of Nature, there is no inherent mystery about consciousness at all. The impression of mystery derives from our own incurable cognitive poverty, not from the objective world in which consciousness exists. There is no real magic in the link between mind and matter, however incapable we are of seeing how the trick is performed. Cold comfort, perhaps, but whoever said that the nature of the mind should be fully accessible to those with a mind?[20]

[19] Genuine externalism therefore requires us to reject the more obvious kinds of physicalism, since the brain cannot incorporate the external in the way the mind can. We have no physical model of how consciousness can lay hold of the physical world in the peculiar way it does.

[20] I am grateful for comments to Thomas Nagel, Simon Blackburn, and various members of an Oxford discussion group.

3

Consciousness and the Natural Order

Cosmologists tell us that the material universe came into existence somewhere between ten and twenty thousand million years ago. The Big Bang rang out across the void, and matter began expanding outwards from a point of infinite density. Biologists tell us that life on earth began about three thousand million years ago. The Soft Rustle of evolving organisms could soon be heard over the surface of the planet. I have never read a scientific figure dating the origin of consciousness on earth, though I suppose it must have been when some of the fancier models of mollusc took up residence in the oceans, or when fish began to roam the depths.[1] The Scarcely Audible Whisper (or Whimper) of sentience reverberated in the seas: awareness was born, quite late in the game. In due course, consciousness followed life onto dry land, where it flourished spectacularly, and in a cosmic blink of the eye the human version of consciousness came on the scene. By this late date the Three Great Upsurges that have marked the history of the universe had come to pass: first matter, then life, and finally consciousness. Loci of conscious living matter now stalked space-time. Whether any further radical novelties lie in store for natural history remains to be seen. Reality may yet accumulate some fundamentally new layer, hitherto undreamt of. Certainly there is still plenty of time left for nature to think up something else that is startlingly innovative, something not prefigured in what is already the case.

---

[1] Consciousness does not leave traces of itself in the way matter and life do. We do not find imprints of it in the fossil record. Its onset is thus essentially conjectural, turning upon what physical facts we recognize as its outward signs. It is as conjectural as those signs. Still, there must have *been* a time when the inner began its career, when the world became conscious of itself. One fine day the mutation occurred, and natural selection never looked back: consciousness worked.

We now know a good deal about how matter and life originated. We can reconstruct the history of these things in plausible outline; we understand how one stage of the universe came from another. In particular, we have a workable theory of how life came from matter: by the replication of clumps of matter modified by explicable kinds of disturbance to the fidelity of the replication, leading to natural selection of the more viable clumps. A basic continuity between the inorganic and the organic can thus be demonstrated. No miraculous jump in the fortunes of the universe need be ruefully accepted. The Soft Rustle could therefore have occurred without the benefit of God's intervention. But in the case of consciousness we have no such understanding: we do not know how consciousness might have arisen by natural processes from antecedently existing material things. Somehow or other sentience sprang from pulpy matter, giving matter an inner aspect, but we have no idea how this leap was propelled. It seems abrupt, unmediated, serendipitous. One is tempted, however reluctantly, to turn to divine assistance: for only a kind of miracle could produce *this* from *that*. It would take a supernatural magician to extract consciousness from matter, even living matter. Consciousness appears to introduce a sharp break in the natural order – a point at which scientific naturalism runs out of steam. It has the look of an irresoluble enigma.[2]

The case is actually somewhat direr than this. For there is a sense in which consciousness has to be created afresh every time another conscious subject comes on the scene. Here consciousness differs significantly from matter and life. When a new material object is created there is a continuity of matter linking the new with the old: the causal processes that produce the new object basically involve the rearrangement of prior material. Matter does not have to be created all over again each time a new mountain is formed or a tree grows; it flows from one thing into another. One Big Bang was enough to stock up the universe with all the matter it needed; we do

---

[2] I do not know if anyone has ever tried to exploit consciousness to prove the existence of God, along the lines of the traditional Argument from Design, but in this post-Darwinian era it is an argument with more force than the usual one, through lack of an alternative theory. It is indeed difficult to see how consciousness could have arisen spontaneously from insentient matter; it seems to need an injection from outside the physical realm. Only something of the same kind could bring it about to begin with, it might be thought. However, as will become clear, I do not really think we need to resort to God here; we need merely to face up to the depth of our ignorance.

not have to posit lots of Little Bangs to account for freshly minted physical objects. It is much the same with life: new organisms are continous with earlier ones, coming from them along unbroken biological chains. Reproduction involves causal processes that are continuously biological: at no stage does the organic lapse into the inorganic, only to regain life further down the line. If there were such a break, then reproduction would have to achieve the equivalent of the beginning of evolution each time a new organism was produced. This would make it a lot harder for organisms to come into existence. (No doubt this is why the idea of spontaneous generation goes so deeply against the grain.) In the cases of matter and life, then, we can say that the generative processes that produce new instances of these types of entity continuously preserve these types: we do not get breaks in the causal chains, periods of absence.

But in the case of consciousness that is exactly what we do get. When one centre of consciousness produces another there is a period during which the continuity of consciousness is interrupted: indeed, the capacity for consciousness is not present during this period. Thus the human sperm and ovum are not capable of consciousness, and it takes a few months before the human foetus is. So when consciousness finally dawns in a developing organism it does not stem from an immediately prior consciousness: it stems from oblivion, from insensate (though living) matter. The causal processes that generate consciousness do not themselves involve conscious states; the consciousness of the progenitor was left behind long ago, and is not essential to the success of the process anyway. New centres of consciousness are not causally continuous with old ones; there is a break in the inter-generational stream. This means that there is a sense in which the origin of consciousness must be recapitulated each time a new locus of consciousness comes along: the world (or a local pocket of it) must go from a state in which there is no consciousness to a state in which there is. The original Whisper was not enough: each new conscious being needs its own individual Murmur to bring it into existence. There is thus not just the one original large miracle to explain; there are billions of smaller ones too. Consciousness has to be recreated every time a new sentient organism springs up – in a way that matter and life do not need to be recreated each time a new physical object or living thing comes into existence. Consciousness could vanish from the universe for ten minutes and then reassert itself after the interlude, so long as the right reproductive processes had been initiated. But if matter or life vanished for that period, there would be a devil of a job getting them started again. Perhaps it is this fact about consciousness that dulls our appreciation of its (apparent) miraculousness: when miracles happen all the time you start taking them for granted.[3]

Yet, one wants to insist, consciousness cannot *really* be miraculous, some kind of divine parlour trick. It must fit into the natural order of things somehow. Its relation to matter must be intelligible, principled, law-governed. Naturalism about consciousness is not merely an option. It is a condition of understanding. It is a condition of *existence*. The only question is how to set about being a naturalist about consciousness – what form the naturalism should take. This chapter will investigate that question: what are the prospects for arriving at a naturalistic understanding of the phenomena of consciousness? I shall argue that they are a good deal dimmer than some people have supposed, at least on the usual understanding of naturalism, and I shall suggest a diagnosis of the difficulty of completing the naturalistic programme. Finally, I shall propose a modified form of naturalism, different from those commonly considered. My overall aim is to steer between what seem to me somewhat glib versions of naturalism, on the one hand, and mystical kinds of anti-naturalism, on the other. I want to recommend a more modest and realistic naturalism than those currently on offer.

Consciousness abuts the physical world along two major axes, which it is natural to picture as at right-angles to each other. The first, vertical, axis connects consciousness to the body and brain: call this the axis of *embodiment*. This axis gives conscious states a physical basis; it links these states to their neural correlates. The second, horizontal, axis connects consciousness to the objects and properties that are represented by conscious states; call this the axis of *intentionality*. This axis gives conscious states a physical content

[3] Imagine if matter and life were continually starting from scratch, as consciousness has to: would we not then regard their origin with the same composure (complacency?) we now feel about consciousness? The more frequently a miracle happens, the less impressed we tend to be by it. Or again, if there were a necessary natural continuity to consciousness, as there is to matter and life, so that the initial miracle did not need to be repeated, would we not then find its origin more spectacular than we do now?

or significance; it links these states t: the world beyond the bound-aries of the subject's nervous system.[4] The intentional axis includes both cognitive representations, as in perception and belief, and conative representations, as in desire and the will. The neural states reached by travelling down the vertical axis are the basis of the conscious states that project outwards along the horizontal axis. These two axes comprise the sum of the involvement of conscious-ness with the physical world.

Philosophers (and others) have long yearned to uncover the na-ture of these axial relations – what it is that constitutes and permits embodiment and intentionality. What *kinds* of relation are involved here? Some philosophers, recently active, have aspired to explain these relations in purely naturalistic terms.[5] In practice, this has meant that they have tried to explain embodiment and intentional-ity by means of concepts that already apply to other aspects of nature, aspects agreed to be uncontroversially natural. These philo-sophers have had a dream in which the phenomena of conscious-ness appear as specific determinations of facts found distributed across a wider natural world. They have wanted to account for the two axes as 'intelligible modifications' (to use Leibniz's phrase[6]) of kinds of property that can be instantiated independently of con-

---

[4]   Of course the physical world is not the only target of intentional states: there are also mental states themselves, my own and others', abstract objects, etc. I think, though, that physical facts are the primary or basic kind of intentional object; this kind of intentionality is presupposed to all the rest. This contradicts the dominant historical tradition in philosophy, in which mental items are taken to be the primordial objects of apprehension (sense-data and so forth), the physical being derivative or secondary. I shall not argue this here, however; nor does anything I say depend on it.

[5]   They thus attempt to reverse the historical trend of philosophical thinking on this subject, since the seventeenth century and before. Naturalism of this kind is a comparatively recent innovation, not unconnected (I should surmise) with the demise of the divine. It would probably have struck the Great Dead Philosophers as an absurd aberration, a procrustean spasm. It is worth bearing this in mind amidst the contemporary naturalistic enthusiasm.

[6]   The phrase occurs in the following incisive passage from Leibniz's *New Essays on Human Understanding* (66–7): 'As for thought, it is certain, as our author [Locke] more than once acknowledges, that it cannot be an intelligible modification of matter and be comprehensible and explicable in terms of it. That is, a sentient or thinking being is not a mechanical thing like a watch or a mill: one cannot conceive of sizes and shapes and motions combining mechanically to produce something which thinks, and senses too, in a mass where formerly there was nothing of the kind – something which would likewise be extinguished by the machine's going out of order. So sense and thought are not something which is natural to matter, and there are only two ways in which they could occur in it: through God's combining it with a substance to which thought is natural, or through his putting thought into it by a miracle.' This seems to me a perfect short statement of the mind–body problem. The challenge to us is to avoid that final 'only'.

sciousness. Then they will have shown how consciousness could have arisen out of a world without consciousness. They will have a naturalistic explanation of emergence.

The notion of *causality* has recommended itself to these visionary thinkers. Thus functionalists have tried to explain the embodiment relation as a matter of the causal role of the underlying neural states.[7] Conscious states are defined by their causal role, say functionalists, and hence are embodied by the bodily states that carry that role. Identity of causal role is what mediates between the conscious state and the neural state; neural states get to be the basis of conscious states because they carry the causal roles constitutive of those conscious states. The embodiment of a conscious state simply consists in the fact that a certain neural state exhibits a particular pattern of (physical) causes and effects. Consciousness emerges from matter when states of matter come to have certain kinds of specific causal powers with respect to other states of matter. Similarly, causal theorists of intentionality have tried to explain that relation as a special kind of causal dependence of mental states on conditions in the external world.[8] Events external to the subject cause changes in the state of the subject's body, these changes acting differentially upon events in the subject's mind; as a result, mental states come to have contents that represent the external states of affairs that initiated the bodily changes in the first place. Or again, there are specific kinds of nomic dependence linking external events with internal ones; these nomic relations are what give mental states their representational properties. The notion of causality, it is thought, brings consciousness into line with our general picture of the world. By ingeniously conjoining causal relations with physical facts we can account for the ways consciousness hooks up to the physical world. Indeed, consciousness just *is* causality linking up the physical in particular complex ways. Causal relations enable us to exhibit consciousness as abutting the physical world in virtue of relations whose naturalistic credentials are beyond question. Causation naturalizes consciousness.

I want to argue that this kind of causal naturalism will not work.

---

[7] See, for example, David Lewis, 'An Argument for the Identity Theory', *Journal of Philosophy* 63 (1966); also many others.
[8] See, for example, Jerry Fodor, *Psychosemantics* (The MIT Press: Cambridge, Mass., 1987); also many others.

In particular, it will not do as a solution to the problem of intentionality. The basic reason for this is that it presupposes a solution to the problem of embodiment, and *that* problem has not (and probably cannot) be solved. The two problems are in fact interdependent, so that naturalism about the one waits upon naturalism about the other. A consequence of this is that the notion of causation (and allied notions) will not by itself do what is wanted. Causation is not the naturalistic talisman it is reputed to be.

In what does this interdependence consist? Consider first the dependence of the embodiment problem on the intentionality problem. Could we have a complete account of how consciousness is rooted in the brain and yet know nothing of the nature of the intentionality of conscious states? Could we, for instance, have an answer to how an experience of red is generated by the brain which did not include an answer to what gives the experience that content? It is hard to see how we could, since *what* is so embodied precisely is a state with intentional content; it is an experience *of red* whose physical basis we are out to explain. The vertical link holds between a brain state and a conscious state that is *defined* by its horizontal relations. Suppose we had a separate account of embodiment, so that it was a further, and undecided, question how the intentional relations in question could be naturalized: we know how conscious states emerge from the brain but we have as yet no idea what the intentionality of these states consists in. That would imply that we can somehow sheer off the intentional aspect of the experience and naturalize only what remains of it. But what might this non-intentional residue be? Would it be recognizable as an experience of red? In fact, no such separation is possible: we cannot hope to explain how an experience with content has a physical basis without explaining how it has that content. It is a condition of adequacy on an account of embodiment that the account slot into an account of intentionality – or else we have not shown how a conscious state *of this kind* can be physically based. We can only satisfy ourselves that we have adequately solved the embodiment problem if our solution is capable of yielding the basis for a solution to the intentionality problem. To hive off the content of experience for independent treatment is too much like detaching the experience from its essence. It is like claiming to solve the embodiment problem for pain without saying anything about what gives pain its characteristic feel or phenomenal quality. We cannot put the very nature of the mental state aside while we attempt to say how *it* arises from physical fact.[9]

The converse dependence might seem less evident. What is to stop as from giving a naturalistic theory of the intentionality of conscious states without venturing upon a naturalistic treatment of their embodiment? Can we not explain the horizontal relations constitutive of intentionality without committing ourselves to any particular view of the nature of the vertical relations connecting conscious states to the body? It might well seem that we can do this, since a causal theory (say) does not need to commit itself on the nature of the mental term of the causal relation it invokes; it restricts its interest to the horizontal axis, leaving the nature of the vertical axis open. A variety of positions on the mind-body problem would thus, it seems, be compatible with advocating a causal theory of intentionality. We could be old-style identity theorists or modern functionalists or unregenerate dualists. We could even be complete agnostics about the embodiment relation and yet claim to have naturalized content causally. Our task is simply to specify the nature of the intentional relation – and it looks like we can do that thing without specifying the nature of the mental relatum of that relation. So, at any rate, it is tempting to imagine.

But I do not think this separation of tasks is feasible either. A fully naturalistic theory of intentionality is possible only if we can also naturalize embodiment. Let us consider causal naturalism about intentionality combined with (say) Cartesian immaterialism with respect to the conscious bearers of intentionality. Can we really maintain that the naturalistic credentials of the former theory are unaffected by the blatant non-naturalism of the latter theory? If we can, then certainly we can completely solve the intentionality problem without solving the embodiment problem. And so any insolubilities attaching to the latter problem will not impugn the naturalism claimed for our answer to the former problem. Intentionality itself is as natural as you could wish; it is just the bearers of intentionality that elude the naturalist's net. What I shall argue,

---

[9] An internalist theory of embodiment will be inadequate if externalism is the correct view of intentionality: so we need to examine that latter question if we are to have any chance of getting the right answer to the former question. The nature of the embodiment of intentional states depends upon (includes) the nature of intentionality itself.

however, is that causal (and allied) theories of intentionality cannot be insulated in this way: their claims to naturalism critically depend upon whether the relata of the invoked causal relations can themselves be naturalized. Even if necessary and sufficient conditions for intentionality can be provided in causal terms, this will not count as a properly naturalistic theory unless the conscious bearers of these causal relations can also be viewed naturalistically. You cannot then be a Cartesian dualist (say) *and* a causal naturalist about content.[10]

It might be thought that this contention of mine is trivially true, since plainly your overall theory will not rate as naturalistic if one component of it does not. But I do not intend here to be making the trivial point that your total theory of the intentional cannot be naturalistic if the ontology of the theory is not: for this is compatible with supposing that the intentional relation *itself* has been fully explained naturalistically. Surely a relation can be inherently natural even though (some of) the entities that satisfy it are not (a ghost may stand next to a tree.) Is not causality just such a relation? Well, no, I do not think it is. What I want to claim is that causal relations *themselves* cannot be regarded as natural unless their *terms* are also agreed to be natural. It is not just the Cartesian's wayward ontology that flouts naturalism; his causal ideology also fails to pass naturalistic muster. My slogan is: CAUSAL RELATIONS ARE ONLY AS NATURAL AS THE TERMS THEY RELATE. The notion of causality is not, as it were, natural in itself: *it* will be spooky in proportion as its terms are. Occult entities breed (and need) occult causation. And occult causation is no comfort to a would-be naturalist. When the terms of the causal relation are straightforwardly physical, then we can regard the causality as mediated by natural physical forces and mechanisms – impact, energy transfer, etc. We know the laws and mechanisms that sustain such an assertion of causality, or at least of their existence. But we cannot think in such homely nomological terms when the relata are not physical. And when they are frankly *im*material a claim of causality cannot be cashed out in this way. The felt naturalism of causality then begins

[10] I cannot cite a causal theorist of intentionality who disagrees with this claim, since the issue is never raised in this form. Materialism (including functionalism) tends to be the assumed background position, which makes the question academic for these theorists. My thesis is that this assumed position is mandatory (as well as unearned: I am taking it, remember, that all such theories of consciousness are radically inadequate).

to wobble and crack; there is a whiff of the occult on the wind. The notion of causality itself is topic-neutral and so does not (analytically) entail anything about the intrinsic nature of what it is claimed to relate; and it is this nature that determines whether the claimed causality can be regarded as spooky or natural, mysterious or explicable. Alleged causal relations between God and his works, or between material and immaterial substances, or between abstract entities and human minds – these are not in themselves natural relations, precisely because their terms are not. If there were such entities, and such causal relations, then we should have to say, not only that there are some mysterious things in the world, but also that there are some funny kinds of causation around, some strange ways in which one thing can influence another. Accordingly, if someone boasts causal naturalism in some area, we have a right to ask whether the causally operative entities invoked meet naturalistic scruples, and to pooh-pooh the boasted naturalism if they do not. Indeed, mystery can be heightened by asserting causal relations between things whose entitlement to such relations is suspect (hence Descartes' problem of mind-body interaction). It is not quite that causation is guilty until proven innocent, but its innocence depends upon the company it keeps. And the reason for this is that we do not regard an assertion of causality as naturalistic unless some account of the mechanism or process of causation is forthcoming or at least in the offing – as it is in ordinary physical cases. This is, of course, why telepathy strikes us as unintelligible, occult. Telepathy is not rendered natural merely by asserting that it is analysable as a causal relation between minds, a relation which is not mediated by any of the known forces of nature. Likewise intentionality is not rendered natural merely by asserting that it is analysable as a causal relation between conscious states and conditions in the world; for we want to know what *kind* of causation is at issue here, how it works. If it turns out that the terms of this causal relation are naturalistically suspect, then intentionality itself will not have been successfully naturalized. The naturalism needs to go all the way down. It follows that we cannot simply leave open the question whether conscious states are themselves natural and hope to naturalize the relation of intentionality; the embodiment problem cannot be left hanging. To put the point differently: psychophysical causation counts as kosher only if psychological events are themselves kosher.[11]

Of course, it is typically simply assumed, in the usual causal accounts of intentionality, that the mental term of the relation is something like a physical state of the organism – a neural state or a symbol in the language of thought (conceived as the 'shape' of a neural state).[12] This assumption is what enables the theorist to regard the causal relations he proposes as scrupulously natural: they link one kind of physical thing (an object in the world) to another (a state of the organism's nervous system). Here we know, or can conjecture, the nature of the mediating mechanism, and we feel no sense of mystery about the claim of causal connexion. We understand well enough how the physical states of one thing can change the physical states of another – how, say, an object's being square could make a neural firing occur in the brain. There is nothing occult about this kind of causal claim. But the crucial point is that this assumption is compulsory if the causal theory of intentionality is to meet naturalistic scruples; it is not optional. An assumed, or unspoken, materialism about intentional states is what makes causal naturalism about intentionality fly. It is an illusion of reason to suppose that the causal relation can be counted on to preserve its naturalness when extended beyond this realm. We cannot simply detach the causal part of the overall theory and expect to leave its naturalness intact, irrespective of the naturalistic status of the entities said to be causally related. That would be like extending a causal theory of action from human beings to angels and then claiming the latter application to be just as naturalistic as the former – despite the fact that we have no coherent idea of the mechanism or realization of such causation for the case of angels. A causal theory of action, linking reasons with bodily movements, is only naturalistic to the extent that reasons and bodily movements are. But in the case of angels these items (or their heavenly counter-

[11] This point applies equally to 'out-in' causation, as in perception, and to 'in-out' causation, as in action. So causal theories of intentional action are not naturalistic unless the causative mental events and states are themselves in the clear naturalistically. No theory invoking psychophysical causation can in good conscience count itself naturalistic until it can clear such causation of the charge of theoretical inscrutability. Such causation has itself to be naturalized before it can serve to naturalize anything else. By what standard is psychophysical interaction between cerebral and conscious events more prima facie naturalistic than intentionality?
[12] See Fodor, *Psychosemantics*.

parts) are not naturalistic; neither then is the causation that alleged-ly connects them. Causation becomes spooky just at the point that its terms do. A naturalistic causal theory of action presupposes a prior naturalism about reasons and their outlying effects. Only with that securely in place can we satisfy ourselves that we understand the nature of the causal relation we have invoked. Billiard-ball causation is limited to the case of billiard balls and their ilk: you do not get the same kind of causation if you replace the billiard balls with less comprehensible entities.

If this is right, as a general metaphysical thesis about causation, then we can apply the same principle to the causal theory of intentionality. According to that theory, external events cause con-scious events to have certain representational features, and these features contribute towards the phenomenal properties of the con-scious events. So the causal relations in question span the physical/phenomenal divide; they connect conscious states, qua conscious states, to external states of affairs. But then these relations can only be naturalistic to the extent that consciousness itself is. We there-fore need to solve the embodiment problem if we are to make good on our naturalistic aspirations with respect to intentionality. If we need God to account for embodiment, then we shall also have need of Him to make sense of intentionality. That is, we shall not be able to make sense of intentionality. And this is so no matter how refined and watertight our causal analysis of intentionality might be.

The argument just given is couched specifically in terms of causa-tion, but the conclusion I am after is meant to apply to any would-be naturalistic theory of intentionality. This thesis can only be proposed as a conjecture, on account of its unrestricted scope, but I think it is a plausible conjecture if what I have said so far is correct. Consider teleological theories, the main naturalistic rival to causal-cum-nomological theories.[13] Teleological theorists hold that content is constitutively dependent upon the world-directed function of a state of the organism. Again, it is typically assumed by such theor-ists that the state with the function in question is itself naturalisti-cally acceptable – a state of the nervous system, presumably. Then

---

[13] See Ruth Millikan, *Language, Thought and Other Biological Categories* (The MIT Press: Cambridge, Mass., 1984); Colin McGinn, *Mental Content* (Basil Blackwell: Oxford, 1989).

ascribing a biological function to that state will not take us outside the realm of the natural. This assumption is what enables the teleological theorist to provide at least a sketch of the mechanism of the function, the kind of physical basis it has. Saying that the heart has the function of pumping blood is naturalistic because the heart itself is, and the notion of function does not itself import anything non-natural. Similarly, if it is the function of a brain state to produce behaviour suitable to a certain environmental stimulus, and this brain state is then identified with a given perceptual state, then too we shall have some conception of how this function might be discharged. But matters take a mysterious turn when this kind of assumption is not made: for we do not know how to conceive of functions allegedly possessed by non-natural entities such as immaterial substances. How is the function in question discharged by a device in the immaterial substance? How does such a substance come to have biological functions in the first place? What kind of raw material is natural selection operating on here? Is not this biological vitalism in another guise? Having a function is a naturalistic property only to the extent that the bearer of the function is itself naturalistic, since only then do we have any idea of what the basis of the function is like, what implements it. My slogan is: FUNCTIONS ARE ONLY AS NATURAL AS THEIR BEARERS. The notion of function, like the notion of causation, is topic-neutral, and so its entitlement to naturalistic status depends upon that of its topic – upon what has it. We cannot legitimately focus on an unproblematic paradigm of biological function, say the function of the heart, and then lift the notion out of this context and hope to make it stand up in application to entities that are not similarly natural. An immaterial substance, if it possesses a function, does not possess a function in the *way* physical organs of the body do. To assert that it has a biological function is to say something mysterious – until it has been explained *how* it does. A reduction of intentionality to functional properties of an immaterial substance is no great coup for naturalism, since the mystery has now been shifted to the reductive basis. Teleological naturalism about intentionality therefore presupposes a naturalistic solution to the embodiment problem.[14]

---

[14] Is what I am saying here just crashingly obvious? I think it should be, on reflection. But it is not trivial, because of its philosophical charge. And it starts to bite once the embodiment problem has been despaired of.

So far as I can see similar considerations are likely to apply to any other candidate theory of intentionality. The analysing relations are going to have to be abstract enough to prescind from the specific physical forces and mechanisms that underlie the usual sorts of causal relations between organisms and their environments. But then those abstract relations will qualify as natural only to the extent that their relata do. It is difficult to see how a putative analysing relation could be both (a) of the right generality to capture intentionality in all its various manifestations and (b) intrinsically natural in the sense that it counts indisputably as natural no matter how spooky its terms turn out to be. Either the relation will be only derivatively natural or it will be too specific to co-extend with the relation of intentionality. Relations like 'colliding with' or 'reflecting light from' are presumably intrinsically natural in this sense – they *entail* the naturalness of their terms, indeed their materiality – but they are scarcely of the right breadth or type to provide necessary and sufficient conditions for intentionality. Whereas the kinds of relations that seem at least potential candidates for analysing intentionality, on the score of their abstractness and generality, seem to be dependently natural relations at best. They need to be topic-neutral to cover the ground, but if they are their naturalism will devolve upon that of the entities they relate. In other words, no analysis of the intentional relation can directly entail that conscious states are straightforwardly physical; but then the naturalistic status of the analysis will turn upon that of the conscious states themselves. No natural intentionality without natural embodiment. We cannot understand how conscious states reach out to the world until we understand how they reach down to the brain.

To ask whether the concepts of causation or function are natural or non-natural is like asking whether the concepts of identity or the part-whole relation are natural or non-natural: the answer wholly depends upon what kinds of entities are taken to stand in these relations. These are all relations that do not take you outside the realm of the natural once you are in it, but they do not guarantee that that is where you are to start with. Using them in philosophical theories, however successfully, is not therefore an automatic stamp of naturalistic approval. Their very topic-neutrality ensures that they are conservative with respect to naturalness or its opposite. Naturalism needs to proceed from the ground up if it is to have a safe foundation. And it must surely seem odd, from an historical perspective, to take it for granted that psychophysical causation, in particular, is in the naturalistic clear, since it has traditionally been regarded as one the greatest of metaphysical puzzles. If we were convinced that states of consciousness were natural products of brain activity, and we could see how they were, so that no mystery attached to their apparent dependence upon the brain, then indeed causal or teleological theories would qualify as naturalistic accounts of the intentional relation. But *only* if this embodiment can be made naturally intelligible do such theories deliver genuine naturalism about intentionality. So: we can solve the problem of intentionality only if we can solve the problem of embodiment. And if it turns out that we cannot solve that latter problem, then clearly we shall be frustrated in our efforts to solve the former problem. There is, I am afraid, no avoiding the problem of consciousness in the theory of content or meaning.[15]

What is it that we should need to know in order to have an answer to the problem of embodiment? What is the location of our ignorance here? This is the same as the question, what should we need to know in order to complete the project of naturalizing intentionality? Some property of the world -- call it property P -- is responsible for the capacity of matter to form the basis of consciousness, or for the capacity of consciousness to take its rise from matter.[16] P is what makes consciousness an intelligible product of brain activity. It does for consciousness and the brain what gravity does for the planets and their orbits, or what kinetic energy does for molecules and the behaviour of the gases they compose, or what the structure of DNA does for parents and their progeny. P is that property,

[15] There is a sense, then, in which the mind–body problem is prior to the problem of meaning: we shall only know how meaning is possible, what its nature is, when we know how the bearers of meaning (ultimately mental states) are possible, what their nature is. We can only give a fully explanatory theory of meaning if we can provide an explanatory theory of consciousness. Meaning things is (part of) what consciousness does, and we shall not know how it does this until we know its nature – in particular, how it relates to the physical world. The theory of meaning cannot then be philosophically prior to the theory of mind. The former theory will eventually run aground on a mystery unless it can call upon an account of consciousness that resolves its problematic status. Philosophy of mind is thus more basic than philosophy of language. We can only take the linguistic turn once we have cleared consciousness out of our path.

[16] Property P makes its appearance in ch. 1, where more is said about what we can and cannot say about it.

whatever it is, currently unknown, that would remove the mystery of consciousness were it to become apparent to us. Now my question is: Where is P instantiated? Where would we need to look in order to light upon P? About what would knowledge of P enlighten us? The answer I want to propose to that question is this: P is a property of the hidden structure of consciousness. What we should need to know in order to understand embodiment is this hidden structure. Not knowing this structure is what leads to our explanatory problems, and hence to our metaphysical perplexities. However, this proposal will need some explaining.

The problem of embodiment is essentially the same as the problem of emergence, seen the other way on.[17] To ask how consciousness can be embodied in the brain is another way of asking how consciousness can emerge from the brain. These two formulations of the problem invite different strategies for trying to solve it, however. We can try a bottom-up strategy: here we seek properties of the brain from which it follows that brain activity can support consciousness. We look for property P in the nature of the brain, hoping then to derive consciousness from this property as an emergent characteristic. We work up from the physical foundation, with consciousness the emergent end-product of our investigation, its final destination. Or we can try a top-down strategy: here we seek properties of consciousness from which it follows that consciousness can be supported by brain activity. We look for property P in the nature of consciousness, hoping then to understand how consciousness can rest upon a physical foundation. We work down to the underlying physical parameters, with consciousness as our point of departure, what guides our enquiry. We want to know what consciousness is such that it can be physically embodied. Proceeding from the bottom up our aim is to remedy our ignorance concerning the properties of the brain; proceeding from the top down our aim is to remedy our ignorance concerning the properties of consciousness. The location of P looks different according to which strategy we pursue. Is it the brain that has an undisclosed aspect or is it consciousness?

Now although these two strategies differ in the manner of their

[17] On the problem of emergence, see Thomas Nagel, 'Panpsychism', in *Mortal Questions* (Cambridge University Press: Cambridge, 1979).

execution, there is a clear sense in which they are equivalent: for whatever we discover from one direction must also hold from the other direction. They must yield essentially the same (metaphysical) result. The property P that explains emergence (bottom up) must *be* the property that explains embodiment (top down). That is to say, P must be a property both of the brain and of consciousness, since its role is to link the one to the other. Strictly speaking, P is a relational property (call it R if you prefer). It is the methods we adopt to identify this property that differ. Heuristically, then, we can distinguish the two strategies, though their metaphysical upshot is much the same. And this upshot, I want to suggest, is that consciousness possesses a hidden structure. The unknown explanatory property P is a property of the hidden structure of consciousness – however we discover this property.[18]

In pursuing the two strategies, different cognitive faculties will be centrally employed in the effort to identify P. The bottom-up strategy will rely upon *perception* of the brain and associated reasoning about what is perceived, since this is how we empirically investigate the nature of the brain. We receive sensory inputs by directing our senses onto the brain as a physical object in space, and then we use our theoretical faculty to reason about what is received. In this way we form a conception of the kind of thing the brain is. It is, thus, a perception-based conception. The top-down strategy, on the other hand, will rely primarily upon *introspection* of consciousness and associated reasoning about what is introspected, since this is our most direct access to the nature of consciousness. What has to be embodied is just the object of introspection, of self-awareness, and our conception of this object is chiefly shaped by the manner in which it presents itself to us inwardly. It is, thus, an introspection-

---

[18]   I shall not fuss over distinctions of type and token, event and state, process and property. I use 'consciousness' to cover all these, rather as I use 'matter' in an analogous way. I do mean to claim that the instantiation of conscious properties involves hidden structure, and not merely that conscious particulars have hidden structure – just as I should say the same about material properties, e.g. being magnetic. The hidden structure of conscious tokens has everything to do with their being of the conscious types they are. Logically, 'consciousness' is a stuff term, as 'matter' is; and I see nothing wrong, metaphysically, with recognizing that consciousness *is* a kind of stuff. At any rate, I shall persist with the intuitive use of the term 'consciousness' without fretting unduly over its proper interpretation. I am sure my claims could be reformulated in the more stilted idiom that has grown up around recent discussions of the mind–body problem. (I think, in fact, that we have become rather obsessed with the distinctions made in this idiom and have lost sight of some of the deeper problems.)

based conception.[19] The success of these methods of investigation will then be constrained by the capacity of the faculties concerned to reveal the full nature of their objects. Notice (what is obvious) that we cannot combine faculties and strategies in the opposite way: we cannot try to work up from the brain to consciousness by introspecting the nature of the brain; and we cannot try to work down from consciousness to the brain by perceiving the nature of consciousness. The brain is not (as such) a potential object of introspection, and consciousness is not (as such) a potential object of perception. Perhaps if we could do these impossible things we would be in a better position to bridge the gulf that separates our conception of one side from our conception of the other: we could juxtapose one perception-based conception with another, or one introspection-based conception with another, instead of having to compare conceptions derived from very different faculties. But we cannot, so we have to live with the conceptions we can obtain, however inadequate and incomplete they may be. We have to accept that our given faculties of apprehension shape the kinds of conception we can form of the brain and of consciousness.

Let us say that these two faculties – sense perception and intro-spection – have different *fields*, meaning by this that they take different kinds of object of apprehension. They are used to detect different regions of reality. They are sensitive to different kinds of property that the world may instantiate. (Alternatively, if we want to make room for some kind of monism, we can say that they present the same reality in different *ways*, from different per-spectives.) Then we can say that the two strategies for solving the embodiment problem, bottom-up and top-down, are geared to dis-joint fields – the fields of perception and introspection, respectively. They are field-specific. Combining them consists in trying to coor-dinate the fields of two different kinds of cognitive faculty. And the two strategies will be successful only in so far as their respective

---

[19] Consciousness is not only presented to us introspectively, of course; we also judge its lurking presence in other creatures, as it is evinced in their behaviour. However, I do think – for reasons I cannot enter into here – that introspective access plays the dominant role in moulding our conception of consciousness: we really do know it best 'from our own case'. We primarily conceive of it as 'that which is known introspectively by its subject'. I doubt, though, that anything I have to say about its hidden structure requires this thesis of the primacy of first-person knowledge in shaping the way we ordinarily think about conscious-ness.

fields somehow yield the property that constitutes embodiment or emergence, namely P. Clearly, then, our prospects of identifying P by adopting one or both of these strategies depend critically upon the scope or extent of those fields (combined with a general reasoning capacity). Do they, in particular, encompass the full nature of the entities towards which the associated faculties are directed? Do the fields exhaust the objects?

Suppose that the fields of the perceptual and introspective faculties somehow fell short of revealing the full nature of the brain or of consciousness, even when conjoined with the general capacity to reason and generate theoretical explanations. Suppose too that these two strategies exhaust our options: we have no other faculty whose field includes what these do not. Then we should simply not be able to solve the embodiment problem: P would systematically elude us. If our perception of the brain did not reveal its full nature – in particular, that aspect of its nature that makes it capable of being the basis of consciousness – then the bottom-up strategy could not work; for the right explanatory property would lie outside of the field of perception (and associated inferential capacities). And if introspecting consciousness did not reveal *its* full nature – in particular, that aspect of its nature that makes it capable of being embodied in a physical system like the brain – then the top-down strategy could not work either; for, again, the right explanatory property would lie outside of the field of introspection (plus inference). In short, we can identify the explanatory P only to the extent that these two faculties have the power (conjoined with a general reasoning capacity) to reveal the full and authentic nature of their objects. For if they do not, then the solution to the mind–body problem will be in principle closed to us. To solve the problem, we have to assume that our faculties of apprehension possess fields that can encompass the explanatory property that does the job. We have to assume that they are *suited* to solving the problem. Their distinctive *modus operandi* must 'fit' the problem. It is not going to be a necessary truth that they do so fit. In fact, I incline to the view that it is a necessary truth that they do not: the faculties are mismatched to the problem.

Now it is not my aim here to argue for this strong closure thesis.[20] I want to make a more modest suggestion: that the field of

[20] I argue for it in ch. 1.

the introspective faculty does not reveal the full nature of consciousness, and that property P lies in the hidden region. That is, embodiment hinges upon a property of the hidden nature of consciousness: consciousness as we apprehend it inwardly can be embodied (or embedded) in the brain only because it has a hidden reality. Accordingly, a top-down strategy founded on introspection alone will not succeed in uncovering P. The key to the embodiment of consciousness lies in its hidden structure, but this structure (by definition) is not accessible to introspection. The field of introspection is thus highly restricted with respect to the entire extent of consciousness. Introspection is confined to the surface of consciousness, as it were, but the secret of embodiment is not legible from the surface. One would have to decipher the deep structure of consciousness in order to understand how it can spring in all its vivid glory from the monochrome convolutions of the cerebral cortex. Introspection does not get one past the outermost vestibule of consciousness.

Is this a possible position? Is there anything about consciousness that positively precludes it? It might seem at first glance that it is not a possible position, because of the special epistemic powers of introspection. Surely, it will be said, introspection provides a uniquely accurate and reliable way of coming to know the properties of consciousness; consciousness is transparent to introspection, self-intimating, infallibly known. The introspective window onto consciousness is singularly clean and undistorting (we can always see the pain through the pane). It lets the truth through far more clearly than the perceptual window, with its illusions, defects, obstacles of size and distance. How then could introspection be as purblind as I am suggesting?

Let me make it clear that I am not contesting these claims about the special epistemic powers of introspection; I am not advocating some kind of anti-Cartesian fallibilism about our ordinary self-ascriptive judgements. What I am claiming is that the properties of consciousness that are so ascribable do not exhaust the properties consciousness has. We can therefore accept the premises of the above argument against hidden structure, but deny that the conclusion follows. For omniscience does not follow from inerrancy, nor from self-intimation of a subset of an object's properties. Suppose we allow that introspection is epistemically perfect within its field: if it tells you that you have a certain conscious state, then you always do; and if you have a conscious state, then introspection will never let you overlook the fact. Is it entailed that introspection reveals the *whole* nature of consciousness to you? Not at all, because introspection may be epistemically perfect only with respect to the surface of consciousness, i.e. with respect to only some of its properties. Take an entity X and a faculty F. F may be inerrant and exhaustive with respect to a subset S of the properties of X and yet be quite incapable of detecting other properties of X – however intrinsic or essential or naturally basic those further properties might be. It is a mistake to generalize from the privileged epistemic status of some of an object's properties to the claim that nothing about it is hidden. From the fact that introspection is remarkably good at detecting some of the properties of consciousness it by no means follows that it is omniscient with respect to the properties of consciousness. And there may be good theoretical reasons to postulate properties of consciousness that fall outside the reach of introspection, despite the natural intimacy of their relation to introspectable properties. It is consistent to hold that introspection tells us infallibly whether consciousness instantiates a certain range of properties and yet tells us nothing *at all* about other sorts of properties it instantiates – not even a hint. I take it that, once spelled out, this point is searingly obvious (and not unfamiliar). Yet I suspect that the fallacious inference in question is one that has been quite influential, at least subliminally, in keeping the idea of a hidden structure to consciousness theoretically unavailable. Bedazzled by the immediacy of consciousness, we are prone to overlook the possibility that there is more to it than what is immediately given – even though there could not *be* the given without the hidden to support it.

Perhaps, too, we are influenced by the difficulty of applying a certain model of partiality of access to the case of consciousness and introspection. I mean that provided by the perception of material objects in space. For our thought about this latter kind of access is shot through with the idea that its objects have unobservable aspects – back sides, occluded interiors, distant parts. We know very well what it is about material objects, and our perception of them, that makes omniscience a pipe-dream, a prerogative of God alone: spatial perspective, roughly speaking. But this general conception of what makes an object of apprehension only partially given does not carry over to the case of consciousness, as we ordinarily understand it. The spatial preconditions for its application do not obtain. We cannot go around a conscious state to get a better look at it, nor can we come in closer, or open it up. We have no clear conception of what it would be for a conscious state to have an unobservable side or part or inside, since we cannot model this (literally) on the case of material objects. Our most familiar paradigm of the hidden does not fit the case of consciousness. We therefore have no ready explanation to hand of what the hiddenness of consciousness might consist in or arise from, and so we are apt to overlook the possibility that a proportion of it might be hidden. Without a picture of the source of our ignorance we naturally suppose there is nothing there to be ignorant about.

But this diagnosis, though it may account for the absence of the idea of a hidden structure from the intellectual landscape, does not, I think, justify that absence. For why *should* the hiddenness of something as (apparently) different from material objects as consciousness is be modelled on the hiddenness of such objects? Why must the hidden be hidden in *that* way? We would look askance at any dogmatic attempt to model the unknown properties of numbers on the case of material objects, these being such different kinds of object; so too we should resist the urge to try to force consciousness into this mould. The point about the hidden aspects of conscious states is that they are not even potential candidates for introspective access – unlike the standard unseen aspects of material objects in relation to perception. But this is not a good reason to deny the existence of these hidden aspects, so long as they perform an indispensable theoretical role. We should not reject hidden conscious structure simply because this structure is not going to mimic the back side of a perceived object or its internal composition. When it comes to consciousness we need to break radically away from this kind of picture. Clinging to it reduces our theoretical options, by hiding the possibility of the hidden.[21]

---

[21] The hidden structure of physical natural kinds typically consists in an arrangement of microscopic or occluded parts. Here we know what it would take to lay the concealed structure bare. But this seems the wrong sort of model to apply to the covert structure of consciousness; so we are less apt to accept the hypothesis of such a structure. We have no clear model of the *source* of the hiddenness. But this should not make us deny the applicability of the idea – which is (definitionally) epistemic in character, and neutral on the metaphysical basis of the hiddenness in question. Compare the case of the hidden structure of meanings or propositions, discussed in ch. 4.

In fact, when you think about it, there appears to be an inverse correlation between the scope of a faculty and its reliability within its field: the narrower the scope, the less prone to error; the more extensive the scope, the more likely to slip up. My introspective faculty tells me about the states of only one object, namely myself, and it confines itself to my mental properties. My perceptual faculties tell me about the states of indefinitely many objects, and they are sensitive to a wide range of properties of those objects. My theoretical faculties vastly extend my ability to come to know truths about the world, taking in the past, the future, the astronomical, the microscopic, the unperceivable. From introspection to perception to theory: exponential epistemic expansion. But if we rank these faculties according to reliability within their fields the ordering goes the other way. Introspection is the most reliable; perception comes second; theoretical inference trails a poor third. Of course, this ordering is rough and unqualified, but it is suggestive: the more you attempt, the more likely you are to fail; the further you reach, the more likely you are to come away empty-handed. Design a device to track more remote traits of the world and you risk falling into error. Introspection may, then, purchase its impressive reliability precisely by playing epistemically safe: it does not venture beyond the surface of consciousness. Its remarkable powers within its narrow domain may then be a reason (though not a conclusive one!) to suspect that it leaves much of that domain unexplored. Going nowhere boldly it leaves its object largely unrevealed. Equipping it with the power to plumb the depths of consciousness might undermine its capacity to report upon the surface, epistemic faculties being what they are – trade–offs between scope and accuracy.

However this speculation may be, the point to keep firmly in mind is simply that from the plain visibility of an iceberg's tip we cannot infer that no part of it is submerged beneath the water line. The thesis of the hidden nature of consciousness is thus quite compatible with granting introspection its traditional epistemic privileges. It is just that those privileges do not extend to every nook and cranny of consciousness. They do not gain you entry to the basement, where the foundation stones are laid.

But what positive reason is there to suppose that introspection has a sharply limited view of its object? Is there anything about introspection as a cognitive faculty to encourage the idea that its coverage of consciousness falls short of the full reality? How power-ful a faculty is it? What are its areas of weakness?

I have already introduced one good reason for doubting the powers of introspection: namely, that consciousness needs some property capable of linking it to the brain, and this property is evidently not accessible to introspection. There must be something about the nature of consciousness that makes it possible for it to emerge from, and interact with, the material world, but intro-spection is not the place to look for that something. If anything, introspection biases us away from this explanatory aspect of con-sciousness, inciting us to believe in miracles. It makes consciousness seem irredeemably removed from the physical world, joined to it only by some supernatural (and disturbingly frangible) adhesive. Introspection seems a very poor guide to understanding how con-scious states mesh with the physical world; quite clueless, in fact, if not downright deceitful. Indirectly, then, we have good theoretical reason for supposing that some properties of consciousness lie on the blind side of the introspective field. Introspection has a blind-spot just where consciousness makes its link with the brain. The chief obstacle to gaining the right perspective on the mind–body problem, then, is a dogmatic insistence on the omniscience of intro-spection. Looked at sideways, as it were, from a standpoint un-occupiable by introspection, consciousness can be seen to have its roots planted firmly in the furrows of the brain. But we shall not recognize the possibility of this if we insist that there is no other perspective on consciousness than that of introspection (and, I should add, our ordinary third-person perspective).[22]

It might be suggested that there is another, less extravagant, explanation of our difficulty. This is that it is not the hidden nature of consciousness that solves the mind–body problem (*de re*, so to

[22] Insisting that the only true perspective on consciousness is through introspection (or ordinary behavioural criteria) is the analogue of holding that unaided perception reveals the only true aspect of material bodies. Refusing to look at bodies through a microscope, or to engage in a bit of theory, is rightly seen as dogmatic and blinkered; while denying that consciousness has any aspect that is not given to introspection (or ordinary third-person ascription) is not apt invite the same charge. There is even a tendency to *define* consciousness as what is introspectable by the subject, thus enshrining idealism about consciousness in its very definition ('to be is to be introspectable'). But we should distinguish *what* is introspected from the introspecting of it, and thus allow that introspection might reveal only one aspect of its object. The side elevation, whether or not we can occupy it, might well exhibit some elaborate cantilevering and joists, not apparent from the introspective standpoint. It might be a lot more complex than it seems (or perhaps a lot simpler: see ch. 1).

speak) but the hidden nature of the brain. The full intrinsic nature of consciousness *is* revealed to introspection; it is rather some essential feature of the brain that is hidden from our (theory-aided) perception of it. If we knew this bottom-up property of the brain, then all would fall into place, without the need for any further knowledge of the nature of consciousness. Matter is what harbours a hidden structure, empowering it to generate consciousness, but consciousness itself is all on the surface. Introspection is thus omniscient about its object: it is our perception-based conception of material objects that is afflicted with blindspots.

It seems to me, however, that this description of our predicament is on the wrong lines, for two reasons. The first reason goes back to something I said earlier: namely, that the proposed alternative explanation is at bottom equivalent to my own suggestion. For suppose we were to discover the fugitive property of the brain that undergirds consciousness. For the sake of concreteness, let it be protomentality as a panpsychist understands this idea. This property would have to connect brain activity in some intelligible way to consciousness. But then it would have to be a property of consciousness: what enables consciousness to emerge from the brain is the same as what allows consciousness to be embodied by the brain. Consciousness would have a protomental hidden structure – that constituted by the particular configuration of protomental properties instantiated by the brain from which it emerges. The property P has to face in both directions; it cannot be a property of the brain and *not* a property of consciousness. Perhaps it will be said that P is, strictly, extrinsic to consciousness, and so not really an aspect of *its* essential nature. But this cannot be right, since if it is thus extrinsic it will not connect consciousness *internally* to the brain: consciousness will still dangle free, failing to be caught in the grip of P. No, P must be intrinsic to consciousness; it must link the very nature of consciousness to its physical basis. Functionalists claim that the causal role of brain states is what sustains embodiment: this is the property of the brain that supplies the link to consciousness. But they also hold – what indeed follows – that causal role constitutes the nature or essence of conscious states. Only because conscious states are held to be defined in terms of causal role can functionalists assert that this is the right property of the brain to provide the necessary link. They are thus rightly committed to a thesis about the nature of consciousness itself. And I think that any proposal as to the identity of P must take this form. It is thus hard to see how the appropriate brain property could fail to count as (part of) the intrinsic nature of consciousness. The property of the brain that explains the emergence of consciousness must be an aspect of the nature of that which emerges. It cannot be a mere correlate.

The second reason for locating P in the hidden structure of consciousness, and not merely in the brain, is this: it is consciousness that cries out for naturalistic explanation, not cerebral matter. Consciousness is the anomalous thing, the thing that tests our naturalistic view of the world. It is what threatens to import immaterial substances, occult forces, weird properties that cannot be instantiated by physical objects. The grey matter of the brain seems mundane by comparison. Consciousness needs to have a nature that renders it incorporable into a world whose fundamental constituents are physical particles and the forces that govern them. Property P (by definition) is what does that; so it had better pertain to the very nature of consciousness. It cannot lie outside of consciousness, on pain of condemning consciousness to inherent inexplicability. The stigma of the occult must be removed from consciousness, and P can do this only if it allowed to penetrate to its heart. Consciousness craves a non-mysterious essence. There must be something about consciousness itself, and not merely its physical basis, that enables it to arise from, and have commerce with, the world of material things. This enabling property is also, of course, an aspect of the brain, and hence of a certain agglomeration of matter; but it is consciousness that has most need of it, consciousness that cannot live without it. It follows that introspection does not disclose the full nature of consciousness.

But what is it about the introspective faculty itself, considered as a method of discovering truths, that makes it as circumscribed as I am suggesting? Do we have independent reason to suspect that introspection casts a narrow beam? Is its incapacity to illuminate the full nature of consciousness predictable in the light of its other limitations? I shall now cite a number of respects in which introspection can be seen to be a rather unimpressive and feeble capacity for discovering truths. Its field is narrow indeed. It tells us precious little about conscious events and their place in the world. These

lamentable limitations should soften us up for the idea that introspection does not even reveal certain aspects of the intrinsic nature
of our own states of consciousness.

The first, and most obvious, respect in which the field of introspection is severely restricted is just this: my introspective faculty
can only be directed onto *my* mental states; it does not extend to
yours. Each person can take his or her own mental states as objects
of introspection but he or she cannot take other people's mental
states as such objects. Concepts deployed in introspective judgements, and knowledge so gained, can apply only to that small range
of mental states possessed by the subject himself. Here the 'inner
sense' differs significantly from the 'outer senses': for no other sense
is such that there is only *one* object in the world whose states it is
sensitive to, that object being identical with the subject whose inner
sense it is. My inner sense is confined to the states of a unique
object: me myself. It is quite blind with respect to the mental states
of other objects: you, her, the dog over there. I can see my own
body, touch it, hear it, taste it, smell it, and I can do the same with
yours, as well as with many other bodies, animate and inanimate;
but I cannot introspect your pain or your thought or your mood.
I can, it is true, come to know these things about you by other
means, namely by perception of your body, but what I cannot do is
register them by means of the faculty by which I register them in
myself. If I want to know your mental states, then I have to switch
faculties: I have to stop introspecting and start perceiving. My
introspective faculty is quite useless to me when it comes to detecting the mental states of people other than myself (this can be
frustrating at times, as we all know). Other people instantiate the
same kinds of mental properties as I do, but I cannot get at those
properties when they instantiate them in the way I get at them when
I do. Same properties instantiated, but entirely different faculties
called for. The field of my inner sense is thus confined to a very
small subset of all the mental states there are in the world. It will
not help me in the slightest when it comes to making psychological
judgements about the vast majority of centres of consciousness. So
far as introspection is concerned, we are all solipsists, however
reluctantly. Only perception can release us from the solipsism built
into introspection. If we had only introspection, we should have to
be practical solipsists, since we should then have no means of

making psychological ascriptions to others, despite the plethora of minds all around us. We can say, then, that introspection is *closed* with respect to the minds of others. Seen from the right perspective, this obvious and familiar truth ought to strike us as a significant fact about the introspective faculty. It shows how narrowly the beam of introspection falls, what a truncated faculty it is. By comparison, the outer senses are untrammelled in their scope. The boundary condition of introspection is co-terminus with the boundary of the subject.[23]

Second, there is a tight restriction on the kinds of mental concept that can be wielded by means of inner sense, and hence a tight restriction on the kinds of mental concept we can have. In brief the restriction amounts to this: you cannot acquire mental concepts for conscious states you do not yourself enjoy. This restriction stands in marked contrast to the conditions governing your possession of physical concepts: here there is no requirement that she who possesses the concept should also instantiate it. Concepts deployed in perceptual judgements about objects, say, are not restricted to those applying to the subject making the judgement. But, according to the restriction, one cannot so much as form psychological judgements, potentially applicable to others, which contain concepts that do not apply to oneself. Only mental concepts we can truly self-ascribe can be ascribed by us to the minds of others. Self-instantiation is a necessary condition of other-ascription. So the mental concepts we can form are limited to those employable by us introspectively; and these, in turn, are determined by the kinds of conscious states we ourselves enjoy. Our own mental life places an upper bound on our

[23] Here there is a striking contrast with the limitations of the senses. We are familiar with the fact that some properties are proper to a given sense and are not detectable by the other senses. Thus colours are visually detectable but not detectable by the other senses: these properties are closed to those other faculties of sense. Call this kind of limitation 'property-closure', and note that it does not imply any limitation on which *objects* are open to the faculties at issue. The various senses can discover truths about the same range of objects (more or less), but there are restrictions on which properties of those objects they can register. But the introspective faculty enforces object-closure as well as property-closure: I can discover truths only about the unique object that is me by use of my introspective faculty. And this is not because only that object instantiates properties of the type proper to introspection: on the contrary, lots of other objects – other people – instantiate exactly the same kinds of property. Introspection is thus like a visual sense that in principle can only detect the colours of a single object, though there are plenty of other coloured objects all around. This makes introspection markedly different from the senses; its limitations cut much deeper than theirs. In a sense, its limitations are more *arbitrary* than theirs.

ability to form a conception of the mental life of others.[24] The introspective faculty cannot deliver up concepts that go beyond the specific character of our own form of consciousness. And this is another respect in which that faculty is impoverished relative to the full extent of consciousness. Introspection-based thought cannot take in forms of consciousness radically unlike our own; yet we know that there are such forms and we expect there to be many more than those we know about. By contrast, perception-based thought can extend to physical bodies whose properties differ radically from those of our own body. We know what a bat looks like, though we do not know what it feels like to be a bat; we can describe a bat's body, but our descriptive resources run out when we try to conceptualize its mind. We cannot form the concept of a bat's sonar experience, since we do not ourselves have such experiences (of anything like them) – just as congenitally blind people (with no visual imagery) cannot form concepts of visual experience. In neither case can the subjects introspect the kinds of experience in question, since they lack such experiences, and nothing they can introspect affords them an adequate basis to project the concept in question. If, *per impossibile*, they could introspect the content of other minds, then indeed they would be able to develop concepts applicable to those minds. But that is precisely what the introspective faculty does not permit. It does not permit what would be necessary in order to extend our conceptual repertoire outside the range of conscious phenomena in which we ourselves revel. So if you want something to blame for your ignorance concerning bat phenomenology, then I suggest you arraign your own introspective faculty. It is the only agency that gives out this kind of information about other minds, and in the case of bats it is sorely inadequate to the task. I know what it is like to be a monkey, I think, because I know introspectively what it is like to be me, and I know that I am a human being and that monkeys are psychologically very similar to human beings. But bats are (at least in one respect) very dissimilar psychologically to human beings, so my introspective knowledge of what it is like to be me (my phenomenological type) will not help me to arrive at a conception of what it is like to be them. The root of my ignorance here is the narrowness of my introspective field:

[24] See Thomas Nagel, *The View From Nowhere* (Oxford University Press: Oxford, 1986), ch. 2.

what it does not include I cannot conceive. My introspective faculty only serves me as well as it does in vouchsafing me a conception of other minds because of the contingent fact that many other minds are similar to my own. Once this condition is abrogated, its powers give out, and I find myself lacking a grasp of the mental life of others. In a possible world in which none of the minds around me were at all similar to my own the feebleness of my introspection-based conception of other minds would be only too apparent. This mode of concept-formation would be impotent in generating a conception of my fellows' mental make-up. In a sense, then, it is only an accident that it works as well as it does.[25] Inherently, it is a puny way to arrive at a conception of the conscious states of others, relying as it does upon a happy coincidence of minds (which is not to say that we have any better way at our disposal). So not only is introspection a sharply limited means of *ascribing* conscious states to subjects (my first point); it is also a far from universal basis for arriving at a *conception* of what might be so ascribed (my present point). Not terribly impressive, taken together. There is something distressingly egocentric about the introspective view of the mental world, but it is an egocentricity we can do nothing to remedy.

If each subject's introspective faculty casts a narrow beam across mental reality as a whole, then it illuminates a still smaller fraction of reality in its entirety. In particular, it tells us nothing about the physical network in which our conscious states are embedded. This network comprises two basic sorts of item: the physical correlates of our conscious states, and the physical causes and effects of our conscious states. Neither sort of physical state is susceptible to introspective access, despite the intimate relationship between such states and conscious states. Introspective data do not (by themselves) provide us with information about the condition of our nervous system. Introspection does not deal in physical concepts. If we want to find out about the physical background to our con-

[25] I mean that the coverage of other minds we achieve in our ordinary thought relies upon the contingent fact of mental similarity between ourselves and the minds around us, and this is apt to disguise the inherent egocentricity of our conception of other minds. Our conceptual self-centredness would soon become apparent if other minds did not oblige us by mimicking our own: we should then not know what it is like to be any mind other than our own. Surrounded by cyphers, we should bewail our conceptual poverty, rue the egocentricity of our method of forming mental concepts. But there would be no escape from such solipsism, since we have no other way of understanding what it is like to be anybody else. Personal relations would be even more fraught than they are now...

scious states, then we have to resort to perception of the brain, aided by theory or apparatus. But this is to admit that introspection is a faculty that can report on certain facts but cannot relate these facts to their causal background; indeed, it cannot tell us what makes the facts it reports so much as possible. Again, we have a contrast with perception: not only can we see that certain properties are instantiated, we can also see (at least typically or in principle) how they came to be instantiated. We see the spilled ink staining the paper, the blow shattering the glass, the fire burning the wood. Perception gives us access to the causal network in which a particular event or state occurs. By its means we can construct a picture of how observable events came to be. But introspection cannot tell us about the causal network in which conscious states are embedded, this being largely physical. It can, of course, tell us which other conscious events are causally involved with a given one, but these only scratch the surface – and are not relevant when the conscious event in question has no conscious cause (e.g. a perceptual experience). Events in the nervous system constitute the predominant causal background to events in consciousness, but all of that whirring causality is concealed from introspection. Introspection is thus a conspicuously impotent means for arriving at causal knowledge about its proper objects. Compared to perception of the external world, which, when combined with appropriate inferential capacities, yields rich and extensive causal knowledge about material objects, introspection must seem blinkered, myopic, tunnelvisioned. Even when supplemented with a general reasoning capacity, it cannot gain access to the most immediate causes and effects of conscious states. You have to gaze (etc.) into the nervous system to get this kind of information. You can introspect religiously from dawn till dusk and you will not figure out the physical causes of the conscious events you experience. It is worse than trying to determine how the picture on a television screen is produced simply by staring at the screen. Introspection is closed with respect to (physical) causal background. It can tell you what conscious states you have, but it is virtually speechless when it comes to saying how you got to have them.

As a consequence, it would be a bad basis on which to try to build a science of conscious events: it could provide descriptions of such events, yes, but it would go almost nowhere towards explaining how those events come about. Such a science would be hobbled by the very faculty it chose to work from. A science should explain how things happen – what the causal regularities are – but an introspection-based science of conscious events could do no such thing: it would be deaf to the underlying causal machinery. So this is one more way in which introspection is a frail instrument for studying consciousness.[26]

It is a consequence of what I have just said that a creature bereft of outer sense, equipped only with inner sense, could never arrive at the idea of the brain and its physical states and processes. Perception is indispensable to arriving at a knowledge of the brain. More exactly, introspective data alone, even when combined with a general science-forming capacity, will never lead to the kind of understanding of the physical correlates and causes of consciousness that we now have. We are familiar with the idea that fragmentary observational data can function as the basis of an elaborate scientific theory of those data, where this theory may mention entirely unobservable entities in its explanations. So it is, familiarly, with the theories of physics. But I do not think that anything comparable to this could happen with respect to introspective data and theories about the brain. Neurophysiological theory is not attainable on the basis of purely introspective data, however ingenious the theorist's capacity for theoretical inference may be. You cannot reason from pain to C-fibres (without ancillary access to concepts of the latter kind). The neuron does not and could not stand to introspective data in the same sort of relation that the atom stands to perceptual data. We can, it appears, reason to the correct theory of the physical world on the basis of perceptual data relating to it, thus transcending these data. But we could not, I think, similarly arrive at the theory of the neuron and its electro-chemical processes by taking our introspective data and asking ourselves what would be the best theoretical explanation of those data. Perception plus inference to the best explanation can take us beyond the perceptual appearances and down into the unobservable world of quarks and charm, but

[26] This is the real objection to pure introspectionist psychology: it could not deliver an account of the causal structure in which mental events are embedded. Psychophysics and psychophysiology are not pursuable under the introspectionist method, as a matter of principle. Complaints of 'privacy' and lack of intersubjective criteria are minor by comparison.

introspection plus inference to the best explanation will not suffice to take us beyond the introspective appearances and down into the unintrospectable world of neurons and acetylcholine. To get to that world we need (unsurprisingly) to be able to apply our senses to the brain; we need to check the thing out perceptually. Opening up the head is, alas, the only way. We cannot spare ourselves this grue-some work by sitting in an armchair and applying our scientific ingenuity to the conscious events that flit into introspective view. This is a marked difference between perception of the physical world and introspection of the mental world. Although we cannot perceive all the causes of what we perceive, we can nevertheless arrive at a theory of these underlying causes by employing our capacity for theory construction. But we cannot similarly arrive at a theory of the underlying physical causes of our conscious states by employing this capacity in conjunction with the deliverances of introspection. It is no accident that scientists of the brain actually look inside heads (I am sure they would avoid it if they could). This is not simply a quick way to find out what they could equally well discover by asking what would be the best explanation of the pain they are now experiencing. Introspection simply does not tell us enough, or the right kind of thing, about conscious states for us to be able to reconstruct, using standards methods of theory forma-tion, the nature of their physical causal background.

Again, I do not expect this point to be very controversial. It is surely obvious enough once the question is raised. Indeed, one might be forgiven for wondering what the point of pointing it out might be. The point, to repeat, is to show the principled limitations of introspection as a source of knowledge about consciousness. After all, introspection does inform us of the occurrence of con-scious events, and these events have their place in a rich causal network. Generally we assume that a causal network can be recon-structed, with enough ingenuity, from knowledge of a subset of the events that make it up: we reason from known effects to putative causes, creating an empirical theory as we go. But in the case of introspection this strategy refuses to deliver the goods: we need *independent* knowledge of the causes, obtained by perception of the brain, if we are to reconstruct the causal network whose tip pokes through to introspective awareness. The introspective data do not direct us out of the mental realm and down into the physical underpinnings, where we need to go. Intuitively, this is because the inferential step from mental to physical would require a move to a different *kind* of reality, a reality not hinted at in the character of the mental data. This step does not consist merely in a smooth(ish) transition within a roughly homogeneous range of entities and properties – as with inferring the hidden properties of matter from its perceived properties. A leap of a different order of magnitude altogether would be required to postulate neurons on the basis of felt experience. This is, I guess, why it is immensely surprising to learn that one's conscious states have the kinds of neural causes that they do have; for this is quite unpredictable from the way those conscious events strike one introspectively. It is the kind of discovery one never quite gets over (or am I too sensitive?). Introspection perforce slides over the surface of the full causal story; it offers no intimation of what lies throbbing beneath this surface. The brain is a machine whose workings are not inferable from the conscious upshot of its activity.[27]

Nor is this closure with respect to causal background confined to causal features of a purely physical kind. As empirical psychologists often observe, there is a colossal amount of cognitive processing that goes on of which we are not aware.[28] This processing is typically described in the language of computation and information-processing; it is not neat neural language. For example, the computational processes that underlie vision, rich and complex as they are, are hidden to introspection. This is why the process of seeing something strikes us as a lot simpler than it really is. Introspection informs us of the final product of these subconscious processes, not of the nature and course of the processes themselves. You would not have the final visual experience without these processes occurring, but you would never guess, introspectively, that they are thus

---

[27] Our readiness to believe in the causal autonomy of the mind, and to be surprised by the dramatic mental effects of localized brain damage, probably stem from the fact that introspection is such a feeble means of deriving causal information about our conscious states. Its lack of causal penetration is what gives rise to the illusion of mental autonomy. If (*per impossible*) introspection revealed the physical causal conditions of our mental events, then we should be less prone to believe in the immortality of the soul and the like. Such beliefs, though false, are not mere superstition; they are encouraged by the partial way in which introspection presents mental events: it generates isolationist illusions.

[28] See, for example, Philip Johnson-Laird, 'A Computational Analysis of Consciousness', in *Consciousness and Contemporary Science*, eds A. J. Marcel and E. Bisiach (Clarendon Press: Oxford, 1988).

necessary. Indeed, it seems essential to successful cognitive functioning that introspection *not* reveal the full extent of the processing
that occurs; for otherwise our consciousness would become clogged
and overloaded, with too much clamouring for our attention. The
operative maxim of the nervous system appears to be this: do not
bring more to the surface of consciousness than is strictly necessary
for informed action. Introspection has (as they say) a limited chan-
nel capacity, so it is wise to ensure that a degree of closure is built
into it; it should not be informed of more than it can handle. Since
conscious space is apparently very expensive, there is a premium on
keeping much of the mind's operation closed to introspection. A
good introspective faculty is therefore one that has been designed
to shine its beam on only the tip of the mental iceberg. Efficiency
lies in economy. Let the bulk of processing stay buried, says introspection, where it will not distract the hard-pressed subject of
consciousness. He is under enough stress already, what with all the
different things he has to think about. Introspection sticks, sensibly,
to the headlines.

    These points about the manifold limits and blindspots of intro-
spection are, remember, intended as propaganda for the more surprising thesis that consciousness itself has a nature that is hidden to
introspection. To sum up: each introspective faculty can only detect
the conscious states of a single subject; introspection is hobbled as a
means of forming a conception of alien forms of consciousness; and
introspection is utterly incapable of informing us of the causal
background of our conscious states. Why then should we so confidently expect that it covers the full extent of our own consciousness? Why assume that the intrinsic properties of conscious states
are all open to introspective inspection? Might not a faculty limited
in the ways cited also be limited in a further respect, namely that
it does not apprise us of certain aspects of the intrinsic nature of
consciousness? Might there not be a natural depth to conscious
states that introspection fails to fathom? As I have argued, there is
good theoretical reason to postulate such a hidden nature – in order
to make sense of the psychophysical nexus. Does not this now seem
like no more than we might have expected, given the generally short
reach of introspection? It is just another respect in which introspection only grazes the surface of what is going on. Of course, the
limits I have identified do not by themselves *entail* the thesis of the

hidden structure of consciousness. But they should make it easier to accept this thesis, given its attractiveness as a solution to the mind–body problem. They should loosen the hold of the assumption that introspection has the full story about states of consciousness. My introspective faculty has a limited purpose; we should not expect that it can deliver a complete science of its object. It is no more privileged in this respect than my unaided perception of material objects – rather less so. Introspectio̱ is good at what it does, yes, but it does not do very much. One of the things it does not do is make us aware of the hidden structure of our consciousness. If I am right, this failing is what underlies our inability to solve the mind–body problem. It is what prevents us from understanding the place of consciousness in the natural order.

I mean the thesis of the hidden structure of consciousness in the same sense as the thesis that physical substances have a hidden structure.[29] Thus liquids, for example, have a hidden structure that explains their characteristic macro-properties: why they flow as they do, assume the shape of their container, turn solid in certain conditions. This hidden structure consists in an arrangement of molecules subject to various forces. The macro-properties of liquids emerge, as we might say, from this hidden structure. And liquids only have these macro-properties in virtue of having such a hidden structure; they are not self-supporting. Now it is not that I think this provides an accurate model for the *way* in which consciousness emerges from the brain; indeed, I think it is quite inadequate in this respect.[30] But it does serve to illustrate the *sense* of the claim that consciousness has a hidden structure. In particular, it underlines the point that this structure is *intrinsic* to consciousness, part of its essential nature. It is not merely extrinsic or collateral, existing *alongside* consciousness. No, I mean to be saying that it is part of what consciousness *is*. It is as intimately related to consciousness as the molecular composition of liquids is related to liquids. Just as a

[29] Or again, in the sense that the meanings of natural language sentences have hidden structure: see ch. 4 for more on this. Introspection is to the hidden structure of consciousness what perception of sentences is to their underlying logical form. Note that to say these are all hidden in the same *sense* is not to say their hiddenness consists in the same kind of thing. It does not.

[30] Principally, this is because the relationship between molecules and liquids is one of spatial composition, whereas the emergence of consciousness from neural aggregates appears to be nothing of the kind: neurons are not the elementary *parts* from which conscious wholes are constructed. See Nagel, *The View From Nowhere*, p. 49f.

casual glance at water reveals only its surface, leaving its deep nature hidden, so introspection of consciousness reveals only its surface, leaving its deep nature hidden. Introspection does not, so to speak, see right into the inner constitution of consciousness, like an X-ray machine. There are, indeed, some properties of consciousness with respect to which introspection is uniquely well-tuned, but there are others of which it has no inkling. These are the properties that enable consciousness to lay down physical foundations. They are, we might say, the naturally basic properties of consciousness.

And why, after all, should a creature with consciousness have ready access to these naturally basic properties? What would be the biological point of that? Why should nature equip us to solve philosophical problems? Nature does not see the point of making property P evident to every subject of consciousness; though it does see the point of making sure that everyone's consciousness has this property (nature abhors a miracle). To design a conscious creature you have to ensure two things: one, that its consciousness can be suitably embodied in a collocation of matter; and two, that there should be properties of its consciousness that it is conscious of, i.e. introspectable properties. You have, then, to build in a deep and a superficial layer. Both demands need to be met, but there is every reason to suppose that they cannot be met in the same way. Different design features will be necessary in order to guarantee that the creature's consciousness meets these two requirements. On the one hand, consciousness has to align itself to the brain; on the other, it has to present itself to the subject. What enables it to do one of these things will not be the same as what enables it to do the other. There is thus no reason to expect that the subject's introspective awareness will take in the design feature that connects her consciousness to its physical moorings. Yet this feature really is an intrinsic and essential property of consciousness. It is simply not a conscious property of it. What is architecturally basic to consciousness, from the point of view of biological engineering, is hardly likely to be uppermost in the subject's mind. In this respect, consciousness does not differ from other organs of the body: how they are constructed is not written on their face for the organism to read. Animals need working organs that can be made from the available materials; they do not need the dubious luxury of an organ that wears its *modus operandi* on its sleeve. Consciousness too is a natural biological organ equipped with a hidden structure. What we get, when we are given consciousness, must be more than what we see, or else we could not be given it in the first place. Lurking benignly beneath the shimmering surface of consciousness is a natural structure on which the very existence of consciousness depends.

In this section I shall compare my approach to the mind–body problem to that of Kant, and contrast it with the approach of Wittgenstein. These two philosophers differ radically in their attitude to the hidden, and it will be instructive to see where they stand in relation to the kind of position I am advocating here. They share a sense of the problem but react to it in markedly opposed ways.

First Kant. Addressing himself to the 'task of explaining the communion of the soul with the body,' Kant writes:

> The difficulty peculiar to the problem consists, as is generally recognized, in the assumed heterogeneity of the object of inner sense (the soul) and the objects of the outer senses, the formal condition of their intuition being, in the case of the former, time only, and in the case of the latter, also space. But if we consider that the two kinds of objects thus differ from each other, not inwardly but only in so far as one *appears* outwardly to another, and that what, as thing in itself, underlies the appearances of matter, perhaps after all may not be so heterogeneous in character, this difficulty vanishes, the only question that remains being how in general a communion of substances is possible.[31]

Kant's point here is that the problem of mind–body communion belongs to the level of appearances – phenomena – and we cannot infer from this that there is any problem in objective reality – at the level of noumena. There is, admittedly, a clear phenomenal heterogeneity, which generates the sense of a deep metaphysical problem, but it does not follow that the heterogeneity, and hence the problem, extends all the way out, or down, to the noumenal level. The heterogeneity may be purely phenomenal. And there is a definite suggestion in this passage that, indeed, the problem does not exist at the noumenal level; there the communion of soul and body proceeds perfectly smoothly. Matter, Kant suggests, may well conceal a hidden nature which is not so heterogeneous with mind that

---

[31] Kant, *Critique of Pure Reason*, trans. by Norman Kemp Smith (St Martin's Press: New York, 1965), p. 381, B 428.

no communion between them is possible. From the perspective of objective noumenal reality, then, matter and mind may not be so disparate as they appear to our limited human viewpoint. Noumenally, there *is* no mind–body problem – beyond that of the interaction of substances in general. The problem is phenomenal only, reflecting our skewed and partial perspective on the world.

Evidently, there is much common ground between my view and Kant's, though it cannot be said that my view was inspired by Kant's statement of the position.[32] But there are two differences I should like to note. First, Kant here attributes the problem-resolving hidden structure to matter, not to mind. He does not expressly rule out attributing such structure to mind, however, and his general position on the noumenal reality of the soul might well allow room for the idea. Still, in this passage at least it is matter exclusively that he credits with hidden structure, and this makes his official position importantly different from mine. Secondly, his formulation in terms of 'heterogeneity' seems to me too restrictive. It is as if the only way he can envisage an unproblematic mesh between consciousness and matter is by these two coming together in a homogeneous unity. They have to be fundamentally *identical* in nature if they are to be linked perspicuously. Now this is certainly one way in which the link might be forged, but we should beware of pressing the problem into this shape. It is not obvious that conscious properties have to be somehow the same as material properties in order for them to be intelligibly linked; it may be that property P links them without assimilating them, perhaps exhibiting both as aspects of a deeper reality. Of course, given my general agnostic stance on the identity and nature of P, I cannot say exactly how the link is effected; my point is just that homogeneity may be the wrong way to think about it. Indeed, it smacks of pretending to a knowledge of the ways of the noumenal that Kant of all people should be chary of. However, with these qualifications noted, I feel able to enlist Kant's illustrious name in my support. We are both defending what may aptly be called *noumenalism*.

[32] Having arrived at the view, and recognizing its Kantian cast, I searched Kant for anticipations, finding (with much satisfaction) the passage quoted in the text. Is it not a little surprising that the view has been (to my knowledge) invisible in later treatments of the mind–body problem, despite its advocacy by Kant? Perhaps it is thought to belong with the wilder excesses of his noumenalism, and hence not to be worthy of serious consideration. That would not be my estimate, obviously.

The Kantian way with the problem may be contrasted with Wittgenstein's way. Wittgenstein writes:

> The feeling of an unbridgeable gulf between consciousness and brain-process: how does it come about that this does not come into the considerations of our ordinary life? This idea of a difference in kind is accompanied by slight giddiness – which occurs when we are performing a piece of logical sleight-of-hand. (The same giddiness attacks us when we think of certain theorems in set theory.) When does this feeling occur in the present case? It is when I, for example, turn my attention in a particular way on to my own consciousness, and, astonished, say to myself: THIS is supposed to be produced by a process in the brain! – as it were clutching my forehead. – But what can it mean to speak of turning my attention on to my own consciousness? This is surely the queerest thing there could be! It was a particular act of gazing that I called doing this. I stared fixedly in front of me – but *not* at any particular point or object. My eyes were wide open, the brows not contracted (as they mostly are when I am interested in a particular object). No such interest preceded this gazing. My glance was vacant; or again *like* that of someone admiring the illumination of the sky and drinking in the light.
> Now bear in mind that the proposition which I uttered as a paradox (THIS is produced by a brain-process!) has nothing paradoxical about it. I could have said it in the course of an experiment whose purpose was to show that an effect of light which I see is produced by stimulation of a particular part of the brain. – But I did not utter the sentence in the surroundings in which it would have had an everyday and unparadoxical sense. And my attention was not such as would have accorded with making an experiment. (If it had been, my look would have been intent, not vacant.)[33]

In this passage Wittgenstein has two main aims. First, he aims to give us a vivid evocation of the feeling produced in us by contemplating the mind–brain nexus – that stunned incredulity that anything like this *could* really be the case. Second, he offers us a totally deflationary diagnosis of the problem we seem to see here, consigning it to the wastebin of philosophical illusion. We peer out over the unbridgeable gulf, a giddy feeling sets in, we exclaim, clutch our forehead, and feel ourselves to be in the grip of a deep metaphysical problem. But the gulf is illusory, produced by a misuse of attention, and the sense of mystery is remediable by reminding ourselves of an ordinary situation in which we might make a statement linking a

---

[33] Wittgenstein, *Philosophical Investigations* (Basil Blackwell: Oxford, 1974), section 412.

sensation with a brain process. Where Kant appeals to a noumenal reality to span the gulf, Wittgenstein counsels us to prevent it from opening up in the first place – by refusing to engage in suspect philosophical practices: gazing vacantly ahead of us, detaching language from its ordinary use, performing logical sleights-of-hand. The suggestion is that the giddiness will go away, and the problem recede, if we follow this therapeutuc advice. That is, Wittgenstein is applying his standard philosophical method to the sense of perplexity we feel about the physical embodiment of consciousness. The philosophical mind–body problem arises, for him, because of a wrong philosophical method; there is nothing about the facts themselves that warrants the feeling of perplexity we so naturally succumb to. The 'gulf' has nothing of the miraculous about it, once we view it aright; it only seems to seem problematic. And to view it aright we need only recall an everyday situation in which we might find ourselves confronted by it – as in performing a psychophysical experiment on the brain. Then everything will seem smooth and ordinary again. The problem arose from getting ourselves into a particular philosophical frame of mind, not from the nature of consciousness and brain, or from our concepts of them. The sense of deep mystery is a philosophical illusion.

Both Kant and Wittgenstein, then, recognize the semblance of a profound mystery here, and they both try to dispel the mystery by diagnosing a certain sort of error we are prone to make: mistaking the phenomenal for the noumenal, according to Kant; taking language on vacation, according to Wittgenstein. Neither philosopher is content simply to accept the appearance of miracle as a brute fact: it must somehow be explained away. But their explanations take very different forms. My own position, of course, tends to agree with Kant's and to be at odds with Wittgenstein's. I shall not here undertake a lengthy critique of Wittgenstein's position, which would require a discussion of his general philosophical method. Let me just remark, dogmatically, that this seems to me about the least plausible case for Wittgenstein to apply his general method. The gulf is not to be rendered innocuous simply by confining it to everyday contexts. For the appearance of mystery palpably does *not* disappear when we remind ourselves of situations in which we might naturally make statements connecting brain processes and sensations. This is because we have no available account of what might explain the truth of such statements. Compare the problem of thought about abstract entities: this problem cannot be made to disappear simply by observing that we often speak unhesitatingly of people doing mental arithmetic. The question is how this is *possible*. In fact, I should hazard the conjecture that it is precisely in such 'everyday' situations as Wittgenstein envisages that the full perplexity of the problem would be most strongly felt. Imagine yourself hooked up in such an experiment, correlating brain stimulations with the felt intensity of sensations: would you not find it astonishing that colour experiences, say, resulted from electrical impulses sent into your grey matter, which you can see reflected in a mirror? I know I should. I should be amazed that this vivid experience of red could result from chemical perturbations in that little bit of wet cortex. The philosophical problem would hit me hardest right then, as I watched the system in operation. So I am not inclined to agree with Wittgenstein on this point.

Wittgenstein set his face against the hidden in the theory of mind, but it seems to me that if nothing is hidden then consciousness is miraculous, and I do not believe it can be miraculous. Naturalism in the philosophy of mind requires that we own up to the hidden.

Then I return, finally, to the issue of naturalism. I argued earlier (pp. 47–58) that to solve the problem of intentionality we must have to hand a solution to the problem of embodiment, and vice versa. The two problems must be solved together or not at all. It has emerged since then that the solution to the latter problem hinges upon the hidden structure of consciousness. So in order to provide, or complete, a naturalistic theory of intentionality we should need to have available a naturalistic account of the hidden structure of consciousness. We should need a characterization of the properties that constitute this hidden structure. And that is something we do not have, even as a glint in the theoretician's eye. But we can still say a bit about the general shape of the overall theory. Our explanandum is the intentional arc – the capacity of conscious states to reach out into the world, grasp its contents, and absorb them into the mental landscape.[34] This capacity of consciousness

---

[34] For more on this see ch. 2.

should not be underestimated: familiar though it is, it is really quite unlike anything else in the world. Through intentionality consciousness ranges out into the past, the future, the very distant, the very small, into other minds, the abstract, the nonexistent, and so forth. And it brings these external things into a peculiarly intimate relation to the subject of consciousness: they are present *to* his consciousness, right there before it, its immediate object. Intentionality brings objects and their properties into a relation of remarkable closeness to the subject, so close that we find ourselves saying that the subject has these things *in* his mind. The world becomes incorporated into the mind. Such a capacity is unlikely to find its *full* explication in the mundane routines of the insentient world. My speculative thesis is that what makes this capacity possible, what confers it on a subject, is the hidden constitution of those states of consciousness in which the capacity is displayed. The intentional arc, as a mode of consciousness, is underpinned by this unknown structure of consciousness.[35] It is this structure that permits a physical system to manifest full-blown intentional relations to things. There is an infrastructure to this arcing out of consciousness, and that is what makes intentionality naturally explicable (along, perhaps, with other kinds of fact). So to take the naturalization of intentionality the whole distance we should need to develop a theory of this infrastructure; we should need to know what it ultimately consists in. All we can say now is that its properties are what *would* have to be ascertained in order to put conscious intentionality on a thoroughly naturalistic footing. Causal or teleological relations may indeed have their place in the eventual total theory, but without knowledge of the hidden structure of consciousness they cannot add up to a complete naturalistic theory. This is not really very surprising in view of the uniqueness of conscious intentionality: something pretty out of the ordinary is going to be needed to make naturalistic sense out of *that*.

And what if this hidden structure is in principle unknowable?

---

[35] We might compare this, metaphorically, to the way a spider's web radiates out to its supports – the spider lodged, ego-like, in the centre. This construction only works because the threads have a hidden structure that enables them to span the chasm over which the spider sits suspended. There is more to the web, in point of engineering, than strikes the eye. Of course, in the case of intentionality there are, literally, no such connecting cables between the mind and its objects. Still, the intentional relation depends upon an unseen structure of some sort, a structure that enables us to summon objects to mind.

What becomes of naturalism under that bleak prospect? Since I am disposed to acquiesce in such bleakness, I must face up to its repercussions as far as naturalism is concerned. Is the third major upsurge in the history of the universe simply not naturalistically explicable? Must it forever remain a mystery to us, alarming in its theological implications? Is giddy awe the only attitude we can hope for towards the fact of consciousness in a physical world? I sincerely hope not, and fortunately there is a way to regain our naturalistic sobriety in the face of the facts. We need to draw a distinction. We need to distinguish between what I shall call *effective* and *existential* naturalism. Effective naturalism is the thesis that we should be able to provide or construct naturalistic accounts of every phenomenon in nature: we should be able actually to specify naturalistic necessary and sufficient conditions for the phenomenon in question. There have, of course, been many successes for effective naturalism: the movements of the planets, the origin of life, reproduction, the weather. No hint of the divine need now be recognized in these areas; the miraculous has given way to the mechanistic. But it seems to me to be a form of idealism to insist that *every* natural phenomenon should be subject to effective naturalism. For this is to assert, dogmatically, that human powers of theory construction are capable of comprehending everything there is: to be natural is to be naturalizable by us. *We* are the measure of nature's naturalness. But there is, I should urge, no guarantee that our powers are thus omnicompetent – that nature is an open book for our eyes to read and our intellects to understand. There may be tales written in that book that we are just not equipped to grasp, however natural and non-miraculous the story being told.

And this is where existential naturalism comes in: this is the thesis, metaphysical in character, that nothing that happens in nature is inherently anomalous, God-driven, an abrogation of basic laws – whether or not *we* can come to comprehend the processes at work. It is, I suppose, an article of metaphysical faith, though this phrase should be stripped of its pejorative connotations.[36] I think

---

[36] It belongs with incredulity over ghosts, telepathy, divine healing and the like. The phenomena alleged to support such hypotheses can always be explained in other naturalistic ways (assuming there are any odd phenomena to start with). This kind of incredulity amounts to more than merely an extensively confirmed high-level empirical theory; it is fuelled by a conviction of deep incoherence in the hypotheses in question.

we know enough about the universe to know that consciousness did not arise by miracle, by a sudden infusion from a supernatural realm. It arose by natural processes from natural materials – ultimately from expanding matter that formed itself into clumps early on in the history of the cosmos. It postdates life and, apparently, there are good naturalistic reasons for this. It is neither a heavenly dispensation nor an inexplicable quirk of organized matter. But it does not follow that we are intellectually equipped to know *how* these natural processes came about, what they consist in. It does not follow, that is, that effective naturalism holds of consciousness. Thus we can be in a position to know that existential naturalism is true of consciousness without being in a position to convert this into effective naturalism; and this is the predicament I strongly suspect we are in. If we are, then the brand of naturalism that is true of consciousness is aptly labelled *transcendental*. The natural facts that enable consciousness to be what, on general grounds, we know it to be, namely a natural phenomenon, transcend our capacity to ascertain these facts. We know there are such facts, but we cannot actually identify them, even in principle. So, even if the bleak prognosis is the right one, we need not despair of holding on to naturalism about consciousness: we always have existential naturalism to fall back on. This option is one that any philosopher of a broadly realist persuasion will want to keep available. Certainly I find it by far the most reasonable, and intuitive, position to adopt in this area. Objectively, consciousness is as natural as anything else in nature, but it is not given to us to understand the nature of this naturalness.[37]

---

[37] Our ignorance is not total, however. We know, if I am right, that the naturalizing properties belong to the hidden nature of consciousness, and we know what it is they have to explain. We also know quite a bit about what they are not. What we do not know is the actual constitution of this hidden structure. But this ignorance does not compel us to lapse into abject non-naturalism, since we can know that something is natural without being able to say how it is. We should be forced into non-naturalism only if it could be shown that there is nothing more to consciousness and the brain than meets the eye. For then we should be confronted by an unmediated and unintelligible brute link, a mysterious joining of incommensurables.

4

The Hidden Structure of Consciousness

The idea of hidden structure has repeatedly proven its value in the history of scientific thought. Indeed, the history of science may be seen as the progressive uncovering of new kinds of hidden structure. These structures feature essentially in our theories of the world. Only by venturing beyond the observable can we develop adequate theories of the observable. Examples abound: the atomic and sub-atomic structure of matter; the curved structure of space-time in relativity theory; the molecular structure of DNA; the logico-grammatical deep structures latent in natural languages; the unconscious processes and structures operating in the mind. In each of these cases the postulation of 'hidden variables' is essential to achieving successful theories in the domains in question – in physics, biology, linguistics, psychology. Unless we recognize the unobservable, the phenomena we do observe will remain puzzling, inexplicable, mysterious. We pay the epistemological price of unobservability because we value the intellectual benefits it brings us, and rightly so. We depart from strict empiricism because it leaves the world unexplained. Scientific realism may make us epistemologically nervous, but it is the only way to bring order to the phenomena.[1]

But there is one phenomenon that we have heretofore refused to view in this way: namely, consciousness. With respect to conscious-

---

[1] Scientific realism also permits us to gain greater objectivity in our representations of the world, by correcting for the relativity built into our original observation-based representations. Postulating hidden structure is a way of suspending the human viewpoint on the world, expelling the subject. What we call hidden is simply what is *there*, irrespective of the biases of our given representational powers. Accessibility is an epistemic not an ontological property. Nothing is intrinsically hidden; hiddenness is relative to our means of seeking out. From God's point of view, the manifest/hidden distinction is empty. This should make us less chary of the hidden: to be hidden is not to suffer any metaphysical etiolation.

ness the idea of a hidden nature has not been met with enthusiasm; in fact, it is rarely considered even as a theoretical possibility.[2] The whole nature of consciousness is assumed to be given to us; nothing about its intrinsic character lurks unseen. When it comes to consciousness we are still unreconstucted empiricists, even idealists. Its reality is a seeming reality.

This idealist conception of consciousness is coupled with a correlative view about the powers of introspection: namely, that introspection provides us not only with accurate but with complete access to the constitution of consciousness. Introspection is a cognitive faculty that sees into every facet of its object; consciousness has no secrets from introspection. It is true that we (fallibly) ascribe conscious states to others on the basis of observation of their behaviour, but introspection is the faculty through which we confront consciousness naked and unadorned. What introspection does not tell us about the essential nature of our own conscious states is not there to be told. Thus our view of consciousness, unlike our view of every other natural phenomenon, is taken to be Godlike: nothing about its intrinsic character escapes our notice. Consciousness ends where introspection leaves off, such are the boundaries of the one and the powers of the other. Nothing can be a property of consciousness unless the subject is conscious of that property.[3]

This conviction about the special epistemic access we have to consciousness is accompanied by a certain picture we are apt to conjur of its inner metaphysical nature. Whereas other natural phenomena – matter, space, life, language, mind (including the unconscious) -- have the character of *depth*, consciousness is conceived as a kind of diaphanous membrane. It lacks that extra third dimension. Those other phenomena have a natural 'thickness' to them, a region that lies beyond our immediate observational access to their superficial properties. They have a surface and an under-

[2] But see Thomas Nagel, *The View From Nowhere* (Oxford University Press: Oxford, 1986), ch. 3. I say more about Nagel's views later.
[3] With respect to the external world, we accept that we have to work at generating a complete and accurate picture of it; we can not just lie lazily back and expect our perceptual faculties to feed us everything we need to know. Knowledge, here, requires effort, physical and mental. But with respect to consciousness it is assumed that no comparable effort is required to arrive at a complete and accurate picture of it; supine introspection will tell us everything there is to know about consciousness. Introspection permits indolent omniscience with respect to consciousness – complete knowledge without lifting a finger. But could any area of reality be so obliging? Is nature ever that considerate? Since when did the natural world start caring about our leisure? Does it not always make us work at it?

side, a manifest appearance and a submerged reality. But consciousness is conceived as exhaustively manifest, as lying wholly on the surface – it has no submerged aspect. We cannot apply the usual distinction of surface and deep properties to consciousness. Consciousness is not a 'layered' thing; it is shallow, gauzy, open. It has a filmy texture, like oil on water, and it refuses to mix with what it floats upon. Ontologically, it is not the kind of thing that *could* conceal a hidden structure. For there is nowhere in consciousness that such a structure could hide: it is much too *flat* for that. So, at any rate, we are inclined (implicitly) to think.

I am going to contend that this natural and traditional picture of consciousness is mistaken. Consciousness does have natural depth, a concealed underside. We need to extend the strategy that has worked so well in other areas to this case too: the demands of theory make the attribution of hidden structure to consciousness unavoidable. Only thus can we explain what needs to be explained. Consciousness is not a diaphanous membrane; it is more like a pyramid only the tip of which is visible – a pyramid equipped with elaborate internal workings, scarcely imaginable from what is given. In a word, we need to become scientific realists about consciousness, as we now are about everything else. Strict empiricism is not even true for its most favoured object. We must reject idealism about consciousness, its final haven.

I shall consider three sorts of reason (there may be others) for crediting consciousness with a hidden structure – that is, a structure not given to introspection (or to the ordinary third-person standpoint). These reasons are: (i) to explain the logical properties of conscious thoughts; (ii) to explain how conscious states relate to the physical body; and (iii) to explain certain empirical data, specifically blindsight. My ultimate interest is in the second of these reasons; the other two I see as preparing the ground for acceptance of the second reason, though they have their own independent interest.[4]

---

[4] So these reasons bear also upon ch. 3. Combining them with my earlier points about the limits of introspection, we arrive at the idea of consciousness as extending way beyond the nearsighted invigilations of the introspective faculty. In fact, consciousness should be conceived hierarchically: there are more or less deep hidden layers, according to their degree of accessibility. Thus I should count the structure needed to explain the logical properties of thought as less deep than that needed to account for the blindsight phenomena, which in turn is less deep than the structure needed to make sense of embodiment. The hidden structure of consciousness is thus like the hidden structure of matter in this respect: it comes in grades, depending upon its proximity to our cognitive capacities.

The first reason, which I shall discuss in this section, is, I think, the least hard to accept of the three, possibly because of its relative familiarity; accordingly, I shall use it to lower the defences of the reader before inviting credence in the other two.

Let us begin by reminding ourselves of some familiar claims about the relationship between the surface grammar and the logical form of sentences of natural language. Speaking of the phrase 'some numbers', Frege writes:

> In fact, these words cannot be taken together at all, and we must not ask for the meaning of this combination. We have here a grammatical pseudo-subject, similar to 'all men', 'no man', and 'nothing' – constructions in which language seems to have indulged in order to mislead logicians.[5]

Russell remarks:

> The *is* of 'Socrates is human' expresses the relation of subject and predicate; the *is* of 'Socrates is a man' expresses identity. It is a disgrace to the human race that it has chosen to employ the same word 'is' for these two entirely different ideas – a disgrace which a symbolic logical language of course remedies.[6]

Wittgenstein says:

> Man possesses the ability to construct languages capable of expressing every sense, without having any idea how each word has meaning or what its meaning is – just as people speak without knowing how the individual sounds are produced.
> Everyday language is a part of the human organism and is no less complicated than it.
> It is not humanly possible to gather immediately from it what the logic of language is.
> Language disguises thought. So much so, that from the outward form of the clothing it is impossible to infer the form of the thought beneath it, because the outward form of the clothing is not designed

[5] Gottlob Frege, 'Peano's Conceptual Notation', in *Collected Papers*, ed. Brian McGuinness (Basil Blackwell: Oxford, 1984), p. 239.
[6] Bertrand Russell, *Introduction to Mathematical Philosophy* (George Allen and Unwin: London, 1919), p. 172.

to reveal the form of the body, but for entirely different purposes.[7]
All philosophy is a 'critique of language' (though not in Mauth-
ner's sense). It was Russell who performed the service of showing
that the apparent logical form of a proposition need not be its real
one.[8]

There are three ideas at play here that I want to highlight. First,
there is the idea that the propositions expressed by sentences of
natural language have a hidden form, not directly revealed in the
apparent grammatical form of the sentences that express them: thus
a surface/deep distinction applies to language. Second, the postulation of deep logical form is motivated, not by how sentences strike
us phenomenologically, but by considerations of logical theory –
the resolution of logical puzzles, the avoidance of baroque ontologies (Meinong), the need to exhibit logical relations between sentences. Third, the apparent form of sentences actively tempts us into
certain kinds of logical and metaphysical error: the surface of
language naturally generates various intellectual illusions, which
can only be avoided by discounting or downplaying the appearances and acknowledging a level of hidden logical structure. We
might put the view collectively expressed by Frege, Russell and
Wittgenstein in this way: Earlier logicians had mistakenly assumed
that the real inner nature of propositions is made manifest in their
ordinary linguistic vehicles, and it was this assumption that
retarded the progress of logic. What has to be recognized is that
language (meaning) possesses a level of structure that transcends, or
underlies, the way it presents itself to us. The way in which we
directly experience language is thus a fallible and partial guide to its
real nature, precisely because our ordinary linguistic experience is
limited to the surface of language and this does not exhaust linguistic reality. Our auditory and visual senses are a poor guide to the
correct analysis of meaning, because they stop at the surface of
language; we must rather employ more indirect methods of theory

---

[7] Ludwig Wittgenstein, *Tractatus Logico-Philosophicus* (Routledge and Kegan Paul: London, 1961), section 4.002.
[8] *Ibid*, section 4.0031. I could also cite many more recent semantic theorists in support of
the same point: for example, Donald Davidson, 'The Logical Form of Action Sentences', in
Essays on Actions and Events (Oxford University Press: Oxford, 1980). Then there is the
whole Chomskyan school.

construction if we are to penetrate to the underlying structure of language, and hence to logical reality.[9]

This general conception is by now familiar enough, making it hard for us to see how radical it really is – how much it alters our view of the *kind* of thing meaning is. Although we appear to speak and understand sentences perfectly well, we are blind to the inner nature of the meanings we so confidently bandy about: these meanings are by no means completely transparent to us – indeed, we are gulled by the way we express them into error and confusion. Meaning has a covert structure, belied by its surface appearance. (Descartes' evil demon had a hand in designing natural languages.) As Wittgenstein says: 'Without philosophy thoughts are, as it were, cloudy and indistinct: its task is to make them clear and give them sharp boundaries.'[10] In an important sense, we do not know how we mean what we do mean; we do not (explicitly) grasp the conditions of meaningfulness of our own utterances. Our meanings come to us through an opaque and distorting medium.

But we can, I think, recover an original sense of surprise (even outrage) by drawing out a corollary of this view of language – a corollary which, oddly enough, does not seem to have been noticed by any of the three revolutionaries cited. Perhaps, indeed, it is a corollary that even they would shrink from (which is why they did not notice it). I mean the following: that the same division of surface and deep structure must apply, *mutatis mutandis*, to *conscious thoughts*. They too must possess a hidden logical structure not apparent in the way they strike us introspectively – in addition to their introspectable surface. For essentially the same considerations apply to the mental vehicle of thought as apply to its linguistic

---

[9]   Thus our ordinary immediate experience of the linguistic vehicles of meaning skews us away from solving logical problems. A correct logic must be striven for, not smoothly derived from the linguistic appearances. This involves giving up a kind of Cartesianism about meaning – the idea that facts about meaning are infallibly given to us. The logical category of a sense may not be marked in our ordinary grasp of it; indeed, this grasp may mislead us as to the sense's logical category. Clinging to such semantic Cartesianism, and denying hidden structure, would impede the solution of logical (and metaphysical) problems.

Just how misleading the surface of language might be is not discussed by the classical authors cited, but they seem not to have recognized any definite limit to the logical malevolence of ordinary language. Presumably, however, its mendacity could not be total, on pain of failing to express propositions at all. Perhaps, then, it is a necessary truth that logical form is only partially hidden.

[10]   *Tractatus*, section 4.112.

vehicle: the mental vehicle, too, fails to display the logical form of the proposition thought.[11] If this were not so, then logic would be a lot easier than it is: we could simply consult our own awareness of the structure of our thoughts and read off their real logical form. We could use introspection to give us the access to the logical form of propositions that our perception of sentences fails to give us. We could simply bypass the misleading outer sentences and go straight to the logically perfect conscious thought. But, clearly, we are not in a position to do this. Introspection of thoughts is not the royal road to logical reality.

Nor can it be that we are somehow prevented from appreciating the real structure manifest in our conscious thoughts by the fact that our spoken language is logically defective – that this language somehow gets between introspection and its logically perfect psychological object. For surely a thinking creature without language would not thereby become an infallible analyser of thought, an effortless logician – by its not being in thrall to a misleading linguistic vehicle. Such a creature would not, for example, be able simply to read the theory of descriptions off its descriptive thoughts; it would still be prone to mistake logically quantified thoughts for subject-predicate ones, just as Russell originally did. The psychological vehicle of propositions is just as imperfect and misleading as the linguistic vehicle; and so introspection is just as inadequate a tool of logical analysis as perception of spoken and written sentences is. Our conscious thoughts do not wear their correct logical analysis on their introspectable face, any more than our sentences do.[12]

Indeed, I suspect that our language is logically misleading *because*

---

[11] This point is easy to state under the hypothesis of a language of thought: the internal sentences admit the same division into misleading surface structure and logically correct deep structure. It is the surface structure that configures the appearance of the thinker's conscious states. But the point is not dependent upon accepting this hypothesis; all we need is the idea that propositions can enter consciousness in a disguised form. Propositions come to us borne by two sorts of vehicle – public sentences and states of consciousness – and both sorts clothe them deceptively. Their fashion sense may not be precisely the same, but they both cover up the body within.

[12] A bridge between sentences and propositional attitudes is provided by linguistic understanding. When we understand a logically misleading sentence our grasp mirrors the two layers of the sentence: the understanding also has its surface features and its deep features. The semantic distinction has its psychological counterpart. Explicitly, we grasp the surface; implicitly, we grasp the underlying structure. Thus we do not introspectively appreciate the real psychological structure of our act of conscious understanding.

our consciousness is, since I believe, as a general principle, that thought is prior to language; language is the way it is, structurally, because thought is the way *it* is, structurally. Language externalizes the disguise consciousness throws over thought. The original obstacle to our doing logic correctly is thus the apparent structure of our conscious thoughts, rather than that of public language. Language gets the blame because of its relative palpability: you can point to the offending portion of the sentence but not to the corresponding component of the thought. There are pseudo-subjects in the stream of consciousness itself, and these are the seed of pseudo-subjects in language. Logicians through the centuries had to contend with the logical malevolence of their own consciousness as well as with that of the language they were raised to speak.[13] It is not that Frege and Russell were gifted with especially acute introspective vision; they had to come at the deep structure of their thoughts from another angle entirely, namely, systematic logical theory.

What, then, is the psychological significance of logical discoveries? I think it is parallel to the linguistic significance of such discoveries; they reveal an additional deep layer of structure. Episodes of conscious thought, like spoken and written sentences, have both a surface and a deep form. Thus the theory of descriptions, for example, has the consequence that thoughts that come to us as subject-predicate in form really have the conjunctive quantified logical form specified by the theory. *What* we think, when we consciously think a descriptive thought, is given by Russell's quantified equivalent; this is the hidden form of the thought, qua psychological item, since it is the real structure of the proposition

---

[13]   We might ask what the reason for this malevolence is: *why* are language and consciousness so intent on deceiving honest logicians? This question seems not to have troubled Frege, Russell and Wittgenstein very much, but it is essential to their position that some account be given of why language should see fit to misrepresent itself. We can hardly take imputations of intentional malevolence literally (what has English got against logicians?), and it would seem on the face of it more sensible to design language so as to be faithful to logical reality. Is it just human ineptitude? My guess is that the misleadingness comes from considerations of economy: ignore distinctions that do not appreciably affect the success of language in practical contexts (similarly for the mind). If so, the vehicles of meaning conform to a general law of biology: do not bother to discriminate between things whose distinctness does not matter practically – save your efforts for what does matter. We could call this the Law of Minimum Discrimination. It derives from the law that proscribes unnecessary expenditure of energy. Logical defectiveness did not prevent language and consciousness from pulling their weight in the perpetuation of the genes; indeed, aiming pedantically at logical correctness might be a disadvantage from that point of view. So do not start speaking and thinking in first-order predicate calculus. Consider what it might do to your genes!

entertained. Since the thought is a conscious state or event, it is the hidden form of a certain conscious state or event. Conscious thoughts thus have concealed logical structures, which are disguised by their surface features. The phenomenal features of conscious thoughts are an imperfect guide to their underlying logical features – which are yet features *of* those very thoughts.[14]

This duality of levels is shown in our practice of ascribing beliefs and other propositional attitudes to creatures. Once one has mastered a bit of logic, one finds no strain in ascribing beliefs to the logically unlettered by using formalized content sentences. One starts with a vernacular ascription of belief, in which the content sentence is left in its original misleading form, and then one substitutes the correct logical analysis of that content sentence; and the result is true if and only if the original was. Thus if the sentence 'James believes that the king of France is hirsute' is true, so too is the sentence 'James believes that $(\exists x)(x$ is a king of France and $(\forall y)(y$ is a king of France $\rightarrow x = y$ and x is hirsute)'. Since the analysing sentence captures the true structure of the proposition expressed by the analysed sentence, we can take it that the subject believes precisely that proposition; for the analysing sentence simply makes perspicuous exactly *what* it is he believes. Belief contexts are transparent with respect to correct logical analyses, even where the original ascription employs a logically misleading content sentence. The case is thus not like substituting referential terms with different senses; here what is believed – the proposition – gets shifted. Even if the believer cannot recognize the truth of the ascription in its logical version, and would even declare it a mistaken analysis of what he believes, the ascription is still true, so long as it *is* the correct analysis of the original sentence – so long, that is, as it succeeds in identifying the proposition believed. I suggest that this can be so only if the psychological state in question actually has the very structure conveyed by the regimented content sentence. (It is the same with reports of speech, where the original utterance is re-

---

[14] I hope it is clear that I am not using 'thought' in Frege's way. Fregean thoughts (propositions) are abstract entities whose only intrinsic structure is fixed as logically correct. I mean to speak of psychological states whose (deep) content is given by specifying such a Fregean thought. These states have an empirical structure that 'fits' the abstract proposition in question, as well as a structure that masks this proposition. Abstract logical form has psychological reality when it is grasped, but this reality is not always made manifest in the surface of that grasp.

placed by its correct logical analysis; the replacement tells you, literally, what was said.) For if the state did not have that structure, the report would have to be false, since it would attribute a form to the subject's state that it simply does not have. Descriptive thoughts really do have a quantified conjunctive form beneath their subject-predicate surface (assuming, of course, that Russell is right). The state genuinely has that form but it is not manifest in the surface phenomenology of the state. So we need to recognize a layer of psychological reality beneath that of the surface phenomenology.[15]

It would not be right to characterize this layer as *un*conscious, akin to the unconscious beliefs and desires of psychoanalysis or the subpersonal states of computational psychology. It is true that the subject is not conscious *of* the deeper layer, at least under its logical description; but it does not follow that this layer does not belong intrinsically to the conscious state itself. Just as F can be an intrinsic property of a perceptible object x without being a perceptible property of x, so conscious states can have intrinsic properties that they do not have consciously. When we re-ascribe a thought using a logical content sentence we do not ascribe a *different* – now unconscious – thought to our subject from that ascribed in the logically misleading vernacular. No, it is the very conscious thought itself (*that* state) that has the logical structure in question, not some other parallel state that fails to qualify as conscious at all; indeed, the thought has that structure as part of its essence. It simply begs the question against the thesis of hidden structure to insist that what is hidden must ipso facto belong to something other than a state of consciousness. And it flies in the face of our common practice of belief ascription. We should stick to our intuitive view that the logical form of our conscious thoughts is not (always) made manifest to introspection. Indeed, this hidden form is just as much a property of those thoughts as is the logical form of thoughts which is not hidden.

It seems to me, then, that essentially similar considerations to

[15] We might here speak of logical natural kinds. Our thoughts present themselves to us in a certain guise, but their 'real essence', logically speaking, may require a different taxonomy from that invited by the appearances. Thoughts which seem to belong together as subject-predicate in form may have to be reclassified in the light of developed logical theory. The appearance, linguistic or psychological, of a logical kind is not the best guide to its theoretically motivated taxonomy. Logic is to the classification of propositional attitudes what chemistry is to the classification of substances.

those moving Frege, Russell and Wittgenstein (as well as later theorists) to discern a hidden structure to linguistic meaning compel us to discern a comparable hidden structure in the propositional content of consciousness. When the stream of consciousness ripples with thought there are patterns beneath the surface – patterns that are only imperfectly mirrored by the disturbances at the surface. Your thoughts go deeper than you know; you are more logical than you seem. Consciousness, like language, disguises its underlying logical structure, and in so doing it tempts us into philosophical error. We avoid such error by declining to be fascinated exclusively by the surface of language or consciousness. We must peer beyond this surface.

Crediting sentences and thoughts with hidden logical structure enables us to explain how they relate to logical reality – the forms revealed in a correct symbolic notation – and hence what it is that their logical relations turn upon. A correct logical notation tells us what the real logical forms are, but these may be different from the apparent forms of our sentences and thoughts; yet it must somehow be in virtue of these real forms that our sentences and thoughts stand in logical relations to each other. How can sentences and thoughts stand in logical relations and yet not have the forms on which these relations depend? The solution to this puzzle is to accept that our sentences and thoughts have concealed logical forms; these then explain how it is that sentences and thoughts as we find them – in the raw, as it were – can be subject to logic as we have discovered it to be. The hidden structures *mediate* between the surface forms and revealed logical reality; the underlying layer acts as a kind of bridge to the subject-matter of logic proper. This layer is what a logical notation aims to capture. In the case of conscious thoughts, the extra layer is a stratum of mental reality, an inner configuration of conscious states themselves, predating the development of the notation that captures it. This layer explains how our conscious propositional states link up to logical structures, i.e. propositions as they are characterized in pure logic. It solves the 'mind-logic problem': the problem of how states of mind relate to the world of logic. In particular, it overcomes the problem posed by the alogical appearance of these states.

Now there is another kind of puzzle about consciousness, similar to the above puzzle in general form, which I think calls for a parallel kind of solution. This is the puzzle of how conscious states relate to the physical world, specifically to the body: the problem of embodiment. Conscious states, we know, depend causally and constitutively on physical states, but the way these states appear to us renders the dependence problematic. The physical sciences tell us about the nature of the body and brain, and this nature seems far removed from the nature of consciousness; yet it must *somehow* be in virtue of physical facts that conscious states come to exist in the first place and have their causes and effects. How can consciousness be physically governed in this way and yet be so utterly unlike that which governs it? How can the subjective have its roots in the objective? What has matter in motion got to do with the way a rose smells? What is it that converts brain 'gook' into visual experience? The solution, I suggest, is to recognize that conscious states possess a hidden natural (not logical) structure which mediates between their surface properties and the physical facts on which they constitutively depend. The surface properties are not enough on their own to link conscious states intelligibly to the physical world, so we need to postulate some deep properties to supply the necessary linkage. Some properties *must* exist to link consciousness intelligibly to the brain, since it is so linked; my suggestion is that these properties belong to the hidden nature of consciousness.[16] The physical governance of conscious states requires a hidden structure to connect those states with physical properties of the body – just as the logical governance of such states requires a hidden structure to connect them to abstract logical forms.

These deep linking properties must meet two conditions: (i) they must be intelligibly related to the surface properties, and (ii) they must be intelligibly related to physical properties of the body. Only by meeting these two conditions can they perform their mediating role. (Similarly, the hidden logical structures of sentences or thoughts must be explicably related both to their surface features, say by specifiable transformations, and to the abstract structures of logic.) My suggestion is that only this supposition of a hidden structure can account for the place of consciousness in the physical world. Nothing overt is up to the job. Without it consciousness

---

[16] For more on this see ch. 3

would be miraculous, impossible (rather as logical thought would be impossible without hidden logical structure). There has to be more to consciousness than there seems to be or else it could not depend upon the physical world in the way we know it does. As it were, nature could not create consciousness out of living matter without first constructing a substructure for consciousness to rest on; levitation is not an option.

It may help to bring this idea into focus if I contrast it with two proposals made by Thomas Nagel – proposals which are interestingly akin to, but importantly different from, the present proposal. The first proposal, made in 'What is it Like to be a Bat?'[17], is that subjective experience might be describable in objective (though nonphysical) terms, and that such an 'objective phenomenology' might put us in a better position to understand the physical basis of experience. Such a mode of description would require us to form new concepts of experience, and to view our experiences differently from our usual subjective view of them; we should come to view them from no particular subjective perspective. This detached objective mode of description might then reduce the distance between consciousness as we *now* conceive it and the physical world. Nagel suggests that 'structural features' of experience might be susceptible to this kind of objective description: 'Aspects of subjective experience that admitted this kind of objective description might be better candidates for objective explanations of a more familiar sort.'[18] This proposal does seem to contain, in effect, the idea that conscious states might have natures that differ from their immediate phenomenal features, yet are not straightforwardly physical, so that there is more to consciousness, and to the psychophysical nexus, than we customarily suppose. These natures are thus at present unknown, though they are perhaps in principle discoverable by means of diligent conceptual effort. It is clear enough, however, that the features Nagel has in mind belong to what I am calling the surface of consciousness, since they are described as 'phenomenological' features. They are abstract features of what is given introspectively. We might compare them to the abstract relations that could be described between colours, phenomenologically understood.

[17] In his *Mortal Questions* (Cambridge University Press: Cambridge, 1979).
[18] *Ibid.*, p. 179.

Nagel's second proposal, made in *The View from Nowhere*,[19] is different from the first, though by no means inconsistent with it. This is that the real nature of conscious states might just consist in states of the brain. Subjective states might fit into the objective order by having straightforward physical natures. Here Nagel is adopting the familiar picture of natural kinds, according to which the concept of the kind leaves open a blank space which may be subsequently filled by science; mental concepts likewise contain a blank that neurophysiology will eventually fill. It might turn out, then, that mental kinds have ordinary physical natures; nothing about the mental concept precludes this possibility. Pain might be C-fibre stimulation in the way water is H_2O. The connexions between the mental and the physical would then only *seem* contingent because the mental concept does not extend to cover the complete nature of the mental kind, this nature being in reality necessarily physical. Nagel calls this a 'dual aspect' theory of conscious states: one aspect consisting in subjective features, the other in brain states. Now this is certainly a conception on which conscious states have a hidden nature, a nature not derivable from how they are given introspectively (nor indeed from ordinary third person criteria); *this* nature cannot be characterized as 'phenomenological' in any sense. It is not an aspect of the appearance of the mental kind, however 'structural'. It lies well below the surface of consciousness. And it takes empirical investigation of the brain to discover it.

If we combine these two proposals, then we reach something like the following position. Conscious states admit of three levels or types of description: (a) purely subjective description, whose essential precondition is empathy or imagination; (b) objective phenomenological description, which is accessible independently of empathy and imagination, but which is still confined to the surface of consciousness; (c) objective physical description, which is not contained in the original mental concepts, and which belongs to a level of mental reality quite removed from introspection and the way consciousness manifests itself to us. The hope, then, is that playing these three modes of description off against each other will enable us to understand how consciousness can exist in a physical organism. In particular, we might hope that level (b) will help us

[19] Ch. 3

mediate between levels (a) and (c). Conscious states have a physical nature in virtue of the fact that their subjective features are linked to that nature via objective properties that obtain at the subjective level. 'Objective phenomenology' is what explains how the subjective can be yoked to the physiological.

This is in many ways an attractive scheme, and one with which I have a good deal of sympathy. My main reservation about it is that it is too conservative about the kinds of properties that characterize the mediating level; as a result, it does not, I think, have the power to solve the original problem. That problem is how to provide an intelligible link between consciousness as it appears and the physical body upon which it depends. It seems to me that neither of Nagel's two proposals can do this, because they stick too closely to properties with which we are more or less familiar. The properties envisaged in the project of developing an objective phenomenology are too close to the surface properties that set the original problem; they are still defined at the subjective level, despite their relative abstractness, floating free of ordinary physical properties – merely bleached out proxies for the problematic subjective features. In so far as one has a clear idea of what these 'structural' properties would be like, they still seem too distant from ordinary physical processes in the brain to supply the desired intelligible connexion. Either they will be only contingently linked to subjective features or they will have the same difficulty making contact with the physical brain. On the other hand, simply positing a physical nature for conscious states seems to leave the original problem entirely untouched; for how do these deep physical properties relate to the superficial properties of the mental state – those that make it the mental state it is? Mental states may have a physical aspect, but the question is: how is this possible? Simply asserting that they do looks too much like trying to solve the problem by main force; it does not remove our initial perplexity. We need to be supplied with a stepping stone to the physical nature; and the idea of objective phenomenology (oxymoronic as it sounds) leaves us still marooned on the opposite bank. The putative mediating properties themselves stand in need of mediation.

The kind of hidden structure I envisage would lie at neither of the levels suggested by Nagel: it would be situated somewhere between them. Neither phenomenological nor physical, this mediating level would not (by definition) be fashioned on the model of either side of the divide, and hence would not find itself unable to reach out to the other side. Its characterization would call for radical conceptual innovation (which I have argued is probably beyond us). Since it would not be characterized by concepts familiar from either side of the psychophysical nexus, however extended, it would not simply raise the same old problem again in a new form. The operative properties would be neither at the phenomenal surface nor right down there with the physical hardware; they would be genuinely deep and yet they would not simply coincide with physical properties of the brain. Somehow they would make perfect sense of the psychophysical nexus, releasing us from the impasse that seems endemic to the topic. They really would *explain* how it is that chunks of matter can develop an inner life. There would be nothing hard-to-swallow or take-it-on-faith about the theory that detailed the powers of these properties.

I should like nothing better than to be able to tell you exactly what kinds of properties these are, but that is something I fear I cannot do. For it is my unhappy conviction that these properties are radically unknowable by us; they are not reachable from the kinds of concept-forming capacities we possess.[20] But this does not, mercifully, prevent me from supposing that such explanatory properties *exist*, and from knowing that they are not identical with any properties hitherto proposed as answers to the problem of embodiment. Our position, I believe, is analogous to that of creatures who are capable of thinking logically but who are constitutionally unable (explicitly) to devise the correct logic governing their thoughts. Such creatures cannot arrive at a reflective understanding of the concepts that characterize the hidden logical structure of their own reasonings; though they may suspect that this hidden level exists and know that nothing they have ever heard from their logicians (a sorry crew) comes close to accounting for the inferences they recognize as valid. Similarly, I believe that the only explanation of the emergence of consciousness in a physical universe is that consciousness has a hidden structure, but I cannot tell you the exact nature of that structure, nor even its general shape. Consciousness must be more than it seems for it to be what it is, but we cannot know what

[20] See ch. 1 on this.

this 'more' consists in. The main obstacle to accepting this is a reluctance to abandon radical empiricism about consciousness – a feeling that consciousness *cannot* be credited with a hidden nature. But I am suggesting that we go right ahead and abandon this assumption (today!), on pain of not explaining what needs to be explained. The example of hidden logical structure already loosens the hold of the assumption, but we need to get yet more radical than this if we are to make any sense of nature as we find it. The assumption is not compulsory, and abandoning it makes a lot fall into place. What I should especially urge now is that our inability to specify the nature of this hidden structure is not a good reason to spurn the philosophical benefits the hypothesis of its existence brings us. Knowing it is there, ticking away, relieves us of the fear that we might have to admit that there is no such thing as consciousness – on the ground that there is no room for the supernatural in this godless world.[21]

I now want to investigate the following question: Does the surface of consciousness actively mislead us as to its real nature? Do we find consciousness essentially problematic, philosophically, precisely because we assume that the surface is all and the surface tempts us into error? Again, let us pursue the analogy with logic and language. In that area, the idea that the surface expression of propositions in language misleads us as to the true nature of propositions is well established; to see things aright, logically, we have to overcome initial impressions, discount the appearances. Ordinary language is not to be trusted. This means, in particular, downgrading our ordinary observational access to propositions, via perceived sentences, and elevating indirect modes of theory construction. Going naively by the linguistic appearances leads not only to logical impasse but also to metaphysical extravagance – as with Meinong's jungle, infested with shadowy Being. Beware the fraudulent singular

---

[21] For strictly philosophical purposes it is enough to know that the mediating hidden structure exists, since this relieves the conceptual (metaphysical) problem of how it is possible for consciousness to be rooted in the brain. This would indeed be an insoluble conundrum if the full nature of consciousness were already revealed to us, but the existence of a covert structure saves consciousness from inherent mysteriousness. The surface properties are not required to make miraculously unmediated contact with the physical underpinnings; they take an invisible, though secure, detour to this destination. Knowing that the route exists makes it possible for us to resist the idea of an impossible journey. There is, in reality, no magic leap across a naturally impassable ravine. The ravine is an illusion, borne of cognitive closure. So that vertigo you feel has no objective correlate.

term, the pseudo-subject, begetter of metaphysical monsters! Fearful of admitting subsistent entities into his logical zoo, Russell advised that 'a robust sense of reality is very necessary in framing a correct analysis of propositions about unicorns, golden mountains, round squares, and other such pseudo-objects'.[22] And the key to preserving this sense of reality, for Russell, is a willingness to attribute hidden logical structure to propositions; we protect our sentences and thoughts from the demons they are apt to conjure up by granting them a covert structure that does not invite a Meinongian ontology; we trade hidden form for extravagant objects. The metaphysical illusions stem from fascination with the surface of language, slavishly taking it at face-value. Philosophically, the way we naturally experience language is a minefield.

Now it is hard not to be struck at this point by the analogy with the kinds of temptations that arise in the case of consciousness. Philosophical reflection on the nature of consciousness has grown its own ontological jungle, led to its own wild flight from common sense. A robust sense of reality has not been characteristic of philosophical (and scientific) thought about consciousness. I refer, of course, to that sorry catalogue of occult entities to which we have become accustomed in these discussions: immaterial substances, disembodied minds, immortal souls, gaseous selves. Consciousness has conjured its own exotic zoo. Then too, there are the many kinds of isolation from the physical world that consciousness has been condemned to suffer: the inverted spectrum, the logical privacy of sensations, complete brainlessness, total solipsism – all the ways in which consciousness has been taken to be merely contingently related to the rest of the world in which it is ordinarily embedded. Consciousness, we are tempted to feel, can live and breathe in its own sphere, totally sealed off from its physical context.[23]

---

[22] *Introduction to Mathematical Philosophy*, p. 170.

[23] Internalism about intentional content might also be included here – the idea that the representational content of consciousness is logically independent of anything objective. Solipsism-of-the-moment is the most extreme expression of this idea of independence: my current conscious state could exist whole and entire without the existence of anything else at all (including a brain). I think this is an illusory possibility, but I recognize that it is nourished by something primitive and compelling about the way consciousness strikes us. Wittgenstein was clearly interested in, and hostile to, such impressions of independence; the opposition to private language is part of his polemic against carving consciousness off from the rest of the natural world, particularly behaviour. My position is that the hidden structure of consciousness contains the machinery to lock consciousness firmly onto the physical world of brain and

Now it is not that all of this is just gratuitous confusion, wilful hallucination, a bad tradition we can freely put behind us. Rather, I think such ideas arise spontaneously in us when we reflect upon our own consciousness; they are positively encouraged by the manner in which consciousness strikes us when we turn our minds to it. In particular, introspection – or a certain philosophical use of it – naturally prompts these flights of imagination in us. Consciousness insinuates its own uniqueness and autonomy, its defiance of the physical. It is not quite that we are under the introspective analogue of a perceptual illusion about the true nature of consciousness, an illusion we can do nothing to dispel; our predicament, rather, is like that of the traditional logician obsessed by the surface of language. The superficial promptings of the phenomena should not be taken for the last word on the nature of what is given; a corrective lies beneath the surface. We should not suppose that the appearances exhaust the reality, nor that the appearances are always to be trusted. On the contrary, the appearances issue invitations to philosophical error.

Meinong's ontology is thus comparable, in point of philosophical aetiology, to Descartes': both are understandable, though mistaken, responses to the appearances. Certain apparent singular terms incite us to seek merely subsistent objects for them to denote. Conscious states, as they are presented to introspection, seem to call for an ontology of nonphysical substances for them to inhere in. And the feeling that consciousness can be radically detached from the physical world is similarly comprehensible, though mistaken; it is a natural response to the way consciousness presents itself. For the surface of consciousness does not contain the materials to demonstrate the nature of its necessary connexion with physical fact. It conceals its physical involvements. We should need access to the hidden structure of consciousness actually to provide such a demonstration. It is in this hidden structure that the necessities that bind consciousness to the physical world ultimately reside. God, knowing the details of the hidden structure, can see quite plainly that

---

behaviour and environment, but that the surface of consciousness encourages us to believe that these links are merely contingent. When you cannot perceive (or conceive) necessary links you are apt to think there are not any, especially when you have racked your brains trying to discover them. This is a mistake, but a natural one. Cognitive closure with respect to necessary links is misinterpreted as contingency in those links.

there are no immaterial substances and the like, and He fully appreciates the nature of the necessities that link consciousness to the body. He has no isolationist leanings and is not prey to ontological temptation. But we, alas, are confined to the slippery surface of consciousness, and this surface does not furnish a rich enough conception of consciousness to allow us to understand how consciousness depends necessarily upon the body and brain. So we proceed to detach it from the body, locating it in a mysterious immaterial substance specially manufactured for the purpose. We fall for the mirage consciousness projects. What we should do is pause and ask ourselves whether the surface exhausts the reality; for if it does not, then the hidden part might well contain what is needed to keep consciousness glued down to the physical world, where it belongs. The cure for these temptations is knowledge of the hidden structure of consciousness – as it is in the analogous logical case.[24]

Unfortunately, if I am right, it is a cure we cannot actually apply, since we cannot know this structure. The mirage will always be there to seduce us. Still, it is soothing to know that the cure exists; it allows us not to take the temptations at face-value. It gives us the confidence to call the mirage by its proper name. We can remain robustly realistic about the physical involvements of consciousness, dismissing the inevitable temptations to the contrary as stemming from ignorance. These temptations arise because we have no grasp of the deep properties that mediate between the surface features we experience and the underlying physical basis. They do *not* arise from a *full* appreciation of a set of *intrinsically* baffling facts. We are like a logically puzzled Russell in want of the notion of a quantifier but justifiably convinced that somewhere in the deep structure the puzzles are all beautifully resolved.[25]

[24] Once apprised of the hidden logical form you are no longer under pressure to concoct a rebarbative ontology to save the appearances: you can Russell away the Meinong. Similarly, I suggest, with the conscious mind: if we but knew its hidden structure we should no longer be tempted by an ontology of the immaterial. Not knowing this structure, but knowing of its existence, allows us to experience these temptations while keeping them at arm's length. God, we know, feels no temptation to subscribe to a Cartesian ontology; His knowledge goes too deep for that. We should try to follow His example, despite the poverty of our understanding.
[25] The further away our conceptual repertoire is from the hidden structure of consciousness the more prey to metaphysical temptation we shall find ourselves to be. The greater the cognitive closure the more the impression of miracle surrounding the psychophysical nexus. The more hidden the underlying structure the less likely we shall be to believe in its resolving

The considerations advanced in the previous section in support of the idea of a hidden structure to consciousness are of a broadly metaphysical character; they concern the philosophical problems that might be solved by accepting that idea. In this section I shall argue that there also exist empirical data that are best explained by adopting the idea; we now have empirical evidence for the thesis that consciousness extends further than it introspectively seems.

If hidden properties are attributed to something, we expect that these properties will play some sort of causal role; they will serve to explain some of the effects that the thing in question has. And observation of these effects, if they are thus explainable, will count as evidence in favour of the attribution of such hidden properties. Of course, it may not be easy to obtain this kind of evidence, given that the deep properties are typically accompanied by the surface properties; for it may be that the surface properties suffice on their own to explain the observed phenomena. What would rule out this possibility would be cases in which the surface properties are absent and yet the usual sorts of effect transpire; then we could attribute those effects to properties other than the surface ones. That is, we have to consider a certain sort of counterfactual question: if the surface properties were removed, would the effects (or some of them) remain the same? If the answer is Yes, as shown by cases in which removal leaves the effects intact, then it is reasonable to assert that the effects in normal cases are not wholly dependent on the surface properties (assuming that no failsafe mechanism comes into operation when the surface properties are abolished.) We shall then have evidence for the presence of causally operative hidden

---

power. I think that the best explanation of these temptations, impressions and incredulities is precisely that the solution to the mind–body problem is deeply closed to us. And given their intensity and persistence I should submit that the closure is principled and permanent. These pathologies of thought, tenacious as they are, are thus powerful evidence that our conceptual resources are fundamentally unsuited to solving the mind–body problem. There is a structural obstacle preventing us from forming the concepts that would release us from the pathologies in question. These pathologies are endemic to our thinking about consciousness; they are not going to be expunged by either therapy or theory. Our cognitive slant drags us willy-nilly into philosophical error, inciting us to impute mystery to what ought to seem as clear as day. We cannot help seeing the objectively natural as supernatural. I *know* there is nothing occult about how the brain secretes consciousness – no more so than the liver's secretion of bile – but even I cannot rid myself of the feeling that something very funny is going on here, that a strange trick is being played on me. My suggestion is that the trick is being played, not by the brain and consciousness themselves, but by my own conceptual/theoretical set: cognitive closure masquerading as mystery in the objects.

properties. The causal powers of the thing in question will not depend wholly upon properties observable at the surface. Hidden causality will commend itself.

Our question, then, is this: Are the characteristic effects of conscious states preserved when the surface properties of consciousness are abolished? That is, does removing the phenomenal features of such states do away with their causal powers? For if it does do away with them, then we do not need any features beyond the phenomenal in order to explain the causal powers in question; while if they persist, we do. This, then, is the question whether consciousness works by hidden causality. Take, for example, visual experience: what happens if we remove the fact that it *seems* to the subject that he is having a visual experience of a certain kind? If it turns out that this does not destroy the characteristic effects of visual experience, then we can assume that in normal cases those effects are produced by properties other than those that are manifest to the subject introspectively: visual experiences pack hidden causality. As a thought-experiment, I suspect most people would be inclined to say that the causal powers of visual experience would not be preserved under abolition of visual seemings – the causality here is entirely superficial. But, remarkably, the empirical facts appear to go against this intuition. A surprisingly large range of the usual effects of visual experience are preserved in cases in which subjects sincerely report having no visual experiences at all. These are the well-known cases of so-called blindsight.[26]

Let me just give a brief flavour of the empirical findings associated with these cases. The subject has suffered damage to certain cortical areas normally involved in visual processing, but not to all such areas; some of the retinal projections to the brain are destroyed, while others remain intact. Asked whether she can still see in a certain portion of her visual field, the subject resolutely denies that she can; she reports having no visual experience with respect to that portion – there are no visual seemings there. However, if she is then tested on various discrimination tasks – involving size, position, shape, movement etc. – she can perform remarkably well: she can reliably tell you what kind of thing lies in the 'blind' part of her

---

[26] See L. Weiskrantz, *Blindsight: A Case Study and Implications* (Oxford University Press: Oxford, 1986).

visual field. As she does this, she claims that she cannot *see* anything at all; she is merely guessing to please the experimenter. She is greatly surprised to learn that she is getting the answers right. Thus she appears to others to be (partially) sighted, but she takes herself to be blind. Behaviourally, she can function much like a sighted person; phenomenologically, she strikes herself as blind. Hence the oxymoron 'blindsight': seeing without seeming to see.

Now my proposed interpretation of these data is as follows. In cases of normal vision two sorts of (intrinsic) properties of conscious experience are causally operative in producing discriminative behaviour: surface properties, which are accessible to the subject introspectively; and deep properties, which are not so accessible. Having both sorts of property functioning together gives you straightforward sightedness (assuming they are produced in the right way by outside stimuli). In cases of simple blindness, where visual discrimination is utterly abolished, neither sort of property gets activated by external stimuli – the capacity for such activation is gone – and so behaviour is not controlled by the internal instantiation of these properties. But in cases of blindsight we have a dissociation of the two sorts of property; here we have the deep properties without the surface ones. External stimuli activate only the deep properties, which do not make it to awareness, while there is no longer a capacity to have the surface properties activated. The result is that the subject seems to herself to be blind, since she enjoys no visual phenomenology, but in fact she still instantiates many of the properties of experience that controlled visual discrimination before the damage happened. The hidden structure of the experience is now operating on its own, unaccompanied by its usual surface aspect. The iceberg's tip has been shaved off, leaving the underwater portion to cause what it can. The causality of consciousness is now all hidden. So it is not that in normal vision the entire causal work of conferring discriminative ability is carried out by the introspectable features of experience, while in blindsight a brand new mechanism takes over; rather, it is part of the old mechanism that is still operative, only now shorn of its phenomenal surface. The old machinery of experience now functions in a darkened room. Accordingly, in normal vision there is more at work than the phenomenal surface; there is also a causal substructure to the experience. The experience causes what it does in virtue of properties which are not manifest to the subject; yet these hidden properties really are intrinsic to the experience. Visual experience harbours intrinsic hidden causality.

I take it that what is most controversial in my interpretation of blindsight is the thesis that it demonstrates a hidden causal structure to conscious visual states *themselves*. It would presumably not be denied that *some* causal structure exists in common to ordinary sight and blindsight; the moot question is whether this structure is intrinsic to experience itself or merely exists alongside it. Is the shrouded discriminative machinery just an accompaniment to the experience rather than a constituent of it? In answer to this, I should say that my interpretation is intuitively more reasonable than this alternative: it conforms better with the way we ordinarily think about experience and its causal powers. For it seems hard to deny that in normal cases of sight it is the experience *itself* that carries the relevant causal powers, not some unconscious (possibly purely physical) subsystem whirring away somewhere else in there. It is in virtue of my having the visual experiences I do that I can discriminate what I can. We explain my discriminative behaviour precisely by saying that I have visual experiences of certain kinds; they are the causal ground of my vision-driven behaviour. We do not say that I have these experiences *and* there is some *other* causal source at work inside me. Attributing the experience to me is sufficient to capture the causal powers being exercised. But if that is really literally true, as I think it is, and if there is a common causal structure involved in sight and blindsight, as I also think there is, then it follows, I think, that (some of) the properties causally responsible for discrimination in normal vision are literally properties *of* the experience itself – though they are hidden to the subject of experience. Visual experiences themselves are what carry causal powers in the production of discriminative behaviour, and blindsight shows that the properties that ground these powers are not all introspectable by the subject. Besides, let us be naive for a minute, do blindsight patients not *look* very much as if they are having visual experiences when they make their surprising discriminations? What they in fact have (if I am right) is a residual component of ordinary visual experience; and this is why they appear (partially) sighted. They do not look the way people look when there is *nothing* experiential going on. So I insist that the hidden causal machinery is integral to conscious experience, not extraneous to it.

It might help to clarify my position on blindsight to compare it with a hypothetical kind of case. Earlier I claimed that conscious thoughts have both a surface 'grammatical' form and a deep logical form; the former is what is given to introspection (and in the shape of the vernacular content sentence in the belief report); the latter is what is revealed by logical analysis and is not (always) evident to the subject in the very having of the thought. Now let us imagine the following syndrome: our subject sincerely claims that he can no longer reason – tell which propositions follow from which other ones – but nevertheless when tested on reasoning tasks gets the answers right above the level predicted by chance. His reasoning capacity is (partially) intact, though he has the impression that his reasoning days are over (I often feel like that). This subject is quite unlike another kind of subject who claims he cannot reason and indeed performs atrociously on reasoning tasks – he is utterly 'logic-blind'. I should say of our first subject that he still possesses the cognitive structures that allow reasoning in normal people, but he has lost the surface features of those structures. He still has the hidden logical forms represented somewhere in his head, which enable him to make logical 'discriminations', but he lacks the surface signs that in normal people accompany the hidden stuff. His predicament is exactly what we should expect if, by surgery, we took away the surface structure of his thoughts and left him with only their hidden logical structure. He is no longer conscious *of* having thoughts, but he still has his share of logical structures mentally represented: logical blindsight is his lot. Now, reasoning back to the normal case, we should say that such abnormal cases, were they to arise, would provide evidence that our ordinary thoughts have hidden as well as manifest properties. Again, it is by having conscious thoughts themselves that we can appreciate what follows from what; so the common element between the normal case and the abnormal case is indeed an intrinsic feature of ordinary thoughts. If such abnormal cases actually presented themselves, then I think they would provide empirical evidence for the thesis, independently recommended on logical grounds, that thoughts have hidden logical structure: there is more to their causal efficacy, in allowing logical 'discriminations', than is comprised in their surface phenomenal features. There is hidden causality in respect of the logical features of conscious thoughts. We saw that thoughts have hidden logical structure; now we see that this structure plays a causal role. The process of reasoning depends upon a system of concealed logical articulation. A person equipped only with the surface marks of thought, in whom the concealed structure was missing, would not be our logical equal – though he would boast that he was.[27]

There are three consequences of the present view of blindsight that I should like to spell out. The first is that, according to this view, the label 'blindsight' is the right label for the condition it denotes; in particular, the use of the word 'sight' is fully justified. On some possible interpretations of the data, this would not be the right word, since the assumption of those interpretations is that nothing *mental* is going on in these cases; the conscious experience is wholly abolished, leaving only mechanisms that at best accompany experiences. The patient is thus not in any literal sense sighted. But on my interpretation the residue is precisely a component of the original experience, namely its hidden component. Thus the mentalistic connotations of the word 'sight' are warranted in these cases. The subject is not merely behaving *as if* he is sighted; there is a clear sense in which he *is* sighted – for he has not lost his visual experiences in their entirety. He still enjoys the benefits conferred by the substructure of conscious visual experiences. The deep properties are still being activated systematically by outside stimuli, and they play their usual role in shaping discriminative behaviour.

My only cavil with the phrase concerns its first part: I do not think it is correct to say that the subjects are *blind*. Rather, they seem to themselves introspectively to be blind – they are, if you like,

---

[27] We might consider the hypothesis that what is true of sight is true of conscious states in general. Namely: their causal efficacy is largely carried by the hidden component, the surface features being responsible for much less than initially appears. In the case of pain, for example, it may be that the quale could be abolished without losing the main functional properties of pain sensations. (No wonder qualia cannot be defined in terms of causal role: pain has a functional role, but not in virtue of its qualitative feel.) If this hypothesis were correct, we should be on the alert for empirical data structurally analogous to those characterizing blindsight: denials of experience accompanied by much of the usual causal profile of the experience denied. If such data were forthcoming, we should have evidence that the *modus operandi* of consciousness is largely a matter of its hidden component. It would not be all that surprising if it were, since there seems no good a priori reason why the features of conscious states that inform us of their presence should also be the features that bring about their effects.

subjectively blind. Objectively, they can discriminate stimuli on the basis of visual inputs as well as many people we should not describe as blind; and they do so in virtue of instantiating the same properties as normally sighted people – or so I have argued. They are partially sighted, but it seems to them (erroneously) that they are wholly blind. It might then be more accurate to refer to the syndrome in question as 'subjective blindness' or (more catchily) 'blanksight'. This would avoid the contradiction involved in describing someone as simultaneously both blind and sighted. That is not a possible condition for anyone to be in, though logic does not preclude someone both *seeming* to himself to be blind while at the same time being perfectly sighted.

The second consequence concerns the alleged epiphenomenalism of consciousness. It is sometimes argued that conscious states must be deemed epiphenomenal because we can imagine systems that are functionally equivalent to conscious systems and yet are devoid of consciousness. Consciousness does no causal work because deleting it need not alter the organism's causal capabilities. Then, applying a version of Occam's razor, it must be redundant to invoke conscious states in explanatory contexts. Now, setting aside other objections one might make to this style of argument, the point I want to make is that it commits a nonsequitur if the position defended here is correct. What the thought-experiment at issue supposes is that there could be a system functionally equivalent to a conscious one that there is nothing it is like to be – a system that lacks subjective phenomenal properties. Absent the qualia and you need not disturb the behavioural dispositions. But, if I am right, it does not follow from this that conscious states are epiphenomenal *tout court*. All that follows (if anything does) is that the *surface* properties of consciousness are epiphenomenal; the deep properties may still be present, doing their usual causal work, in the functionally equivalent system there is nothing it is like to be. Consciousness is causally efficacious all right; it is just that its uppermost layer is given to idleness (not that I should agree even with this latter claim).

And the same point goes for the weaker thesis that consciousness is partially or largely epiphenomenal: that its efficacy in respect of behaviour is minimal or nugatory. For if the causal powers of conscious states depend to some degree on their hidden properties, then qualia-free virtual functional equivalents do not prove semiepiphenomenalism about consciousness all the way down. They do not prove that consciousness packs a negligible causal punch: they prove only that the surface of consciousness is not the main authority from which the motor system takes its orders. To prove the stronger claim it would be necessary to show (at least) that you could have functional equivalents without the instantiation of the hidden properties of consciousness; and this is by no means entailed by producing cases in which there are no properties for the system to introspect. For the same reason, syndromes such as blindsight do not show that conscious visual experiences are largely epiphenomenal in respect of visual discriminations; they show only that the surface properties of consciousness play less of a causal role than we might naively have supposed. Indeed, it may be that the main causal burden of consciousness is borne by its hidden properties – these still being properties precisely of consciousness. Most of what consciousness does may be under the control of its subsurface constitution. There is thus less of an epiphenomenalist threat if consciousness is awarded a hidden causally active structure. In fact, awarding it such a structure seems the best way to reconcile the evident causal potency of consciousness with the apparent ease of retaining its causal powers while doing away with qualia.[28]

The third consequence concerns the science of psychology. The view that has become standard is that psychology treats of two fundamental kinds of property: conscious properties and unconscious ones. These are conceived as, respectively, accessible to the

---

[28] That is, hidden causal structure seems like a nice way to resolve what amounts to an antinomy about consciousness. On the one hand, there are excellent reasons, biological and observational, to credit consciousness with major causal heft: it seems as causally vital as any organ of the body. On the other hand, there are distressing intuitions of a philosophical nature that seem to cast doubt on the causal power of consciousness: it seems all too easy to imagine an insentient robot equipped with all the same causal powers as a conscious creature – just remove our consciousness and leave our brain intact. Now there are two points to make here. First, we may be under an illusion when we imagine deleting consciousness while leaving the brain fully intact – an illusion spawned by not knowing the hidden structure of consciousness. If we knew this structure, then we might see that there is no way to remove consciousness without degrading the brain's physically-based causal potential, i.e. removing some of the physical machinery. Second, it may be that the causal powers of consciousness are preponderantly carried by its hidden structure, in which case we have a resolution of the antinomy: consciousness has causal heft all right, but not principally in virtue of its qualia-constituted surface. The way to build a robot approximating to the causal powers of a conscious creature would be to install only the hidden structure of consciousness. The existence of such a robot would not constitute a proof that consciousness *tout court* is epiphenomenal, only that its surface marks are.

subject by means of introspection and inaccessible to him by these means. Psychological properties are either present to the subject or instantiated in some subpersonal system within him: they are either right here or somewhere over there. Observable behaviour is typically the joint upshot of both kinds of property, working in tandem. But in the view I am advocating we need to recognize three levels – or a twofold distinction within one of the levels. The conscious level needs to be bifurcated into the surface and the deep, both layers operating together, along with the genuinely unconscious states and processes, to produce behaviour. In the case of vision, say, we need first the unconscious subpersonal modular computations that eventually generate a conscious percept, and then we need to divide that conscious percept into its hidden component and its manifest component. Vision-directed behaviour thus has a threefold psychological aetiology. The subject is not conscious *of* either of the first two of these, but the hidden properties of the percept are nevertheless aspects of the conscious experience itself, not of its subpersonal antecedents.[29] A full and adequate psychology would thus need to employ concepts appropriate to each of these three levels. A science of mental causation requires knowledge of the factors operative at each level.

Psychology must, therefore, if it is to frame adequate laws and explanations of behaviour, find a way to characterize the hidden properties of consciousness – it must actually identify these properties and develop a theory of them. For psychology seeks (among other things) causally relevant traits of mind, and the infrastructure of consciousness contains such traits. The question must then arise as to whether it *can* discover these traits: for if it cannot, then it must remain at best an incomplete science. If the hidden causal structure of consciousness proved noumenal for us, then the correct psychological science would be closed to our understanding. And

---

[29] This suggests a rough criterion for distinguishing unconscious states from hidden features of conscious states. F is a hidden property of conscious experience E iff (i) F is a property of E, (ii) F is not a manifest (to the subject) property of E, and (iii) F is not part of the aetiology of E. Intuitively, the difference between a hidden property of a conscious state and an unconscious state is that the hidden property does not belong among the causes and effects of the conscious state. Various unconscious computational states lead up to a visual experience which has a hidden aspect: the difference is that the former but not the latter are implicated in the causal production of the experience. This is a way of getting at the idea that the hidden aspect is intrinsic to the experience.

given that there has to be a close connexion between, on the one hand, the properties of consciousness that explain (physical) behaviour and, on the other, the properties of consciousness that explain its (physical) embodiment – behaviour consisting in movements of the body – the quest for the basic laws of behaviour will be about as difficult as the problem of what makes consciousness relate intelligibly to the body and brain. Both depend upon the existence of intelligible psychophysical mediation. Since the properties that confer causal powers on conscious states with respect to physical behaviour must somehow overlap with those that give conscious states a physical basis, the task of identifying the former properties must be about as difficult as that of identifying the latter properties. The problem of unearthing the fundamental laws of behaviour cannot be separated from the problem of emergence. How conscious events cause (and are caused by) physical events cannot be divorced from how conscious events arise from physical events. Basic psychophysical causal laws will be as obtainable (or unobtainable) as principles intelligibly linking conscious states to their realizing brain states. Put differently, the puzzle of psychophysical supervenience infects the project of devising psychophysical laws, or accounting for psychophysical causation. Both require knowledge of the hidden natural structure of consciousness. Without this knowledge we shall not be able to progress much beyond crude psychophysical correlations.[30] A psychology of behaviour is thus in the end as hard and frustrating as the mind–body problem; they are, indeed, aspects of the same basic question. And since I think the mind–body problem is *very* hard, terminally so, the science of psychology must also be. (Science turns out to be as hard as philosophy.) If we are cognitively ill-equipped to solve the mind–body problem, as I have suggested we are, then we shall be correspondingly limited when it comes to developing a deep science of behaviour: the psychophysical nexus will baffle us whichever way we come at it. Our thirst for causal explanation may here remain forever unquenched. We shall never have God's knowledge of why we do what we do. We can, of course, come to know something of

---

[30] Such correlations would allow prediction, but they would not be accompanied by the kind of understanding we seek and expect in other areas. They would have a brutish feel to them. They would be like the generalizations of Mendelian genetics without detailed genetic theory to back them up. There is more on the inferior theoretical status of psychophysical generalizations (as we are able to formulate them) in chs 5 and 6.

a superficial nature about the mental antecedents of behaviour; but we may not be able to penetrate to the ultimate underlying principles. At any rate, if we can, it will be because we have got a lot better at understanding how consciousness seeps from organic material lumps. Not a prospect to stake one's life on, I should say.

I began this chapter by extolling the virtues of hidden structure in general, citing some examples in which the idea has proved indispensable. But in those examples we can actually specify aspects of the hidden structures in question: we can say what *kinds* of properties are instantiated at the hidden level. This is what permits us to develop detailed theories in which the hidden structures play an essential explanatory role. No doubt we believe in the existence of such structures (in part at least) because we can identify the properties that define them. However, in the case of the hidden structure of consciousness, I have said nothing about which properties define that structure, and so have done nothing to further the project of constructing a real theory of embodiment.[31] This may be found objectionable: how can I enthusiastically postulate the existence of such a structure and yet confess myself unable to say anything about its constitutive characteristics? I am voluble on behalf of something whose nature reduces me to silence. I seem like an agnostic theist.

My answer to this objection is that we can have theoretical reason to postulate the existence of a level of reality whose actual constitution we admittedly cannot specify. We can know that something exists without knowing its nature. We can assert that a gap is filled without being able to say how it is filled. When the surface properties of a system are insufficient to explain its workings, we can reasonably suppose that there must be other properties, instantiated somewhere in the system, that transcend the surface – and these properties explain what the surface properties fail to. That is to say, we can reasonably suppose that our own modes of

---

[31] But let us remind ourselves of what we do know (if I am right). We know what the unknown theory would be a theory of, namely the hidden structure of consciousness. We know what kinds of property would *not* solve the problem (see ch. 1). We also have the beginnings of a theory about why we cannot arrive at a theory of embodiment – because of the conceptual confinement imposed by our given concept-forming capacities. And we know how to soothe our metaphysical anxieties about the occult appearance of the mind–body link – by recognizing the existence of transcendent facts. Even if the embodiment relation itself is radically incomprehensible to us, still we are not in *such* bad philosophical shape. I can think of other areas of philosophy where our position is much worse.

epistemic access to the nature of the system do not exhaust its reality. Thus we might for a while have been in the position of knowing that the observable properties of matter do not explain its behaviour, so that we need to postulate further unobservable properties that do, without having any inkling of what those unobservable properties might be like. This is really no more than to admit that our theories are fundamentally incomplete. So it is with consciousness: we know that what we introspect of consciousness (and grasp from the third-person perspective) is insufficient to explain how consciousness relates to the physical world; so we have reason to think that consciousness has properties that go beyond this mode of access to it. We know there is a theoretical gap, and we know that nature does not tolerate gaps. We are like thwarted logicians who know that the surface structure of sentences is inadequate to explain their logical properties but who cannot for the life of them develop the logical concepts needed to account for these properties: they know that a hidden logical structure must exist, since the surface of sentences will not do the job – and there must *be* an answer to their puzzles, however elusive it may be. Similarly, our position with respect to the hidden natural structure of consciousness should be one of agnostic realism – and I see nothing intellectually disreputable about this kind of position. So I am not embarrassed by my failure to specify the nature of the hidden structure that links consciousness to its physical basis. It is enough, for my philosophical purposes, to know that this structure exists – and I think I have good theoretical reason to believe that.

But just how hidden is this hidden structure? So far I have been suggesting that it is hidden to introspection, as well as to our ordinary third-person perspective on conscious states. But I am strongly inclined to believe that it is a good deal more hidden than this. As I have argued elsewhere, there are principled reasons for suspecting that our concept-forming capacities are not up to developing the kinds of concepts necessary to understand the nature of the psychophysical link.[32] Roughly speaking, this is because the required concepts need somehow to straddle the gulf between matter and consciousness, but our concepts of matter and consciousness are constrained, respectively, by our faculties of perception and introspection – and concepts so constrained will not be capable of

[32] See earlier chs.

explaining the psychophysical link. Our perceptual access to material things, including the brain, sets limits on the way we can conceive of these things; and our introspective access to consciousness sets limits on the way we can conceive of it. We need a manner of conception that abstracts radically away from these two fundamental ways of apprehending the world, but we simply have no such manner at our cognitive disposal. We have no faculty that would enable us to form concepts of consciousness and the brain capable of solving the mind–body problem. Our empirical faculties bypass the place in reality where the solution lies. They are wrongly targeted, so far as the true nature of the psychophysical nexus is concerned. That nature does not reside in the catchment-area of those faculties. It is the wrong shape for them to take a grip on. Our concepts are infused by our basic modes of apprehending the world, and these modes of apprehension are unsuitable foundations for the kinds of concept needed to make sense of the link between consciousness and matter.[33] Thus I am prepared to embrace a kind of *noumenalism* about the psychophysical link; and since this link hinges upon the hidden structure of consciousness, I am ready to accept noumenalism about that structure. There can be no delving down into it. But – and this is the central point I want to make now – I do not think that even this extreme degree of hiddenness is a good reason to doubt that such a hidden structure exists: I can know that the structure exists (*has* to exist) even though I cannot even in principle identify any aspects of its intrinsic constitution. For I know that if it did *not* exist then consciousness would not be

---

[33] It is no easy task to formulate the nature and strength of this shaping and constraining. Philosophers since time immemorial have been trying to spell out the nature of the necessary link between concepts and experience (both perceptual and introspective). The link must not be made so strong that none but the most observational concepts have genuine content, but nor must it be made so weak that no substantial constraint is imposed. The intuitive thought is that empirical concepts (those applicable to the non-abstract world) must have *some* kind of contact with possible experience or else they will have no content for us: we shall have no colourable conception of what it would consist in for them to be instantiated. My conviction is that the concepts needed to resolve the mind–body problem fail that condition, vaguely formulated as it is. To put it differently: the property that objectively resolves the problem is not such that the concept of it meets the condition of intelligibility (to us) enshrined in the traditional intuitive thought. That property is experience-transcendent to a degree, and in a manner, that defies comprehension in terms of the concepts to which we can give content. If our concepts are boxes into which properties fit, then we cannot manufacture a box of the right shape to fit the property that solves the mind–body problem. For experience always plays some role, however indirect, in determining the shape of the boxes. Experience, moreover, is exactly the wrong place to look for the property that joins consciousness to the brain.

possible in a physical world – and I know that it is possible, because I have a piece of it myself. It is either eliminativism or miracles or hidden structure: and the first two possibilities are not to be entertained. Absolute noumenalism is preferable to denying the undeniable or wallowing in the supernatural.

If the present view of consciousness is correct, then consciousness posseses a unique combination of characteristics, so unique that it has proved difficult to countenance their combination. On the one hand, consciousness possesses properties to which we have immediate introspective access; on the other, it has properties of which we have no knowledge at all, and perhaps cannot have knowledge. It is simultaneously the best known thing and the worst known thing, the most manifest and the least manifest. This can seem odd, rebarbative even, but it is not inconsistent, since the properties in question form disjoint sets (or are brought under disjoint concepts). Knowledge, remember, is always under a description. Furthermore, I think it is the only way to explain our intellectual predicament: the introspectable surface of consciousness needs an unknown substructure to link it intelligibly to the physical body – or else it floats miraculously free of what we know to be its necessary basis. Perhaps it is the felt difficulty of seeing how these contrasting epistemic features could be combined that has disposed people to make consciousness an exception to the rule that natural phenomena need to be credited with a deep structure in addition to the face they present to observation. The phenomenon of consciousness presents *such* an accessible face that it is hard to believe it could conceal a highly secretive underside. If people have been so moved, then this is yet another illustration of the pernicious effect of letting your metaphysics be dictated by your epistemology. My position would be that the metaphysical merits of the present conception should be allowed to overrule any discomfort it may induce in the epistemologically sensitive. That discomfort is only temporary anyway – at least so I have found. Consciousness now strikes me as *exactly* the kind of thing that might be *expected* to combine these opposite epistemic features. For, on the one hand, it must be intelligibly related thus-and-so to the body, this requiring some truly remarkable covert constitution; and, on the other hand, it must be directly given to introspection, this calling for a rare degree of epistemic proximity. No wonder, then, that it appears completely transparent from one angle, while from the other it could hardly be more opaque. Why, after all, should what makes the embodiment of consciousness possible *also* be a potential object of introspection? Consciousness must possess a face that enables it to slot into the physical make-up of the brain, but it also presents a face upon which introspection gazes: and these are not going to be the same face. That is just the way consciousness *is* – and indeed has to be. By virtue of its position in the world, consciousness must possess a dual nature. Yet it must also be a unitary thing, since what is introspected has also to be embodied. The contrasting epistemic features stem from these two simultaneous demands.

The relative epistemic distances of the surface and the deep properties of consciousness may also explain why our ordinary mental concepts are so closely tied to the surface. These concepts do not operate in the way typical natural kind concepts do, by containing a blank space to be filled in by subsequent empirical discoveries about the hidden make-up of the mental kind in question.[34] Rather, they present the essence of the mental kind as already contained in the concept: she who masters the concept thereby knows the nature of the kind. This may seem in some tension with the idea that conscious states harbour a hidden structure, since this structure might be taken to be analogous to (say) the physical structure of chemical kinds. But in fact there is no irresoluble tension here: conscious states have a hidden structure, but our mental concepts do not purport to advert to that structure. They are content to stick to the surface of consciousness, promising nothing about its deeper layout. The criteria for their application do not therefore reach beyond our ordinary methods of ascribing conscious states to ourselves and others. The individuation of mental kinds takes place at the surface. Our mental concepts are happily superficial, while that to which they apply possesses natural depth.[35] Perhaps if a creature had

---

[34] See chs 5 and 6 on this.

[35] In chs 5 and 6 this is not recognized as a possible position. There I assumed that any hidden structure to the mind would perforce play a controlling role in our use of ordinary psychological concepts. Now that I no longer make this assumption, I am free to combine the hypothesis of a hidden structure with the denial that ordinary psychological concepts function as natural kind concepts directed towards the covert structure of their reference. Thus the mind itself is not inherently superficial, but our ordinary concepts of mind are confined to the surface. This should change the emphasis of the position advocated in those chapters, though it does not disturb the main points at issue there.

partial access to the deep properties of its consciousness, comparable to our partial knowledge of chemical substances, then it might organize its mental concepts in ways that are sensitive to the underlying mental reality, making them less chained to the surface. Its concepts might then be construable as hypotheses about a partly hidden reality, attempts to map the underlying natural categories. But these concepts would differ profoundly from ours: using these concepts, our curious creature would treat the phenomenal features of its sensations, say, as merely defeasible guides to the kind of conscious state it was in. Our mental concepts, by contrast, are more like concepts for observable properties of material things, such as shape and colour: objects which have these properties no doubt harbour a hidden structure, but that structure is not gestured towards in the employment of the corresponding concepts. The concept *square*, say, does not care what the microscopic structure might be of objects to which it applies, so long as it latches on to the right gross geometry.[36] Somewhat similarly, our mental concepts apply to something that has a hidden structure, namely consciousness, but they do not attempt to delineate consciousness in ways that reflect that structure. They are oblivious to the underlying natural principles governing the workings of consciousness.

In fact, given our total lack of access to this structure, they could hardly aspire to plumb the depths: they are wise to content themselves with the surface. There is no point in trying to make our concepts go deeper than our knowledge can extend. A sensible concept does not attempt to reach out for the noumenal, since its reach would then exceed its grasp. Mental concepts are thus unlike ordinary natural kind concepts, not because consciousness objectively lacks a hidden structure, but rather because that structure is

[36] This is consistent with insisting that the instantiation of conscious properties is only possible because of the existence of an underlying structure. The physical realization of conscious properties necessarily involves a hidden structure, though this structure is no concern of the concept of those properties. Compare the instantiation of shape properties by physical objects: for an object to be round its constituent atoms have to be arranged in a certain pattern and be subject to certain forces, but the concept *round* contains nothing of this. We might say that the property of being round is instantiated in objects by virtue of a hidden structure of atoms, without wishing to assert that the concept in any way adverts to this structure. It is not a natural kind concept, in the standard sense, but it only gets to apply to things in virtue of properties that are hidden from ordinary observation. Concepts of consciousness are a bit like that, only in their case the story of their instantiation is inscribed in a locked book.

too noumenal for them to get their talons into. Our mental concepts have application only because the hidden reality exists, but they are not answerable to this reality and do not gain their point from it. Folk psychology is thus not a naive and pitiful attempt to carve out the natural kinds and laws that obtain at the hidden level; its business is strictly superficial. So it is not in danger of falsification from that level, and its superficiality is no reason to regard it with contempt. What it does not strive for, it cannot be criticized for failing to achieve. It is protected by its (relative) humility. No doubt knowledge of the hidden structure of consciousness would be a fine and powerful thing to possess — as scintillating as any science we now have — but it may be that knowledge of the surface is all we are ever going to get. Perhaps we should be grateful that we know anything at all about consciousness. Folk psychology is not something to be taken for granted: it encapsulates a form of knowledge we might have had to do without.

5

Mental States, Natural Kinds and Psychophysical Laws*

Suppose (i) that there are causal relations between mental and physical events, (ii) that where there is causality a (strict) covering law exists which subsumes the events under some of their descriptions, and (iii) that there are no (strict) psychophysical laws, known or unknown. Then, Davidson argues, physicalism with respect to particular mental events may be deduced.[1] The third premiss has proved to be the stumbling-block, and Davidson admits that his defence of it is less than decisive. However, I think the case for (iii) can be substantially strengthened, and my main aim in this chapter is to show why the claim should be accepted. Davidson's own reasons for denying the possibility of psychophysical laws, or something close to them, will emerge as corollaries of the considerations I adduce, but my arguments will make use of doctrines and principles foreign to his own defence of (iii). The issue is important beyond its role in establishing an identity theory: for a demonstration of the in principle unavailability of psychophysical laws would have repercussions for such matters as the unity of science, the irreducibility and autonomy of psychological explanation, determinism with respect to human action, the prospects for psychophysiology as a science like others, and quite generally what the relation is between mental states of a person and physical states of his body.

*Previously published in the *Proceedings of the Aristotelian Society*, Supp. Vol. 1978. Appears with permission of Basil Blackwell Ltd.
[1] See 'Mental Events', in *Experience and Theory*, eds L. Foster and J. Swanson (Duckworth: London, 1970).

At first I thought that the absence of psychophysical laws would have interesting consequences for the question whether mental states should be conceived of as natural kinds, whose real essence is specifiable in physical terms of the brain. For, if there were no such laws, then mental states could not be so conceived, since the necessary co-satisfaction of mental and physical predicates required by that conception would be incompatible with the demonstrated lack of nomological tie between the two types of predicate. But I now think it is the other way about: it is precisely *because* mental predicates can be shown not to denote natural kinds, but rather to express concepts of a fundamentally different character, that authentic psychophysical laws can be ruled out in advance. So my strategy is to argue for that first claim and then try to show how, on that basis, the impossibility of psychophysical laws falls out as a consequence. The reasons for the grounding claim come in two parts which are strictly inseparable – the first denying that mental terms denote physically circumscribable natural kinds, the second intended to suggest some more positive rationale for that denial – and expository order should not be taken to indicate any assertion of logical priority. I also evaluate briefly the impact of these considerations upon whether there could be psychological laws of intentional action and upon physicalism. My guiding aim throughout is to urge a certain *contrast* between standard natural kind terms and psychological terms. In so doing I presuppose a certain well-known conception of natural kinds and their terms.[2] Those who reject that conception are unlikely to appreciate the intended contrast; they should not read on.

Mental States and Real Essence. For it to be true that a mental state ψ (propositional attitude or sensation) has a physical real essence ϕ, it must hold that a creature cannot instantiate ψ without thereby instantiating ϕ, and *vice versa*; that is, 'ψ' and 'ϕ' have to be necessarily co-extensive. Kripke,[3] following Descartes,[4] asked us to

---

[2]   That advocated by S. Kripke in 'Naming and Necessity', *Semantics of Natural Languages*, eds D. Davidson and G. Harman (Reidel: Boston, 1972), and by H. Putnam in *Mind, Language and Reality*, Philosophical Papers vol. 2 (Cambridge University Press, 1975), *passim*.
[3]   Kripke, *op. cit.*
[4]   See especially Descartes' *Principles of Philosophy*, Principle LX.

envisage an inductively established 'correlation' between such states ψ and ϕ, taking pain and C-fibre stimulation as his example. Then, in order to refute an identity theory for ψ and ϕ, he insisted that ψ and ϕ might conceivably come apart; and the possibility that they should is inconsistent with their being identical. So also is it inconsistent with ϕ constituting the real essence of ψ, even if this relation is not construed as identity. Now I wish to agree with Kripke on this point: if it is possible that ψ and ϕ should come apart, as seems evident enough, then ϕ cannot, as a real essence must, determine the existence and identity conditions for ψ.[5] So the 'correlation' cannot be construed on the model of the relation between a natural kind – e.g. water, being hot, being magnetised – and its a posteriori real essence, as articulated in the vocabulary of some special science. More especially, no mental state or kind of mental event has a brain state or kind of brain event as its underlying essence.

What is chiefly remarkable about this argument is not so much its conclusion as its epistemic status. For, if sound, it shows a priori that the relation between mental states and their 'correlated' physical states cannot be that of identity; and it might well be thought that establishing a theoretical *non*-identity is just as empirical an exercise as establishing a theoretical identity. Thus it might earlier have been conjectured (falsely) that solar heat and solar light are one and the same phenomenon, and it might now be wondered whether intra-atomic force is the same as gravitational force; no amount of a priori reflection can decide such questions. But the Kripke-Descartes argument apparently relies upon no empirically established premiss: the possible coming apart it envisages seems to issue from nothing other than our ordinary grasp of psychological concepts; and this already sets mental states apart from those other

---

[5]   Kripke in fact exploits a pair of intuitions against the identity theorist: (a) that the mental state could exist without the physical, and (b) that the physical state could exist without the mental. I endorse (a), but am committed to the denial of (b), or a close relative of it, by my later acceptance of the thesis that mental facts are supervenient on physical facts. To motivate this asymmetry of attitude, I need a reason for not taking (b) at face-value. My reason is that the following form an inconsistent triad: (i) if creatures x and y differ with respect to possession of a mental state ψ, then they differ in their behavioural dispositions; (ii) since dispositions to behaviour are precisely dispositions to bodily movements, x and y cannot differ in their behavioural dispositions unless they differ in their (internal) physical states; (iii) x and y could be exactly alike physically, yet differ in respect of possession of mental state ψ. Since I take (i) and (ii) to be virtually self-evident, I reject (iii). No parallel argument can be constructed against (a).

states whose relation to the world as described by fundamental science does not admit of such a priori decision. If Kripke's modal intuitions are really veridical, we know in advance of empirically established psychophysical correlations, or the lack of them, that no set of terms drawn from the physical sciences can characterize a real essence for any mental state.

What now is the nature of this contingent relation between mental and physical states? Nothing so far conceded to Kripke precludes its being the *realization* relation, in Putnam's sense.[6] The important property of realization is that the range of physical states fit to realize a given mental state can be indefinitely various, subject perhaps to the condition that they preserve the causal powers and dispositions of the realized mental state. Because distinct physical states can realize the same mental state in different creatures or at different times, no physical condition could qualify as the real essence of a mental state. It is this feature of mental states, I suggest, that lies behind Kripke's intuition of contingency. It also appears that the variable realization point is itself a fact about the mental, in its relation to the physical, excogitable a priori – we do not need to observe actual cases of distinct physical realization to know it (the reason will be made explicit later, see pp. 146–52).

The non-rigidity of the realization relation prevents us applying a familiar model of reference-fixing for natural kind terms to mental predicates. The model has three elements: an ostensively (or otherwise) distinguished paradigm sample of the kind, an equivalence relation as between its members, and an empirically discoverable underlying real essence definitive of the kind in question. The canonical (but idealized) procedure for conferring reference to a kind K on a term F is to stipulate: an object x belongs to the extension of F (is of a kind K) if and only if x is equivalent in point of some real essence E to objects comprising a (supposedly) paradigm sample S of K. What is notable here is that we may, at the time of such reference-fixing, have no inkling of what E consists in, or hold erroneous beliefs about it. Nevertheless, the actual essence E determines whether any given object belongs to the extension of F; so that our initial criteria for classifying objects as of kind K may be

---

[6] Putnam, *op. cit.*, passim. In appropriating the realization relation I intend no commitment to a functionalist construal of mental states: the final section, in effect, offers a different account of why mental states can be variously realized.

radically in error, perhaps because the superficial properties of the observed sample are deviant in K. In fact the real essence of the kind, and hence the kind, can diverge widely from our initial criteria of identification and recognition: whether an object really qualifies as a member of the kind may, and typically does, require a measure of advanced science to determine reliably. Now suppose we try to apply this familiar picture to mental predicates and their corresponding kinds, taking their real essence to consist in some indefinitely specified hypothetical brain state. We select a sample of creatures known to instantiate some given mental state – let it be pain, or the belief that snow is white – and stipulate that a creature belongs to the extension of the corresponding predicate if and only if its nervous system satisfies that physical condition which 'correlates with' the given mental state in the selected sample of creatures. Then plainly, even if all *actual* creatures realized the mental state in the same way, the procedure would, because of the possibility of variable realization, go wrong in possible cases: the stipulation would have the clearly unacceptable consequence that any creature realizing its mental states differently from the creatures comprising the sample could not instantiate the given mental state. It follows that we cannot construe mental terms as denoting their corresponding mental kinds in virtue of members of the kind satisfying certain conditions specified in the vocabulary of the physical sciences (or in extensions of it): because of variable realization.

This claim about mental predicates should be sharply distinguished from certain other judgments as to whether a given term denotes a natural kind. It is true that a term is necessarily a natural kind term if it is, and necessarily not if it is not, but there are differences in the *epistemic* status of such judgments. Standardly it is an a posteriori question whether a given term specifies a natural kind: it might, for example, have turned out – it was epistemically possible – that 'water' not be the natural kind term it actually is, and it might turn out that 'cancer' is actually not. Now my contention is not that we don't know a priori that mental predicates denote (physically definable) natural kinds, but rather that we know a priori that they do not. Unlike other terms whose semantic status is currently in doubt, we do not have to wait upon empirical investigation to decide the matter; we already know the answer to be negative, by dint of our present mastery of psychological concepts (or so I am in the business of claiming). It is important for me to insist upon this contrast, because my thesis is to be that we have a priori knowledge of the impossibility of tight psychophysical laws, not that the empirical evidence makes it highly improbable or even actually false.

Not that mental predicates are unique in this respect; something similar holds of artefact kinds, e.g. chairs, clocks and thermostats. Being defined according to function, anything that discharges a given function qualifies as of the corresponding kind. Since, in general, physically distinct kinds of object or mechanism can perform the same function, artefact properties, like mental properties, admit of variable realization. In consequence, we are antecedently sure that such predicates cannot be construed as endowed with sense and reference in the canonical natural kind style; for that would be – recognizably – alien to the sort of concept we, a priori, know them to express. Artefact kinds, like mental kinds, are not possessed of an a posteriori physical real essence constituting them as of the kind they are.[7] I think the same must be said of semantic predicates too, and not just analogously but connectedly. Any attempt to identify (or otherwise correlate by necessity) a semantical property of an utterance with a physical property of it, or with a physical condition of the speaker's brain, would be vulnerable to Kripkean contingency intuitions and to the evident possibility of distinct physical realizations. No doubt when a man says that snow is white some physical state of his brain corresponds (realizes that semantic property), but it does not follow, and is known a priori not to be a necessary truth, that whenever anyone samesays with that man he instantiates the same physical property. Satisfiers of semantic predicates are not collected together by virtue of a hidden physical essence, and any attempt to determine the extension of such a predicate by adverting to some corresponding (realizing) physical condition would be destined to go amiss in possible, if not actual, further cases. (We shall appreciate better why this should be later; for the moment I take is as given.)

The denial that mental terms denote natural kinds defined by physical real essences has certain consequences and corollaries, arti-

---

[7] *Pace*, I think, Putnam at pp. 242f. *op. cit.* It may indeed be epistemically possible that (actual) pencils are organisms, but that would not exclude there being inorganic pencils; nor does the fact that pencils are artefacts exclude there being organic pencils. (Think of chairs.)

culation of which will serve to confirm the contrast I am harping on. I mention three.

(i) Putnam[8] observes that, in respect of natural kind terms, there typically obtains a certain 'division of linguistic labour'. A term may gain universal currency in a speech community on the basis of there being, within that community, a sub-group competent reliably to classify objects as belonging to the kind in question, the rest of the speakers being linguistically parasitic on, and deferential to, this group of 'experts' in the term's use: mastery is collective, not individual. Such division of labour is of a piece with the fact that natural kind terms refer to sorts of entity distinguished by possession of an arcane real essence, whose nature may be only locally known. The experts, if there be such, are relied upon in difficult cases, while the normal speaker classifies rudely, if at all. Now I think it manifest that no such linguistic phenomenon attends the use of mental predicates; the grounds of their application are exoteric and humdrum. Nor is this merely an interim stage in the history of our language, to be superseded by eventual expertise in brain science or the like; it is, rather, an essential feature of our use and understanding of psychological terms. It is well that our operation of these predicates anticipates no such revision in our linguistic practices, since the variable realization point blocks any principled and systematic deference in the attribution of mental states to (say) specialists in neurophysiology.

(ii) It is characteristic of terms for natural kinds that there is implicit in their use a possibility of significant *regrouping* in our classifications, if that be demanded by our best scientific theory of the world: our original naive divisions, prompted by surface appearance, may not conform to the more accurate classifications invited by advanced science. Thus we have, on the one hand, fool's gold[9] and, on the other, Putnam's example of two kinds of 'jade'.[10] Upon discovery of the underlying essences we withdraw the term from masqueraders, or detect an ambiguity. But, as has already become evident, we do not envisage *such* regroupings of psychological kinds in response to investigations revealing differential physical realization. Indeed I doubt that our naive psychological

8　In 'The Meaning of "Meaning"' *op. cit.*, pp. 227 f.
9　Discussed by Kripke, *op. cit.*
10　*Op. cit.* p 241.

classifications could be overturned in the aforementioned ways under pressure from *any* sort of scientific theory of the mental, so well grounded are the groupings we commensensically effect.

(iii) For much the same reason a standard style of theoretical elimination is not to be expected either. Quine[11] remarks that natural kind terms and dispositional predicates tend to give way, in the presence of mature science, to theoretical descriptions of underlying explanatory traits. Such terms are programmatically introduced, and expected to lapse. The dispositional idiom, in particular, along with the subjunctive conditional, is a welcomed (by Quine) casualty of the progress of science. Now, irrespective of the general merits of that conception, it is clear enough that it cannot threaten our o.dinary psychological terms (and the explanations they feature in). For, first, there is no physically statable similarity standard capable of capturing a given mental kind, for reasons already given and yet to come; and, secondly, it is extremely plausible that the dispositional properties of mental states, notably beliefs and desires, especially as they are reflected in subjunctives linking them to actions, are nothing less than constitutive of our mastery of mental terms, so that the contemplated reduction would have to be accounted a straight change of subject. Mental terms are not merely promissory notes hitherto unredeemed; they make no promises and are beyond redemption.

What these three points of contrast drive home is that toward mental kinds, as not toward natural kinds in general, a certain attitude characteristic of scientific realism is not to be (and is not) entertained: the attitude, namely, that our commonsense intellectual organization of a given subject-matter might be substantially modified by, and be defeasible in the face of, a projected scientific theory. More specifically, we cannot conceive of mental states as endowed with an unknown physical essence whose detailed revelation might turn out to require just such revisions in our naive psychological scheme as I have been considering.

Thus far physicalist construals of the real essence of mental states have been rejected. But I wish to claim something stronger, and correspondingly harder to prove: that mental states enjoy no sort of

---

[11] See, e.g., 'Natural Kinds' in *Essays in Honour of Carl G. Hempel*, ed. N. Rescher (Reidel: Dordrecht, 1969).

real essence whatever. The case for this is inductive, and tentative. If the claim carries, we can conclude that mental states are no species of natural kind at all. Of course, it may be felt that the case is already proved by default, because no prima facie plausible candidate for a non-physicalist real essence suggests itself; and I have some sympathy for that attitude. Nevertheless, I think there are a number of proposals we can profitably consider. Thus it may be suggested that a mental state's real essence could be identified with its supposed causal or functional role. Ill-formulated as that suggestion is, the following can be said against it. First, it is doubtful that each mental state has associated with it a distinctive causal role it can call its own, for the causal dispositions of mental states – as they mediate sensory input and motor output – operate holistically. Second, real essences paradigmatically pertain to the constitution or internal structure of a kind, but functional role is not like that. Third, it is hard to see how any specification of the constitutive causal or functional role of a mental state could be other than a priori and definitional, which descriptions of real essence are not.[12] This last point applies a fortiori against the suggestion that a definition of one type of mental state in terms of another – e.g. the Grice-Grandy definition of belief as a certain sort of complex desire,[13] or a definition of intention in terms of beliefs and desires – could supply an appropriate real essence: such definitions, if successful, may be in some sense explanatory, but they are scarcely a posteriori. Essences of that sort would be nominal, not real.

A second candidate for mental real essence might be extracted from the writings of Descartes, Locke and Berkeley, among others. This is the idea that mental states, capacities and events 'inhere' in a purely *mental* substance. According to that idea, garden variety psychological properties are to the inner and covert workings of their mental substance as the superficial properties of (say) metals are to atomic structure. It will be admitted that we have as yet no notion of the *modus operandi* of such mental substances, but it may be questioned how such a picture can be excluded a priori. I believe any such conception can be eliminated by considerations parallel to

---

[12]   Insistence upon these disanalogies between functional role and real essence apparently puts me in disagreement with Putnam at p. 450, *op. cit.*

[13]   See R. Grandy, 'Reference, Meaning and Belief', *Journal of Philosophy*, 1973, pp. 439–52.

those that told against the corresponding physicalist suggestion, where the central nervous system played the part of underlying substance. For if such a picture were correct, then the three features lately denied of mental predicates – division of linguistic labour, possible regrouping and theoretical elimination – *would* hold of them, only now transposed from the physical to the recondite mental: but as they do not, it is not. To see this, conduct the following thought-experiment. Suppose a scientific theory of the alleged mental substance to be verified in respect of a group of persons, in such a way that we become apprised of its hidden ways and mechanisms. Now consider a (by hypothesis epistemically) possible situation in which some other group of creatures, theretofore reckoned as mentally endowed as the first group, are found to be equipped with a radically different kind of mental essence, or with none at all. Would we then declare 'fool's persons', or discern an unsuspected ambiguity in our psychological terms? I think we would not; so the original supposition must be rejected. (The case is only strengthened by invoking an introspective basis for mental attributions.) The consequences of taking such an hypothesis seriously simply don't hold; our ordinary psychological concepts rule it out a priori. We thus seem headed for the conclusion, to be finally reached later, that mental terms do not denote natural kinds of any sort.[14]

I have been speaking of terms for mental states and types of event, but parallel considerations apply to psychological sortal predicates, *i.e.*, 'person' and restrictions thereof. In fact, what we already have implies that persons do not comprise a natural kind. For (as I take it) a person is precisely an individual sufficiently richly endowed with mental traits, and if these do not qualify as natural kinds, nor can persons. Persons have no real essence; their essence is nominal, and analytically defined. In this respect, the concept of a person does not coincide with that of a human being, though they may be *de facto* co-extensive: for, by contrast with persons, to qualify as a human being an individual must instantiate the appropriate empirical real essence – genetic structure, evolutionary origin, and the like. The relation between personhood and

[14] I hope it is clear that by 'natural' kinds I do not mean all and only those kinds whose members are not the product of human contrivance. The intended notion pertains not to provenance, but to the presence of an empirical real essence, with all that that implies.

humanity is a contingent one, analogous to realization; and the contrasts so far remarked seem to hold equally of persons.[15] God did not have to make persons out of human beings nor beliefs from patterns of synaptic connexions; but he had no choice in the making of human beings and heat and lightning.

Psychophysical Laws. The burden of the last section consisted in claiming, incompatibly with a certain physicalism about mental states, that mental and physical predicates are never necessarily co-satisfied. My question now is whether such inductively established correlations as there are might rank as *lawlike*, i.e. whether universal conditionals linking mental and physical predicates would, if true, be laws of nature.

A short way to return a negative answer suggests itself. It might be argued, familiarly, that all natural laws are in fact metaphysically necessary, since the entities of which they treat are defined (a posteriori) by the actual laws to which they conform; but we have already shown there to be no psychophysical metaphysical necessities; so, contrapositively, there are no psychophysical laws. There are three reasons why I shall not take that short way: first, I am not persuaded of the first premiss; second, the initial assumption is commonly maintained because of the allegedly intimate connexion between natural kinds and their laws, but psychophysical laws would mention *non*-natural kinds, so the motivating principle would be inapplicable; third, I think it possible to argue for the desired conclusion without dependence upon any such doctrine, and more illuminatingly. (Not that anything I say will be actually inconsistent with that strong view of nomic necessity.)

Consider first unrestricted psychophysical bridge laws (true lawlike biconditionals) containing predicates 'ψ' and 'ϕ'. Now we have already dealt with the case in which a statement of that form might aspire to lawlikeness by dint of the identity of ψ and ϕ; there are no such identities. So let us assume that ψ and ϕ are distinct and enquire whether they might yet be lawfully co-instantiated. It is uncontroversial that to rate as lawlike a generalization must be, in Goodman's word, *projectible* to unobserved, future and indeed non-

---

[15] This seems to contradict the tendency of J. L. Mackie's view of persons in *Problems from Locke* (Oxford University Press, 1976), pp. 200f.

actual cases; it must be confirmable by its positive instances and supportive of subjunctive and counterfactual claims.[16] The crux, then, is clearly this: is the meeting of such requirements by a psychophysical generalization compatible with the variable realization point? Evidently not, it seems to me. Observation of some proper subset of all the creatures to which the law purports to apply should make us willing, given a sufficient number of positive instances, to project the generalization to all other cases. But we know a priori that it is perfectly possible for other unobserved creatures to realize their mental states differently from those we have so far happened to encounter. The contingency of the realization relation therefore precludes nomologically necessary correlation between mental and physical predicates. Comparably, we shall not expect the physical realizations of artefacts, e.g. clocks, we have not observed to conform by natural necessity to those we have, as it happens, observed in the past. (Of course whether such generalizations are extensionally *true*, at least of all actual individuals past, present and future, *is* an empirical matter; what is a priori, according to me, is that they are not strictly *lawlike*.) So I conclude that there are no exceptionless psychophysical bridge laws, and that this seems owed to mental states wanting physical real essences.

That diagnosis receives support from the following thesis about natural laws. For a generalization to qualify as a law the properties specified by its contained predicates must not only be universally co-instantiated, they must be *connected* in some way. Now a plausible account of what such modal connexion might consist in is that the observed co-instantiation must result from the presence of some underlying generative mechanism or structure, whose detailed elucidation would serve to *explain* the coincidence of properties.[17] That is: if a property P is assigned to a kind K, then the corresponding generalization is a law just in case K has some real essence (generative mechanism) E whose characteristics are responsible for, and theoretically explain, why it is that Ks have P. Granted such a view, we can see why there could not be psychophysical laws. For suppose K to be the mental kind ψ, and suppose some physical property ϕ is regularly co-instantiated with ψ. Then the correspond-

---

[16] See N. Goodman, *Fact, Fiction and Forecast* (The Athlone Press, 1954).
[17] Cf. R. Harré and E. H. Madden, *Causal Powers* (Basil Blackwell, 1975); and Quine, more mutely, in 'Necessary Truth', *The Ways of Paradox* (Random House, 1966).

ing generalization does not affirm a connexion of ψ and ϕ that
could be explained in the style just adumbrated, because ψ, as I
have argued, has no physical essence E which might be 'responsible
for' instances of ψ satisfying ϕ. The realizing physical state cannot
fill the bill, on account of its variability. The psychophysical generalization lacks a ground for the necessity that would qualify it as a
law.

This point bears upon something Davidson says.[18] It appears that
he, like me, believes that the anomalousness of psychophysical
generalizations is a matter decidable a priori, presumably by mere
reflection on the concepts involved. But he offers an analogue of the
case which seems to me unfortunate: in point of lawlikeness, he
says, psychophysical statements resemble such sentences as 'Emeralds are grue', in contrast with 'Emeralds are green'. The analogy is
poor for two reasons. First, there are, as Davidson himself insists,
(manufactured) predicates relative to which 'grue' is lawlike; but
Davidson also holds that mental predicates are *absolutely* anomalous. Second, it is highly doubtful that Goodman's sentence is
unlawlike a priori; indeed his own account of what it takes for a
predicate to be projectible, in terms of entrenchment relative to
prior scientific and commonsense theory, would seem to make it
come out a posteriori.[19] I think the source of the disanalogy traces
back to the non-natural kind status of the mental. To see this, let
'grue' mean 'green before t and blue thereafter'. Then, although
'Emeralds are grue' is actually anomalous, it seems epistemically
possible that it should have been lawlike: for we can imagine being
possessed of a theory of emeralds according to which their colour
will change from green to blue at t; so that, relative to that (empirically false) theory, 'grue' *is* projectible over emeralds. But then it
is hardly a priori that 'Emeralds are grue' fails of lawlikeness. By
contrast, we cannot say of psychophysical statements that they
might have turned out to be lawlike, for it is a priori that they are
not. It is because emeralds have a real essence of which we may
be so ignorant as not to know which predicates are lawlike over
emeralds that a judgment of anomalousness in their regard cannot be
counted a priori; and just because mental states lack such a hidden
essence there is nothing about them with respect to which we could

[18] In 'Mental Events', *op. cit.*, p. 93.
[19] Goodman, ch. 4. *op. cit.*

be thus ignorant. Inasmuch as we do not need to wait upon the revelation of the real essences of mental kinds to judge of their nomic incongruity *vis-à-vis* the physical, a better analogy is afforded by the case of artefact predicates.

It may now be conceded that for *unrestricted* bridge laws there is no hope, but urged that the prospects for certain restricted psychophysical biconditionals are much brighter. Thus someone might suggest that generalizations restricted to biological species, or to individuals, or even to individuals during intervals, would rank as genuinely lawlike. Of course, such restrictions could not be party to any identifying theoretical reduction of mental to physical properties, not without some sort of relativization of identity anyway; but yet it might be claimed that the restrictions satisfy the usual criteria of lawlikeness. Now I think we can safely dismiss the second two proposals, if only because they offend against the usual condition that a law not contain ineliminable mention of particular objects.[20] The restriction to species is more interesting. Actually such empirical evidence as there is discourages hopes even for such species-specific laws, but I shall place no weight upon this merely empirical fact. The point to be emphasized is that, although observation of a psychophysical correlation in a number of creatures of a given species may give us *some* inductive reason to expect others to follow suit, we do not think it at all nomically *impossible* that a new creature of the species might exhibit a different physical realization of the mental state in question, particularly if the state is a propositional attitude. This is vividly, if luridly, brought out by consideration of prosthetic replacements for neural (or whatever) structures and mechanisms: for any mental state ψ we can conceive of surgically replacing its neural realization with some other physically distinct type of device, of appropriate functional properties, capable of sustaining ψ. It is otherwise in respect of non-mental characteristics of members of an animal species: there are no such physically distinct prosthetic substitutes for blood and bone that are still blood and bone. And it is surely not sufficient for lawlikeness, however weak our grip on that notion may be, that observation of positive instances of a generalization make it merely probable, other things (what things?) being equal, that further cases will conform. If

---

[20] See C. G. Hempel, *Aspects of Scientific Explanation* (The Free Press, 1965), p. 268.

it were sufficient, then there might be similar laws for clocks and chairs and thermostats. Even if we were thus undemanding of a law, a deep contrast would abide between the (by sufferance) law-like status of psychophysical generalizations and authentic scientific laws (of which more soon).

The preceding arguments have tilted at *bi*conditional psychophysical laws, and the operative point has been that possession of a mental state does not, of necessity, determine which physical state will realize it. But what of the converse determination? That instantiation of a physical state ϕ, which realizes a given mental state ψ in a creature x, implies instantiation of ψ in any other creature y which instantiates ϕ seems strongly suggested, if it is not actually entailed, by the thesis of the supervenience of the mental on the physical. Consequently, a supervenience conditional – composed of a (possibly complex) physical antecedent and a mental consequent – would seem, *prima facie*, to have some claim to lawlikeness: it seems supported by its instances and empowered to sustain strong subjunctive projections. I have no decisive rebuttal of this contention, but I offer the following considerations. First, we cannot immediately infer to the lawlikeness of a psychophysical supervenience conditional from its necessary truth and empirical status, since for other cases of supervenience – of the aesthetic on the physical, the moral on the descriptive, the semantic on the psychological – we should not wish to press a parallel claim, even though in these cases too confirmability and projectibility appear to obtain. Second, knowledge of the truth of a finite number of such supervenience conditionals, containing a common mental consequent, provides no effective way of identifying the set of physical predicates on which the mental predicate may in principle supervene. Third, and most significant, the possible heterogeneity of physical conditions realizing a given mental condition prevents any theoretical *unification*, in non-psychological vocabulary, of the instances of the mental property: we should be given no general explanation, in physical terms, of the mental condition and the mental events that condition circumscribes. Thus, though it may be in principle possible to state a sufficient physical condition for the application to an agent of the predicate 'x (intentionally) signed a cheque for £100', this would not provide any substitute, of equivalent explanatory power, for conditions stated in psychological terms (this is just the irreducibil-

ity of the mental to the physical again). If supervenience conditionals be laws, they are not the sort to comprise a unifying and
integrated theory of the mental.

What Davidson's argument for a token identity theory expressly
denies is the existence of psychophysical *causal* laws, for these are
the kind that might be offered to back singular causal statements
relating particular mental and physical events; and of such laws we
have so far been silent. In discussing laws of this type I shall follow
Davidson's account of the logical form of a causal law: a causal law
consists of a conjunction of conditionals quantifying over individual
events, one conjunct affirming sufficiency, the other necessity.[21] It
seems clear at once that we cannot expect the same type of mental
event to be caused, under that description and as a matter of law,
by the same type of physical event, since the antecedent physical
type may vary according as the mental condition determining the
succeeding mental event's type is variously realized in a creature's
physical states. But it may be thought that a *sufficient* causal condition for the occurrence of events of a given mental type could be
stated in physical terms, in virtue of supervenience. For, if ψ supervenes on ϕ in respect of a particular event e, and it is a causal law
that events of type ϕ are brought about by events of type ϕ', then it
looks as if we can say that if an event of type ϕ' occurs there
follows, by causal law, an event of type ψ, since an event of type ϕ
follows by law and ψ supervenes on ϕ. This reasoning assumes that
the supervenience relation, as between properties of objects at
times, preserves lawlikeness, and so inherits any doubts we already
had about the nomic propriety of that relation. But it faces another
objection too: while we might thus be able to make out a case for
causal sufficiency we cannot conjoin a *necessary* physical condition
for the mental type in question, just because a given mental property may supervene on ever so many physical conditions, and hence
mental events circumscribed by that property may be caused in
various ways between which there need be nothing (physically) in
common. For this reason (among others perhaps) the causal law
that backs a psychophysical singular causal statement cannot do so
under a mental description of the denoted mental event – unless,
that is, we see fit to think again about the proper form of a causal

---

[21] See 'Causal Relations', *Journal of Philosophy*, LXIV (1967), pp. 691–703.

law, and be ready to give up on the necessity part. What seems certain is that mental predicates will have no place in that theoretically organized body of strict laws whose existence is required by an appropriately strong interpretation of the principle of the nomological character of causality.

Psychological Laws. Though the announced topic is psychophysical laws, I should like now to indicate two ways in which the conclusions thus far reached bear upon the possibility of purely psychological laws of intentional action; it will become apparent that this involves no real digression.

It is a familiar point that a statement relating an agent's reasons (desires and beliefs) or intentions to his actions has some sort of a priori or constitutive status. In particular, the propositional attitudes that prompt an action are canonically specified by describing their intentional objects, namely, action-types. This feature of the mental antecedents of intentional action permits us to read off from them which type of action is to be performed, and plays an essential part in the capacity of beliefs and desires to rationalize actions. And when we explain a particular action by citing the mental events and states that caused it we must at some point employ descriptions which thus intentionally relate those events and states to the action they cause. But here a difficulty has been descried: for, so the doctrine goes, a statement can only qualify as causal if it identifies each of the causally related events in 'logically independent' ways; yet the intentionality (object-directedness) of mental causes seems to flout this requirement. Now in the case of *singular* causal statements linking beliefs and desires (or the initiating mental events in which they participate) to actions there is a handy solution of this difficulty. For if we already subscribe to a token identity theory – and the present problem may give us stronger reason to – we know there to exist non-intentional descriptions, namely physical descriptions, of the mental causes of action, and that substitution of these into the original, apparently nonempirical, statement will yield a clearly a posteriori and explanatory truth, giving no hint of any 'logical connexion' between the identifying descriptions. But this solution seems unavailable for *general* reason-action conditionals. Here we cannot remove the whiff of analyticity by redescribing the mental *types* in physical terms, because an identity theory for types is false. And if we cannot turn that trick, then, by the Humean doctrine, such generalizations cannot count as causal laws. It follows that human action explanation is not deductive-nomological, and that the practical syllogism cannot be regarded as a (homonomic) sketch for a causal law. This is not, of course, to deny that there are causal laws covering intentional actions: but not *as* intentional actions. Given the variable realization point, the laws that back the singular reason-action statement will not only fail to be psychological; they will cut across, and not coincide with, the explanations afforded by psychological rationalization.

A second point of impact is this. To supply a law linking reasons and actions we require conditions on the former nomically sufficient for the latter. Two obstacles arise: (i) Attitudes capable of rationalizing an act of ϕing might be present in an agent (and other conditions be fulfilled) yet no bodily movement which is a ϕing occur; (ii) the rationalizing attitudes may succeed in causing a ϕing, but in such a way that the ϕing is not intentional (deviant causal chains). In both cases, unpacking the usual *caeteris paribus* clauses which save such generalizations from outright falsification would seem to require (*inter alia*) specification of certain *physical* conditions, whose satisfaction is necessary for the consequent of the alleged law to hold. Thus, in respect of (i), the agent must be physically able to ϕ, where this will consist in such facts as that his efferent nerves are intact and functioning. But actual provision of such physical conditions would show the 'law' to be, upon full formulation, psychophysical – and we have already seen that there are no proper psychophysical laws. Similarly, if we tried empirically to isolate the nondeviant causal chains, by describing what sequences of physical events (physically identified) from attitudes to bodily movements preserve agency, then incorporation of such physical conditions into the antecedent of the putative law would render it psychophysical – and then again our old considerations apply. It might seem that this argument could be blocked, for both types of case, by refusing to descend into physical (physiological) vocabulary: why not simply say 'has the power to' in the first case, and in the second volunteer only abstract conditions on the structure a nondeviant chain must exhibit? But then it would be plain that we are not dealing with empirical causal laws at all, but with philosophical analyses.[22] Such a conditional analysis might cease being a priori if we spelt these (topic-neutral) conditions out into terms of the physical properties that realize them, but only at the cost of sacrificing their claim to be empirical causal laws for different reasons. We have, in effect, the same dilemma here as arose in the previous paragraph, but now a different horn does the impaling.

Physicalism. Everything I have written so far commits me to rejecting an identity theory of mental and physical states.[23] But how significant a concession to dualism is this? I think that a firm distinction of tokens from types, of events from their properties, serves to defuse any reasonable physicalist scruples about what is thus conceded; in particular, endorsement of Kripke's argument for non-identity of types does not, in itself, entail the anti-physicalist claim that there are entities of which no (nontrivial) physical predicate is true. For consider a structurally parallel argument concerning functional properties of artefacts. Suppose that for some observed class of clocks satisfaction of the predicate 'x records that it is noon' is correlated with (realized by) a certain physical condition C of the clocks' mechanism. We could then say, truly, that that chronometric property might have been correlated with (realized by) some distinct physical condition C' of some quite different kind of mechanism: and that possibility would entail, according to Kripke, that there is no identifying chronometric properties with physical ones. He would be right to reason so; but what does such irreducibility, and hence non-identity, show to worry a sensible physicalist? Very little, since all individual clocks are identical with physical objects, as all chronometric events are identical with physical events, and the (chronometric) properties of clocks are supervenient upon physical properties of their mechanisms. Within the class of mental events, intentional actions illustrate this point vividly. While it is true that no physical predicate picks out a property identical with that expressed by 'x (intentionally) signed a

[22] Cf. Davidson in 'Freedom to Act', *Essays on Freedom of Action*, ed. Ted Honderich (Routledge, 1973), p. 154.
[23] I have taken states to correspond to predicates, i.e. as properties or universals rather than particular individuals. If you think that states admit of a type-token distinction, interpret me as speaking of types throughout.

cheque for £100', we have no difficulty in seeing that each such action token is identical with some bodily movement or other, and that that mental description supervenes upon some physical description of each such movement. We can call up a Kripkean intuition in this case too, but no conclusion follows to the effect that there are entities which elude physical description. Quite generally, the property that qualifies an event as mental is identical with no physical property, though each individual mental event can be identified with a physically describable event, and mental descriptions may nevertheless supervene on physical ones. I suspect we are inclined to think more is at stake in distinguishing mental from physical states because we are in the grip of the natural kinds picture of mental properties; which is why the analogy with artefact properties seems so unsatisfyingly deflationary. But I have argued that we should free ourselves of that picture.

The following theses are compatible with the denial of type identity: supervenience; an identity theory for particular mental events; and the necessity that, for any mental property ψ, and for any object x which is ψ at a time t, there exists some physical property ϕ such that ϕ realizes x's being ψ at t. Actually, however, something yet stronger is compatible with a dualism of types. It has been insisted that, from the fact that object x's being ψ is realized by its being ϕ, it does not follow, and is not a necessary truth, that *any* object y's being ψ is similarly realized. But that is no bar to acceptance of this claim: if x's being ψ is realized by its being ϕ, then it is a necessary truth that *its* being ψ is so realized. Indeed the claim seems true, at least if x is essentially ϕ. Moreover, in the cases that interest us, the antecedent of this conditional appears to hold. I am necessarily human and my being human realizes my being a person; so it couldn't be that *my* being a person was differently realized, though other persons could be realized in biologically distinct ways. Or again, if an event's being a pain is realized by its being a C-fibre firing and, what is very plausible, being a C-fibre firing is essential to that event, then the event could not exist unless its having that mental property were realized as it actually is. Once more, suppose a particular action of signing a cheque is identical with some bodily movement: though other actions of that type could have been realized by different sorts of bodily movement, *that* action could not have realized its mental description otherwise. If this is right, there is a strong, indeed necessary, connexion between (some) mental predicates of events and individuals and the physical predicates that specify their realizations: but the necessity doesn't generalize.

Psychological Attributions. Earlier I appealed to certain intuitions about when we would judge that a creature satisfies mental predicates. It seemed that these judgments were indifferent with respect to physical realization, so that possession of a mental state could be prised off any particular physical condition. It seemed also that our use of psychological terms does not carry the assumption of an arcane real essence, in principle discoverable, which would, in a case of conflict with our ordinary exoteric criteria for mental attributions, be preferred as deciding the case one way or another. My question now is what the ultimate basis for mental attributions is and what its distinctive features.

The basis is, indisputably, twofold: behaviour and introspection – however these may subsequently be construed. I shall not discuss the interrelations of these bases, nor the question of their relative priority. Instead I shall concentrate my remarks on the former, because it seems to me the more instructive. However, I think that much of what I am going to say about the behavioural basis goes over, *mutatis mutandis*, to the introspective basis: both afford a means of access to mental states and events which is the common property of every master of psychological terms and concepts, and with respect to which there is no proleptically conceiving a science of the mental capable of overturning their authority. To be sure, the demonstration of this, though structurally parallel for the two sorts of basis, differs in that we are to imagine ourselves, in adjudicating cases of conflict, the recipients of different sorts of information – introspective and behavioural – against which other conceivable items of information might be brought in rivalry: but I think that no actual distortion of our psychological concepts will result from concentration upon third-person attributions.

The central claim I wish to make about the application of mental predicates to another on the strength of his behaviour, verbal and non-verbal (where this may, if you like, be understood as non-inferential causal prompting) is this: we cannot correctly construe such behaviour on the model of those 'identifying marks' or 'criteria of recognition' which, in the case of natural kinds, function as mere rough and ready preliminaries to a precise statement of necessary and sufficient conditions, themselves independently recognizable, for membership in the kind concerned.[24] The behavioural basis is indefeasible, in that sense, simply because there is no other conceivable ground for attributing mental states to a creature save its observable behaviour – or at any rate, no other basis that could *systematically* replace behaviour. In contrast with natural kinds, we do not think of behaviour as putting us (defeasibly) on to a mental reality to which other and superior modes of access are possible, and whose constitutive properties might come apart from their behavioural manifestations in such a way that the behavioural basis may eventually be discarded when theory develops and be overridden in a case of conflict: for there is just no other basis for a mental attribution to another save his behaviour.[25] We might be tempted to suppose otherwise by the thought of an identity theory for types, but the hope of restoring the analogy with natural kinds that way would be vain, since: (a) we would need a prior interpretation of behaviour before we could arrive at a set of psychological ascriptions with which to redescribe the correlated brain states; and (b) such a correlation for a given interpreted creature could not thereafter substitute for the hard work of behavioural interpretation, because we should be back at the first square when confronted by a creature exhibiting, incompatibly with type identity, different physical realizations. (Notice that this claim is not inconsistent with a realist view of mental states and events, where these are taken to be causally responsible for, and therefore quite distinct from, their behavioural manifestations: the fact remains that the mental states of another cannot be presented to us otherwise than through his behaviour.)

Moreover, if behaviour had no more intimate connexion with mental attributions than the initial identifying marks of a metal had with our sophisticated metallurgical classifications, then the follow-

---

[24] Putnam, in 'Brains and Behaviour' *op. cit.*, compares instantiating a mental state with suffering from a disease. The analogy is crucially imperfect, because symptoms do not afford the *sole* means of identifying a disease; at some stage we can detect its presence more directly—say by microscopic examination of the blood. Sensing a possible disanalogy, Putnam suggests that direct inspection of the brain might replace overt behaviour in the attribution of mental states. But his own insistence upon variable physical realization shows that the replacement could not be thoroughgoing. So his comparison is importantly misleading.
[25] Cf. Wittgenstein in *Philosophical Investigations* (Oxford, 1953), especially 149 and 158.

ing thesis would not hold good: mental attributions are *superven-*
ient upon behavioural facts, in the sense that we cannot justifiably
count two creatures as psychologically discernible whose behavioural dispositions, as evidenced in their actual behaviour, perfectly
coincide (note that this is neither a definability nor a conceptual
priority thesis). But that thesis constitutively governs our psychological ascriptions; so behaviour *is* indefeasible in the intended sense.

Given the constraining rôle of behaviour in psychological (and
semantic) interpretation, we can see the variable realization point in
a fresh light. Since, evidently, the same range of psychologically
interpretable behavioural dispositions could be induced by instantiation of physically distinct underlying states, and since mental
attributions supervene on (dispositional) behavioural facts, we can
readily envisage interpreting two creatures the same because of
coincidence in behaviour, despite divergence in their internal realizing physical properties. It is as if mental state and physical realization come apart at the level of behavioural dispositions: behaviour
is the *locus* of contingency between mental and physical states.

It will deepen appreciation of the crucial rôle of behaviour in the
application of mental terms to consider briefly three related features
of psychological interpretation and explanation, features which set
mental concepts off from others. All three stem directly from the
constraining behavioural basis of psychological attributions.

The first is a certain *holism* in a theory of interpretation. Interpreting a given behavioural event, or sequence of events, by
ascription of mental states – centrally beliefs and desires – has repercussions for what other behaviour is apt to occur and how
further behaviour may be plausibly interpreted. Ultimately, indeed,
each psychological attribution must face the tribunal of behaviour
as a whole. We must always stand ready to revise the psychological
theory of another accepted hitherto, for the theory is perpetually
and in principle open to test by new episodes of behaviour.[26] It is
not as if we can at some stage abandon the behavioural evidence in
favour of evidence bearing less holistically on the total theory,
because no other sort of evidence is available. Holism is ineliminable because of the exclusively behavioural basis of all mental
attributions. Matters would be different if mental states had a real

---

[26]   Cf. Davidson, 'Mental Events' *op. cit.*, pp. 96f.

essence, detectable independently of behaviour; for then the holism would be partially eliminable: having once verified a psychological theory by the usual holistic methods, and identified the neural correlate of each ascribed mental state, we could proceed to interpret a new creature by direct inspection of it cerebral states. But again variable realization blocks any such short-cut; we shall ultimately be forced to resort to behaviour. Holism with respect to behavioural evidence and the denial of physical essence are thus of a piece.

The second feature is *indeterminacy*, to which parallel remarks apply. It is precisely in the light (or dark) of evidence of behavioural dispositions that indeterminacy of psychological (as well as semantic) attributions threatens. If, contrary to fact, a type physicalism were true, then the indeterminacy would be at best epistemic – there would be a fact of the matter, detectable or not – since physical properties are not held to be indeterminate and, *ex hypothesi*, are *identical* with mental properties. But this way with radical ontic indeterminacy is unavailable, given the falsity of such physicalism. And even if the indeterminacy were merely epistemic, it is significant that it arises essentially out of the exclusiveness of behavioural evidence. Indeterminacy, the sovereignty of behaviour, and rejection of type physicalism thus go hand in hand.

Thirdly, the over-arching ideal of *rationality* in psychological interpretation is a constraint that has application only to behaviour: our explanations of behaviour are governed by the condition that the agent be represented as largely rational and intelligible. But a rationality constraint simply gets no purchase in the description and explanation of physical states and events in a creature's brain. We could not set about psychologically interpreting brain conditions independently of behaviour, even though those conditions realize the mental properties we end up ascribing by more orthodox means. Rationality connects mental attributions with behaviour, not with internal physical states.[27]

---

[27]   Davidson seems to be saying something similar about the connexion between rationality and the absence of psychophysical laws: see his 'Psychology as Philosophy', in *Philosophy of Psychology*, ed. S. C. Brown (Macmillan, 1974). On the significance of the behavioural basis to the issue compare his remark, 'There cannot be tight connexions between the [mental and physical] realms if each is to retain allegiance to its proper source of evidence.' 'Mental Events', p. 98.

My point in all this is that mental concepts, informed as they are by these three features of their use, obey their own distinctive principles of application: and that these principles are inconsistent with the idea that mental states have physical essences or are strictly nomologically correlated with physical states; inconsistent too with the thought, not unconnected with that first idea, that behaviour is a defeasible means of access to psychological descriptions of another, analogous to our rude criteria for sorting natural kinds, and susceptible of replacement by some more scientific and streamlined basis for mental attributions. These features of mental concepts, I suggest, complement and confirm the negative contentions of earlier sections. Indeed, it seems to me not implausible to claim, at least for third-person ascriptions, that what lies behind the intuitions and theses of those sections is precisely the key rôle of behaviour in the application of mental predicates to a creature. Mental kinds point outward, so to speak, to their behavioural manifestations, not inward to the physical conditions that sustain them. (Semantic concepts too, as hinted earlier, share such answerability to behaviour and heedlessness of the physical substratum; which is unsurprising seeing that semantic and psychological seamlessly interlock in the interpretation of what a creature does.)[28]

I said earlier that an attitude of scientific realism (which I distinguish from plain realism) is inappropriate to mental states, events and individuals. That claim receives support from a further, and important, contrast between mental terms and standard natural kind terms; the contrast concerns an asymmetry in the way such terms relate to the theory we hold of their denotations. It is very plausible that the platitudes of commonsense psychology, as they relate mental states to each other and to behaviour, *implicitly define* the terms contained therein: it is thus a necessary, indeed analytic, truth that entities are mental if and only if they satisfy those platitudes. In consequence if (*per impossibile*) the commonsense theory should be false, then mental states would simply not exist − for the corresponding terms have no meaning, and hence no denotations, beyond their rôle in that theory. Now this feature of mental terms stands in striking contrast with typical theoretical terms as they occur in scientific theories. For it is not plausible, and goes ill with

---

[28]   See Davidson's 'Belief and the Basis of Meaning', *Synthese*, vol. 27, 1974, pp. 309−24.

scientific realism, to claim that such theories implicitly define their theoretical terms: it could turn out, and frequently has, that a scientific theory once accepted is largely false of the entities of which it treats.[29] There is always, it seems, the epistemic possibility that our current theory of a certain natural kind of entity be false, compatibly with its terms remaining denotative. Yet this is exactly what does not hold of commonsense psychology and its terms: we reel at the thought that its platitudes are false.[30] What is the source of this asymmetry? The answer lies, I suggest, in the lack of empirical depth of mental states consequent upon their not being natural kinds. For suppose they did have real essences distinct from, and possibly prepotent over, the characteristics by which we commonly identify them. Then we *could* contemplate the possibility that untutored commonsense had got their properties radically wrong: that in their essence they conformed to quite different principles, to which the old platitudes were at best approximations. But in fact we contemplate no such thing: the essences of mental states are right on the surface, comprised in our ordinary means of identification. Again, our understanding of psychological terms confirms, because it is in part explained by, the thesis that such terms do not denote natural kinds.

The constitutive status of commonsense psychology, as against scientific theory at large, connects with certain other aspects of the mental worth remarking. First, claims about mental states will typically attach to their nominal essence, and hence be philosophical not scientific – much of the philosophy of mind consists of just such claims. Second, though we may be sceptical whether our ordinary theory of persons applies to another creature, we cannot coherently entertain scepticism about what is psychologically true of a creature, by way of general principles, if it does so apply. Third, market-place psychological truths speak of the connexions between mental states and behaviour: if these connexions are nothing short of constitutive, then our recent observations on be-

[29] See Putnam *op. cit.*, especially 'Explanation and Reference'.
[30] David Lewis, in 'Psychophysical and Theoretical Identifications', *The Australasian Journal of Philosophy* (December 1972), pp. 249–58, takes the analytic status of psychological platitudes as a reason for construing commonsense psychology as a species of term-introducing scientific theory, because he thinks standard theoretical terms are similarly implicitly defined. Since I agree with Putnam on theoretical terms, I see a deep contrast where Lewis avers a similarity.

haviour and mental attributions are borne out – and without commitment to any form of reductive behaviourism. What is also suggested by the definitive character of commonsense psychology is that something spiritually akin to the description theory of reference applies to mental terms. Indeed, the contrast just drawn with scientific theories turns crucially on rejection of that theory for theoretical terms, and acceptance of some sort of causal theory. It seems clear, at least, that a causal theory of reference – initial baptism, socially transmitted mastery, *etc.* – does not apply to mental terms: one more reason for refusing to their denotations the title of natural kinds.[31]

[31] For many useful comments on earlier drafts I should like to acknowledge Anita Avramides, Malcolm Budd, James Hopkins, Jennifer Hornsby, Marie McGinn, Christopher Peacocke and Arnold Zuboff.

6

Philosophical Materialism*

Suppose, to sharpen ideas, that we have devised a regimentation of vernacular mental discourse into a first-order theory.[1] According to some acceptable semantics for this theory, its singular terms (including variables) will be assigned appropriate mental *objects* from the intended domain: these objects will comprise persons and various sorts of mental events and states such as sensations, thoughts and actions. The objects thus referred to and quantified over make up the ontology of the original mental discourse. The predicates of the theory, on the other hand, will be interpreted as expressing *properties* attributed to the objects in the domain of the theory.[2] The intuitive notion of the 'subject matter' of mental sentences is then to be understood in terms of such an assignment of objects and properties to terms and predicates of the regimented theory. Now consider a like regimentation of physical discourse relating to the body and brain, containing scientific vocalulary, extant and future. The ontology of this physical theory comprises organisms and physical events and states – neural and behavioural let us suppose – while its predicates are taken as attributing properties to such physical entities. Then, supposing all this, the question as to the

* *Synthese* 44 (1980) pp. 173–206. Appears by permission D. Reidel Publishing Co., Dordrecht, Holland, and Boston, U.S.A.
[1] The supposition of first-orderness is not esential to what follows, but it is the clearest way to keep straight on the distinction between objects and properties, and this *is* essential to what follows.
[2] We need not construe the semantic interpretation of predicates as consisting in an assignment of entities (namely properties) to the predicates; we can interpret them by means of the usual disquotational satisfaction axioms in which no singular terms for properties occur. Doing so removes the temptation to take property distinctness as *ontologically* significant.

relation between mind and body can be formulated in two parts: (a) what is the relation between the respective ontologies of the mental and physical theories? and (b) in what kind of relation do the properties ascribed by the theories stand? In this chapter I shall offer some considerations in favour of the following answers to this pair of questions: mental objects are identical with (or are composed of)physical objects, and mental properties are neither nomologically reducible to physical properties nor (in a sense to be explained) lawfully correlated with them. This composite thesis is familiar from the writings of Donald Davidson as *anomalous monism*;[3] my supporting considerations will be less familiar.

Before presenting these considerations, a word is in order on the epistemological status of these claims. It is commonly supposed, on the model of theoretical identification in science, that materialist theses (and their negations) have the status of scientific hypotheses: they are to be decided by means of a posteriori procedures, specifically experimental investigations of a psychophysiological sort.[4] On that view acceptance or rejection of anomalous monism will perforce wait upon the prosecution of such researches; a philosopher can only distinguish the possible outcomes and indulge in more or less unfounded empirical speculation. The contrary view, which I wish to endorse, is that questions (a) and (b) admit of a priori resolution and fall therefore strictly within the province of the philosopher (hence my title). This difference of methodological view can be brought out as follows. Suppose that you have resolved, by the usual criteria, that a certain creature (or species of creature) is endowed with the psychological properties typical of a human person, and that you know the creature's complete mental description. But suppose also that you know next to nothing of the physical properties of the bodily organ which is 'responsible for' its mental activity: perhaps it is some species of extra-terrestrial person totally unlike us physically, or perhaps you are back in the days

---

[3] See his 'Mental Events', in *Experience and Theory*, eds, L. Foster and J. Swanson (Duckworth: London, 1970), 'The Material Mind', in P. Suppes *et. al.*, eds. *Logic, Methodology and Philosophy of Science IV* (North-Holland Publishing Company, 1973), 'Psychology as Philosophy', in *Philosophy of Psychology* ed. S. C. Brown (Macmillan, 1974). Something close to anomalous monism is tentatively endorsed by Thomas Nagel in 'Physicalism', *The Philosophical Review* 74 (1965).
[4] See, for example, U. T. Place, 'Is Consciousness a Brain Process?', reprinted in *The Philosophy of Mind*, ed. V. C. Chappell (Prentice-Hall, Inc., 1962).

before the human sensorium was identified and investigated. Nevertheless, you are enough of a materialist to believe there to be such
an organ and that there are causal and other relations between
events in it and mental phenomena. You are, then, in a position to
wonder how exactly the objects and properties invoked in your
mental description of the creature relate to the physical objects and
properties a theory of the creature's organ of mentation would
introduce. You wonder, in particular, whether the ontologies can be
identified and whether there are psychophysical laws. Now those
who think the mind–body problem, construed in my bipartite
way, to be empirical or scientific in character would claim that so
far you are in no position at all to pronounce upon the truth of this
pair of theses; certainly you do not, in the specified state of ignorance, have any rational ground for accepting anomalous monism.
If you are to have any justified opinion on the matter, you must
undertake appropriate empirical research, delving into the creature's mental organ and hunting for psychophysical correlations. To
suppose otherwise is to be guilty of 'apriorism' of the worst kind.
I want to claim, in opposition to this, that you *already* possess
sufficient knowledge to return rational answers to these questions:
you can produce good reasons for accepting an identity theory for
mental particulars, as well as for doubting any strict nomological
correspondence between mental and physical properties. That is
(roughly) the sense in which the questions admit of (and I think
require[5]) a priori resolution. Accordingly, the arguments I shall
produce exploit general features of mental and physical concepts of
which we can be credited with implicit knowledge. Just because my
considerations are thus metaphysical in character they are available
to one in the state of psychophysiological ignorance I described.

A number of philosophers have recently claimed, very plausibly,
that certain terms of our language – the so-called natural kind terms
– display a characteristic syndrome of semantic features which
distinguish them from certain other terms, aptly labelled nominal.[6]

[5] I say this for two reasons. First, and familiar, observed psychophysical correlations would
be consistent with nomological dualism, and so could not *establish* monism. Second, the
empirical method of seeking correlations would make anomalous monism unknowable if
true, since it is true just on condition that the only means of establishing it yields negative
results. The mind-body problem had better, then, be decidable in some other way.
[6] See the collection, *Naming, Necessity and Natural Kinds*, ed. S. P. Schwartz (Cornell
University Press, 1977) for some key papers.

Here, by way of reminder, is a summary list of such features, related in various ways: (i) our initial criteria of recognition for membership in the kind are epistemically contingent; (ii) our original naive classifications of objects into natural kinds are susceptible of revision in response to scientific investigation of the kinds; (iii) there is the prospect of eliminating (ordinary language) natural kind terms in favour of nomenclature drawn from a scientific theory of the kinds; (iv) the equivalence relation that collects objects into a given natural kind is a theoretical relation; (v) we can construct plausible 'Twin earth' cases for natural kind terms; (vi) the extension of a natural kind term is not fixed by the concepts speakers associate with the term ('meanings are not in the head'); (vii) natural kind terms exhibit a high degree of division of linguistic labour; (viii) a causal-historical theory of reference seems applicable to natural kind terms; (ix) the extension of a natural kind term is typically fixed by ostension (natural kind terms are indexical in some way).[7] It is not to my purpose to scrutinize or defend these theses now; what I want to note is the source of the claimed features. Their source resides, I think, in a conception of natural kinds appropriately designated *realist*: i.e. realism about what constitutes a natural kind of object is what underlies our acknowledgement of the listed features of the associated terms. For we think of what determines a natural kind as independent of our conventions and knowledge: it is fixed, rather, by possession of a hidden real essence (to use Locke's term) or nature whose proper characterization it is the business of empirical science to labour to discover. It is this realist idea, I suggest, that generates the syndrome of features (i)–(ix).[8] The basic point is simply that, natural kinds being deter-

[7] This is a somewhat eclectic list of theses: (i) and (ii) are associated chiefly with Saul Kripke's 'Naming and Necessity', in *Semantics of Natural Languages*, eds D. Davidson and G. Harman (Reidel: Boston, 1972); (iii) is suggested by W. V. Quine in 'Natural Kinds', in *Essays in Honour of Carl G. Hempel*, ed. N. Rescher (Reidel: Dordrecht, 1969); and (iv)–(ix) can be found in Hilary Putnam's 'The Meaning of "Meaning"', in *Mind, Language and Reality* (Cambridge University Press, 1975).

[8] The realism implicit in this view of natural kinds fits Michael Dummett's characterization of realism in general: see his *Truth and Other Enigmas* (Harvard University Press, 1978), *passim*. That characterization decrees a view realist if it allows that the facts in question be (possibly) recognition-transcendent. The conception of natural kinds sketched in the text makes natural taxonomy depend upon conditions in the world possibly transcending our epistemic capacities. On such a conception one anticipates the rise of *scepticism* about our knowledge of the fundamental kinds of nature. Both themes – realism about natural kinds and the associated scepticism – run through Locke's *Essay Concerning Human Understanding* (1690).

mined by nature, terms introduced by speakers to denote such kinds do not carry in their sense a characterization of what in the world constitutes the denoted kind. This real constitution may or may not be discoverable by speakers, but it is certainly not comprised in their ordinary use and mastery of the term. The essence of a natural kind is real not nominal.

Now, turning to the realm of the mental, we are driven to enquire whether mental predicates are natural kind terms in the foregoing sense. The issue is significant for determining the nature of mental properties and (hence) the shape of a science of psychology, or whether indeed there can be such a thing. It will be useful to divide the enquiry into two parts, according to the type of mental term in question. The objects of mental discourse are of two broad categories, which I shall distinguish as *sensations* and *thoughts* (or equivalently, experiences and propositional attitudes). We are to take these objects as mental particulars (events or states) instantiating properties which qualify them as the specific kind of sensation or thought they are – as a particular pain or thought that the sky is blue, for example. The mental kinds thus circumscribed appear to enjoy different sorts of essence. Roughly speaking, it is of the essence of a (type of) sensation to have a characteristic phenomenological quality; and there is no grasping the concept of such a mental type otherwise than ostensively: being felt in a certain way is necessary and sufficient for being an instance of that sensation type.[9] On the other hand, a thought does not appear to be thus defined; its essence consists rather in a certain psychological relation to a specific propositional content: what it is to have a thought is not (essentially) a matter of undergoing a particular kind of qualitative experience.[10] (I shall say more on the distinctive features of sensations and thoughts later; these remarks are intended as a crude delineation of territory.) So we now ask: are the mental kinds belonging to these categories possessed of a real essence? In an earlier chapter[11] I argued for a negative reply, concentrating on the

[9] Cf. Kripke, *op. cit.*, p. 339, and M. T. Thornton, 'Ostensive Terms and Materialism', *The Monist* 56 (1972).
[10] I do not, of course, mean to suggest that thoughts and sensations in a creature possessed of both enjoy a totally insulated existence. Sensations may acquire a thought component, and thoughts may be qualitatively tinged. Nevertheless, they are I think essentially distinct kinds of mental state, contingently co-possessed.
[11] 'Mental States, Natural Kinds and Psychophysical Laws', in *Proceedings of the Aristotelian Society*, Supp. Vol. LII (1978); now ch. 5 of this book.

suggestion that physical states of the brain might constitute the underlying real essence. The argument converged on this conclusion from two directions: firstly, the relation between mental properties and their correlated brain states seems to be highly contingent, unlike the relation required between a natural kind and its real essence; secondly, attention to our understanding and use of mental terms fails to disclose the syndrome of semantic features listed above, revealing instead a quite different family of characteristics. Moreover, the picture seemed unaltered by the postulation of some suppositious immaterial real essence: still the mental concepts refused to behave as they would if the supposition were true. I will not repeat these arguments here – the reader can probably get the drift of them by reflecting upon (i)–(ix) and asking himself whether they apply to his mental concepts – but it may be worth confirming the contrast with natural kind terms by trying to construct a Putnamian Twin earth example involving mental terms for sensations or thoughts.[12]

Imagine two linguistic communities – one on earth, the other on Twin earth – whose languages contain the terms 'pain' and 'the thought that the sky is blue', and suppose them equally ignorant of neurophysiology. They apply the terms on the strength of the usual behavioural and introspective evidence. Now suppose that the mental states denoted by these terms are (as Putnam would allow) differently realized in the neurophysiology of the people on earth and on Twin earth, but that they have no inkling of this. We should not then say that the mental terms are ambiguous, having distinct extensions for the two communities; and the reason is that meeting the commonsense criteria for possession of a mental state like pain or the thought that the sky is blue cannot come apart from possession of those states. The case is unlike terms for substances, e.g. 'water', where the hidden nature of the denoted substance fixes extension independently of the speakers' dispositions to apply the terms to presented samples. In the case of different physical realizations it is no *mistake* to apply the terms indifferently to people in the two communities, as it is for speakers on Twin earth to apply their term 'water' to H_2O given that it actually refers to a chemical-

---

[12]   See Putnam. *op. cit.*, pp. 223–7, for a more detailed account of what these examples involve.

ly distinct substance XYZ. The point is that chemical substances are constituted by an underlying nature which may not be manifest in casually detectable features of the substance, whereas mental properties are not so constituted by a hidden nature which may come thus radically apart from our ordinary tests for applying them. (Try to conceive of two communities whose dispositions to use the word 'pain' coincided but in one of which the word did not denote pain at all, denoting some other sensation instead.) So one cannot construct a Twin earth example for mental properties: in a case of divergence between underlying properties and surface features the mental kinds go along with the surface features. As Putnam would put it, the extension of mental terms *is* determined by the concepts speakers associate with them – the meanings of mental terms are 'in the head'. In this respect they belong to the family of nominal terms of which 'bachelor' is the hackneyed paradigm. If this is right, it is easy to see that the other features peculiar to natural kind terms will be absent from our mental vocabulary. It follows that the sort of realism appropriate to natural kinds is not in place with respect to mental kinds. In short, they have no real essence.

Now this contention is apt to meet with resistance, and reasonably, on the basis of a certain conception of what it is to be a particular entity. This conception can be formulated as a general metaphysical principle about particulars which would, independently of the preceding reflections, command our assent and which apparently conflicts with my doctrine on mental kinds. The principle has not, to my knowledge, been explicitly enunciated before, but I think it has informed philosophical enquiry on various topics, including the nature of the mental.[13] A bald statement of the principle is this:

(P)   Every particular is of some natural kind.

The import of (P) is that any entity that qualifies as a particular – that is, on the traditional explication of that notion, as an entity located in space and time, a potential object of ostension, and endowed with causal powers – any such entity must be a possible subject of empirical enquiry in something like this sense: it has some

---

[13]   Locke seems to operate with some such principle in the *Essay*; cf. n.8 above.

intrinsic nature *qua* member of a kind, where this nature can be given some theoretical description in a department of what is recognizably a science. In other words, (P) requires any particular to belong to the extension of *some* predicate which displays the characteristic syndrome of features set out above. The motivation behind acceptance of such a principle is again, I think, a certain *realism* about the notion of a particular. We are prone, realistically, to conceive of particulars as possessed of an intrinsic nature independently of our concepts and knowledge; we think of them as classifiable into kinds such that terms for those kinds do not admit of nominal definition. We have the picture of bringing each particular under some general term which stands for a property the possession of which consists in something which further investigation, typically of a scientific character, will, we hope, eventually reveal. That is, all particulars must have a nature *qua* some kind which is not already comprised in the content of the concepts under which we commonsensically bring them: they have an 'inner constitution' transcending surface appearance. This realist view of particulars is also assumed by a certain (broadly nonHumean) view of causality. Save perhaps at the most fundamental level of scientific explanation (if there is such a level), we expect to be able, in respect of any observed causal nexus, to supply an answer (or at least we believe that there should *be* an answer) to the question *in virtue of what* the causal nexus obtains, in particular how and why the cause brought about the effect: we take it, that is, that there exists some underlying causal mechanism whose operations account for the brute causal relation we have observed.[14] (An example is the explanation chemistry might give for why a particular event of salt dissolution was caused by immersion in boiling water.) And what is thus responsible for the observed causal nexus of particulars is, precisely, the intrinsic nature of the particulars involved. This seems to imply, given that particulars are causally active, that every particular has the sort of real essence *qua* some kind, which we saw to be demanded by the realist view of particulars articulated above. Nor is this surprising if a scientific description of particulars explains their causal powers: the real essence required by realism will just *be* that

---

[14] R. Harré and E. H. Madden, in *Causal Powers* (Basil Blackwell, 1975), seem to have their heart in the right place on this issue, but they underestimate event causation in this connexion and neglect also to discuss the nature of *mental* causation.

which furnishes the explanatory causal mechanism. If we wish to preserve this picture of the metaphysical status and causal powers of particulars, then we must assent to (P). Since I am inclined to accept this view of particulars at large, it may now seem that I am embarrassed by an inconsistency in my views. Before discussing this seeming conflict, however, let us see how (P) applies to specific classes of particulars.

The principle is straightforwardly satisfied by particulars of the animal, vegetable and mineral sorts: the natural kind terms that restrict these general sorts – 'horse', 'cabbage', 'gold' – apply to any particular of those general categories; it is thus easily verified that such particulars are always of some natural kind. Abstract objects, such as numbers, are the exception that proves the rule: their properties are not natural kind properties, but then they are not particulars.[15] The category of artefact particulars is instructive. Consider the class of clocks and the chronometric events and states associated with them. These are certainly particulars, yet the clock kind is not a natural kind: clocks come in indefinitely various physical mechanisms, and the class is defined nominally according to function. However, clocks are still clearly in conformity with (P); for (P) does not say, absurdly, that *every* kind or class to which a particular belongs is natural – it says only that there must be at least *one* such. Plainly artefact particulars do fulfil *this* condition, because they are always made up of some material or kind of object for which (P) straightforwardly holds. So each artefact particular will possess a real nature under *some* description, but not under the description by which we initially classified it, e.g. 'clock'. (Actually artefacts do call for a minor modification of (P), hitherto suppressed, to allow for the possibility, relevant in other connexions also, that the individuation effected by the artefact term not be matched by any natural kind term applicable to the particular: thus, for example, a crown of diamonds is not itself a diamond. To take care of such cases, let (P) be disjoined with a condition allowing particulars to have *parts* of some natural kind.)

As observed just now, adherence to (P) seems to collide with my claim about mental kinds, for that claim was precisely that the

---

[15] Of course nominalists, identifying numbers with particulars (inscriptions, say), *will* take these objects to fulfil (P); in which case *all* entities would be of some natural kind. But I am not now advancing that stronger thesis.

mental properties under which mental particulars fall are *not* natural kinds. Must we then infer that either my claim or (P) is false? The case of artefacts should teach us otherwise. What is needed to reconcile the two claims is *some* description of mental particulars, not itself mental, which denotes a natural kind. And one view of mental particulars that delivers the needed natural kind is the token identity theory: for if each mental particular is identical with (or possibly is composed of) some physical particular, then each will instantiate some physical kind – and physical kinds (e.g. neurophysiological kinds) clearly do fulfil (P). As with artefacts, mental particulars, granted a token identity theory, will fail to meet (P) as initially classified, but yet satisfy other predicates – namely physical – which ensure their conformity to the principle. (Notice that a type identity theory does *not* reconcile the claims, since it is tantamount to the thesis that mental kinds do have a physical real essence.) So it appears that a token identity theory would allow us to preserve the realist view of particulars and would, as a consequence, supply the materials for a satisfying explanation of the causal transactions into which mental particulars enter; while not going back on the claim that mental terms do not denote natural kinds.

Anomalous monism, as a token identity theory, can, then, *reconcile* two claims that seemed individually plausible and in tension. But I want to suggest, further, that we can construct a sound *argument* from them to it, as follows:

(1a)   Every particular is of some natural kind
(2a)   Mental kinds are not natural kinds

So

(3a)   Mental particulars must be of some nonmental kind; by elimination this kind must be physical; which is to say mental particulars are identical with physical particulars.

This argument is good if (and only if) three conditions are met: first, the premises are intrinsically plausible; second, neither of them already contains the conclusion in a question-begging way; and third, anomalous monism is *uniquely* capable of reconciling them, thus permitting the step by elimination at (3a). I think it is reasonable to claim that the argument does indeed meet these three conditions. I have already contended that (1a) and (2a) are plausible taken separately and begin to engender doubts only when considered together. On the second requirement, neither premise seems obviously to presuppose the conclusion. Premise (2a) clearly does not. Nor, I think, does (1a): its motivation did not speak explicitly of the physical, and indeed some philosophers have held views tantamount to the claim that mental particulars have an immaterial real essence (incompatibly with (2a)).[16] What leads to physicalism is the *conjunction* of the two claims. As to the third condition, it may be objected that mental particulars might satisfy nonmental descriptions which are not yet strictly physical, e.g. functional descriptions. Even allowing that possibility the argument would still be interesting, showing in effect either a physicalist or a functionalist identity theory. But the suggestion does not in fact block the argument, since functional properties are not, almost paradigmatically, natural kind properties (compare artefacts here). In the absence of plausible alternatives to physical natural kinds, the elimination step seems legitimate. In sum, anomalous monism – or rather its monistic part – seems derivable from the claims it was invoked to reconcile. So the ontology of mental discourse can be identified with a subset of the physical ontology, chiefly comprising events in the brain.[17] As promised, the considerations implying this identification are of an a priori character, relying only on very general features of the concepts concerned. The generality can be seen in this, that the reasons supporting token identity are completely general across actual and possible mentally endowed creatures, and so are not confined, as inductive psychophysiological researches would be, to psychological creatures of a specific physical constitution.

The structure of the argument just advanced was this. The objects of mental discourse seemed to have properties between which a

[16] See Locke's *Essay*, esp. at III, 6, 3: both spiritual and material substance are credited with an underlying knowledge-transcendent *modus operandi* or real essence.
[17] Two kinds of mental particular – namely persons and intentional actions – seem less in need of elaborate argument to establish their identity with physical particulars. For it is easy to appreciate that each person is of some natural (biological) kind, e.g. human being, and that each action is (in part) a movement of the body, and hence of some physiological kind. Thoughts and sensations differ in being physical particulars hidden (in part: see p. 182) *within* the body.

certain tension exists: on the one hand, they are particulars and as such must fulfil the conditions attaching to that status; on the other, they are objects of mental kinds and those kinds do not fulfil the required conditions. The solution was to relieve the felt tension by letting mental particulars satisfy other descriptions, namely physical descriptions, which allow them to meet the stated conditions on particularhood. Now I shall draw attention to another pair of concepts, applicable to mental particulars, between which an analogous tension exists, and suggest in resolution that it be treated similarly.

Thomas Nagel has written illuminatingly on what he calls the subjectivity of conscious experience.[18] In brief, his idea is that to undergo an experience is for there to be *something it is like for* the subject of the experience; and the concept of this something is such that it can be grasped only by a being whose own subjective phenomenology matches that of the given experiencer. That is to say, what it is to enjoy a given type of experience can be comprehended only from a single (type of) point of view, that conferred by being oneself visited with such (or similar) experiences. This feature of experiences poses, he thinks, a problem for physicalism, since physical facts are essentially objective in the sense that they can be understood from *any* point of view irrespective of the specific phenomenology of the understander's own experiences. Thus Martians whose sensory modalities are very different from our own may be prohibited from forming an accurate conception of the nature of our experiences, but there is no such principled obstacle to their achieving full comprehension of the physical workings of our brains. This categorial difference – between the subjectivity of the mental and the objectivity of the physical – makes it hard to see, Nagel suggests, how states of the brain could constitute the 'real nature' of conscious states.[19] Yet, as he also acknowledges, these subjective particulars also find their place in the objective world of

18 See his 'What is it like to be a Bat?', 'Panpsychism', and 'Subjective and Objective', all in *Mortal Questions* (Cambridge University Press, 1979).
19 In fact, as Nagel sometimes suggests (e.g. in 'Subjective and Objective', *op. cit.*, p. 201) the problem is equally acute for Cartesian dualism, since a *mental* substance would present the same difficulty. The difficulty might be stated dilemmatically: either we try to explain subjective properties objectively (in terms of a physical or mental substance), in which case we falsify their nature; or we admit their *sui generis* character, in which case we cannot explain their relation to the objective world. If so, physicalism not *distinctively* afflicted by the fact of subjectivity.

physical things: they are spatio-temporal entities and they enter into relations, causal and other, with physical particulars. There is a sense, then, in which we can conceive of experiences from both the subjective and objective standpoints: they seem to enjoy both modes of accessibility.[20] If so, they must have *some* sort of objective aspect. But, recognizing this, we generate a tension between two theses about these mental particulars: that they are essentially subjective, and that they have some objective aspect. The question, then, is how to reconcile and integrate these two ways of conceiving experiences. Well, predictably, one way would be to bring anomalous monism to bear again: mental particulars have a foot in both the subjective and objective spheres because they are entities that satisfy both mental and physical descriptions: they are subjective *qua* mental and objective *qua* physical. Put differently, epistemic accessibility is always under a description: when we conceive a mental particular subjectively we put ourselves (if we can) into the subject's position; when we conceive it objectively, as an item in the all-inclusive spatio-temporal order, we take up a standpoint independent of our own phenomenology by supposing the particular to satisfy some physical description. In this way, then, anomalous monism can explain the dual status of subjective particulars.

Does this reconciliation run up against Nagel's denial that the physical can constitute the nature of essence of the subjective? No, because that is a thesis about mental *properties* and anomalous monism is so far silent on their relation to physical properties; it asserts only that any particular satisfying a mental predicate satisfies a (nontrivial) physical predicate – it does not say that the latter gives the essence of the former, indeed it denies as much.[21] Not being a reductive thesis it does not try to *assimilate* the subjective to the objective.

[20]   Cf. Nagel, *ibid.*, p. 201.

[21]   Nagel puts this question to the physicalist: 'if experience does not have, in addition to its subjective character, an objective nature that can be apprehended for many points of view, then how can it be supposed that a Martian investigating my brain might be observing physical processes which were my mental processes (as he might observe physical processes which were bolts of lightning), only from a different point of view?' 'What is it like to be a Bat', *op. cit.*, pp. 173–4. Care about the distinction between objects and properties helps us see what a physicalist must accept and what he can reject in this: for it does not follow from the fact that subjective *properties* have no objective real essence that a Martian physiologist cannot observe physical *objects* in my brain which are in fact identical with mental particulars, since he need not be investigating those physical objects *as* instances of subjective properties, i.e. investigating the *nature* of those properties.

It is natural now to wonder whether the principles thus reconciled can be converted, along the lines I discussed earlier, into an
argument for what reconciles them, as follows:

(1b)   Every particular has some objective aspect
(2b)   Mental kinds are essentially subjective

So

(3b)   Mental particulars must have some nonsubjective descrip-
       tion; by elimination this must be physical; which is to say
       mental particulars are identical with physical particulars.

Again there are three conditions on the success of such an argument: the premises must be individually plausible; they must not be
question-begging; and they must be uniquely reconciled by a token
identity theory. It seems to me not entirely outrageous to suppose
these conditions met. I have given reasons, apparently endorsed by
Nagel, for accepting (1b) and (2b) – hence the tension Nagel himself hints at. Nor is it at all obvious that either premise is trivially
equivalent to the conclusion. This is plain for (2b), and (1b) says
nothing explicitly of the physical – indeed someone might suggest
that the required objective description relate to some underlying
*im*material substance. This, however, seems to conflict with (2b),
since, like type physicalism, it would imply that subjective properties have an objective nature. One might try to claim that the
properties of such a substance do not exactly constitute the *nature*
of subjective properties, but this just adds an extra mystery to the
already mysterious idea of an objective immaterial substance. But
the suggestion does seem to point to a possible weakness in the
argument, namely its assumption that all objective descriptions are
physical. Though I cannot prove this assumption, I find it prima
facie plausible, and so am inclined to construe (1b)–(3b) as a
genuine argument. At the least, these considerations make anomalous monism an attractive theory of mental particulars.

The persuasive force of the above argument can be increased by
noting a connexion between it and the previous one employing
(1a) and (2a). Nagel makes a point of contrasting the usual theoretical reductions, directed upon natural kinds, with a putative physi-

calist reduction of subjective properties; the contrast concerns the relation between appearance and reality in the two cases.[22] In the case of a theoretical reduction of a natural kind we have the following picture: the manner in which the kind is presented to us results jointly from *its* intrinsic nature and *our* mode of perceptual receptivity, e.g. in the case of heat. The reduction consists in prescinding from its manner of appearance to us, assigning that to our sensory peculiarities, and developing a more objective conception, suitable to a scientific theory, of the independent intrinsic nature of the kind – where this conception is in principle available to *any* being of sufficient intelligence. But, Nagel observes, this picture seems exactly wrong in respect of subjective kinds: we cannot correctly (or even coherently) conceive of their mode of appearance to us in introspection as the joint upshot of an independent mental reality and our own peculiar mode of receptivity to it, in such a way that the essence of the experience would be accurately revealed by bracketing the appearance.[23] On the contrary, moving to the physical correlates of experience takes us not nearer but further away from the essence of the subjective. That is precisely what is meant by saying such states are essentially subjective. Now then, if we agree that a kind is a natural kind only if it admits of this sort of distinction between appearance and reality – and this seems required by the realist view of natural kinds adumbrated earlier – then (2b) is seen to entail (2a); for being a natural kind just *consists* in possessing an objective nature. With respect to (1a) and (1b) we get an entailment from the former to the latter, since again to be of a natural kind is to have an objective aspect. So (1b) acquires whatever plausibility (1a) had. Indeed, one would expect the properties that meet those two conditions to coincide, as indeed they do under anomalous monism. We cannot, it is true, straightforwardly derive the second argument from the first (nor the first from the second), but putting both together yields a more comprehensive picture of mental particulars in the light of which the attractiveness of anomalous monism is significantly enhanced.

---

[22] See Nagel, *ibid.*, pp. 173–4.
[23] This is in effect another way of stating Kripke's point about the difficulty of explaining away the impression of contingency associated with mental-physical correlations: see Kripke, *op. cit.*, pp. 339–40.

It is time to make explicit (what has no doubt by now dawned on some readers) that the tensions, reconciliations and resultant arguments of earlier sections instantiate a pattern whose original is due to Davidson.[24] He enunciated three apparently inconsistent theses relating to mental events and showed how anomalous monism could reconcile them; he then converted the theses into an argument for that theory. The theses were: (i) mental events causally interact with physical events, (ii) causal relations are backed by strict laws, (iii) there are no strict psychophysical laws. The argument proceeds by requiring mental events to have a certain property – that they be governed by laws – and then claiming that they fail to have that property *qua* mental. They must, then, have the property under some other description, and the argument is under way. The structural parallel between this reasoning and my earlier arguments is most clearly exposed by reformulating Davidson's argument in two premises, collapsing (i) and (ii) into a single thesis, thus:

(1c) Every mental particular is of some nomological kind (i.e. instantiates a strict law under some description)
(2c) Mental kinds are not nomological kinds (i.e. anomalism of the mental)

So

(3c) Mental particulars are of some nonmental nomological kind; by elimination that kind is physical; so mental particulars are identical with physical particulars.

I want now to spell out some connexions between this argument and my earlier argument and to offer some considerations against the possibility of psychophysical laws.

What, to begin with, is the connexion between the requirement that mental particulars be of some natural kind and the requirement that they be of some nomological kind? The connexion resides in this principle: to be a natural kind is to be such that there are natural laws definitive of the kind. That is, articulating the stuff of the world into natural kinds involves settling upon a system of laws

---

[24] See the papers of his cited in n.3.

in which the kinds identified play a systematic explanatory role. This implies that for any natural kind there are laws that determine the existence and identity conditions of the kind: nothing could qualify as an instance of the kind and fail to conform to the prevailing laws of the kind.[25] (Note that this is not to say that *every* law applying to a given natural kind is thus definitive of its identity.) So mental particulars, since they are of some natural kind, must instantiate laws whose appilicability to the particular is constitutive of its being of that kind. Thus it is that (1a) implies (1c), which is hardly surprising in view of the scientific realism about natural kinds we accepted earlier. Now if (1a) requires there to be laws of that constitutive status under which mental particulars fall, then the relevant question for deriving the identity theory is whether mental descriptions feature in such laws. For, if they do not, then mental particulars will be constrained to satisfy nonmental descriptions, and the argument will be set to go through. This amounts to the question whether universal generalizations containing mental terms are metaphysically necessary. So, with respect to psychophysical singular causal statements, we enquire whether the corresponding psychophysical generalization is of the required status (and similarly for noncausal psychophysical correlation statements). As I argued in chapter 5, on the basis of some claims of Kripke and Putnam (among others), it seems that no psychophysical generalization is thus necessary: statements relating mental properties – sensations or thoughts – to the brain are metaphysically contingent.[26] Since, therefore, the mental kinds can exist in worlds in which they do not fall under those putative laws, mental descriptions do not yield laws definitive of mental kinds. Accordingly, mental particulars must belong to *other* kinds whose laws do thus define them, and then token physicalism seems inescapable. What this account of Davidson's principles brings out is that his argument can succeed even allowing psychophysical generalizations to possess *some* degree of nomologicality; what matters is that this does not measure up to what we are entitled to expect. However, that said, I do not myself believe the implied concession should be granted; for I think there

---

[25] Cf. Putnam's 'Is Semantics Possible?', *op. cit.*, pp. 140–1, and David Wiggins, 'Essentialism, Continuity and Identity', *Synthese* 23 (1974), pp. 55–6.
[26] See Kripke, *op. cit.*, pp. 335ff. and Putnam, 'Philosophy and our Mental Life', *op. cit.*, p. 293.

are good reasons for denying that psychophysical statements have the characteristics proper to genuine laws of *any* degree of nomologicality. To the elucidation and defence of this claim I now turn.

Davidson has argued that, because of the distinctive character of mental and physical concepts, there cannot be tight nomological connexions between mental and physical properties, either lawlike correlations or causal laws. His official reason for this claim is that the mental and physical schemes of explanation and description operate under 'disparate commitments': 'physical change can be explained by laws that connect it with other changes and conditions physically described,' whereas psychological explanation is answerable to 'the constitutive ideal of rationality'.[27] The basic idea here is that physical theory proceeds under constraints and aims in which the notion of rational intelligibility has no place: this controlling ideal of psychological interpretation has proper application only to the explanation of behaviour, and finds neither foothold nor echo in the description of a person's brain. In consequence Davidson feels able to say 'complete understanding of the workings of body and brain would not constitute knowledge of thought and action'.[28] I think it is fair to report that many philosophers have been perplexed by this reasoning of Davidson's; the perplexity might be expressed in the following way. Suppose we agree with Davidson that mental concepts afford a species of understanding not supplantable by physical concepts, so that psychological theory, being thus *sui generis*, is not reducible to physical theory. Why should it then follow that mental and physical properties cannot be lawfully correlated: why should they not occur in generalizations that are confirmed by their instances and support subjunctive claims, thereby allowing prediction and explanation of mental events? Why, in other words, should the fact that mental concepts cannot be reductively *explained* by physical concepts entail that the two cannot be in lawlike relation? One might trace the felt non-sequitur here to an equivocation on the phrase 'tight connexions' as it occurs in Davidson's claim that there are none of those between mental and physical properties.[29] Davidson's points may indeed show that there are no 'tight connexions' in

---

[27] 'Mental Events', *op. cit.*, pp. 97–8.
[28] 'The Material Mind', *op. cit.*, p. 715.
[29] See 'Mental Events', *op. cit.*, p. 98, for this formulation of the claim.

the sense of nomological reducibility entailing replaceability without explanatory and descriptive loss, but it does not obviously follow that there are no 'tight connexions' in the sense of confirmable and projectible correlations. I think that Davidson makes the first of these senses of the claimed 'nomological slack' very plausible but that he does not present us with a notion of law that warrants the inference to the second sense. However, I want to suggest that the correct conception of law does corroborate Davidson's position, though I have no direct evidence that he in fact subscribes to this conception. We can come at the matter by turning to an analogous claim made by Nagel.

Davidson addresses himself to what I am calling thoughts; Nagel's concern is with sensations. Davidson finds a feature of the attribution of thoughts – namely, the constraint of rationality – which governs understanding another by means of such psychological concepts, and which cannot be extracted from concepts involved in understanding the world physically. Nagel, for his part, finds in concepts for sensations a formally analogous feature itself not capturable in physical terms – namely, subjectivity – and which therefore precludes comprehending the character of another's experiences by way of physical concepts. The claimed features are different, but both are exploited to warrant the denial that knowledge of physics can *constitute* knowledge of psychology, in its attitudinal and experiential departments, respectively; that is, to deny the possibility of psychophysical reduction. But now one wants to ask how the truth of such a claim for *sensations* could show them anomalously related to the physical, in the sense that there are no such lawlike correlations or causal laws. Some remarks of Nagel suggest that he does regard the categorial difference he discerns as reason to rule out psychophysical laws of sensations, but he is more explicit than Davidson about what notion of law is needed to justify this consequence.[30] The idea at which he gestures is roughly this: a generalization counts as a law just if either it is itself an intelligible principle of necessitation or it can be explained by some other generalization possessed of that property. This conception of lawhood is radically nonHumean in two respects: it

---

[30] See his 'Panpsychism', *op. cit.*, pp. 186–7.

requires that a law state necessary connexions (of some strength), and it requires that the necessary connexions be themselves in a certain way intelligible or explicable. The two characteristics are related in that if a generalization is thus intelligible it will present itself to the intellect as affirming a necessitation. A soberer statement of the idea is this: a law must be backed with a theory.[31] Now suppose we accept this view of the nomic, and ask whether psychophysical generalizations conform to it. Then it seems, granted the irreducibility theses of Davidson and Nagel, that such uniformities as might be disclosed by empirical research into psychophysical correlations do not have this property of intrinsic intelligibility: one does not see *how*, by what mechanism, the mental and physical properties are so correlated.[32] Because of the categorial difference between mental concepts (for sensations or thoughts) and physical concepts one is at a loss properly to *explain* the observed correlations: they remain, in a certain sense, brute. Even if we are prepared to project the generalization over some range of creatures and circumstances, the necessity that sustains this is visibly (or *in*visibly) opaque. This apparent incommensurability of the concepts would disappear if, *per impossibile*, the mental were physically reducible; but the whole point is that it is not. So if psychophysical laws require theoretical explanation, and theoretical explanation requires reducibility, then the impossibility of reduction implies the unavailability of genuine psychophysical laws. My suggestion is that some such view of laws is needed by Davidson (and Nagel); moreover, the view seems to me an independently attractive one.

Once we demand of a putative law that it meet this condition of intrinsically intelligible necessity, we establish an intimate connexion between laws and natural kinds. For, the underlying theory that renders the necessity of the law transparent will concern itself precisely with the real internal essence of the kind of which the law treats. What exhibits the necessity of the law is just the theoretically articulated nature of the kind in question. So if nomologicality requires explicability, then the kinds lawfully related will be natural

---

[31] The view of laws here advocated follows William Kneale's (I think) sound and sensible discussion in *Probability and Induction* (Oxford University Press, 1949), §§ 13–20.
[32] This last formulation is taken from Nagel, 'Panpsychism', *op. cit.*, p. 187. One might detect a related point in Davidson's claim that 'mental and physical predicates are not made for one another', 'Mental Events', *op. cit.*, p. 93.

kinds in our original sense.[33] But then the nomologicality of mental kinds would imply their naturalness; the falsity of the consequent yields the anomalism of the mental.

This position is open to challenge by anyone who sees fit to reject the notion of law it presupposes. A Humean about laws, taking them as mere *de facto* uniformities, will dispute the need for (indeed possibility of) the sort of intelligibility we required above; he may even dispute the very idea of natural necessity. I should reject the latter position outright, but an intermediate position occupied by a more moderate Humean calls for comment. The position I envisage waives the requirement of intrinsic intelligibility but accepts that laws involve necessity; the accepted form of necessity is thus taken as brute and inexplicable. I am not myself attracted by this idea of opaque necessitation, but it is worth enquiring whether we can still exclude psychophysical laws a priori under that conception of what it is to be a law. It is clear right away that the necessity could not be absolute (hold for all possible creatures in all possible worlds) for reasons already given; but what of species-specific laws true in a proper subset of all possible worlds? As far as I can see, no a priori arguments can confute this hypothesis in respect of primitive sensations such as pain, but I think that thoughts can be argued to fail of lawlike correlation with the physical even in this attenuated mode. Here is the (or a) reason.

Consider the following platitudes about belief attribution. Suppose, as a representative example, that we attribute a belief to someone whose content is given by the sentence 'Hollywood is seedy', on the basis of the person's utterance of a sentence tantamount to that content sentence made while standing on a Hollywood street. Allow that the belief was formed, and the utterance prompted, by the impact of various sensory stimuli received by the person under these conditions. Now compare this first person to a second who invites the same belief attribution on the basis of utterances made in response to observations from an aeroplane flying over Los Angeles. Or again, compare a third person whose

---

[33] Someone may object that since the explanation of laws must stop somewhere – for not *all* laws can be made intelligible by other, more fundamental, laws – it is left open that psychophysical laws should be thus primitive. I reply that I expect such fundamental laws to possess a degree of intrinsic intelligibility not exhibited by psychophysical correlations (if there are any), and that it seems absurdly *ad hoc* to claim that such correlations could rank as *basic* laws of nature, in view of their manifest friability.

belief that Hollywood is seedy is derived from perusal of travel
books or by talking to acquaintances. Let us call the condition
under which the belief is formed the *input* to the resulting belief
state. Then what these examples platitudinously show is that the
same belief can be possessed – the same thought entertained –
under quite dissimilar, indeed disjoint, input conditions. For beliefs
about concrete objects (and perhaps for other kinds of entity too)
we can introduce the idea of a *physical mode of presentation* of
an object to a person at a time. This corresponds (roughly) to the
notion of a perspective, and it can be explained in various ways. I
shall define it as a pattern of (physical) stimulation impinging on a
person's sensory receptors, as a result of which (in conjunction no
doubt with many other factors) a specific belief is formed. The idea
can be generalized to the intermodal case: the same belief is very
commonly attributed in circumstances in which the modes of presentation of the object(s) concerned relate to distinct senses. What is
notable here is that the content clause that identifies the belief is
insensitive to these variations in input conditions. We find such
physical heterogeneity on the output side too; the behaviour we
take as expressive of a given belief can itself be indefinitely various.
Moreover, the physical modes of acquisition and manifestation of
a belief are often systematically correlated: the circumstances and
manner of manifestation of the belief can depend upon its conditions of acquisition. Let one man believe that Everest is hard to
climb as a result of viewing it from its north side, and another form
the same belief by surveying its south side. The first man may be
disposed to attempt the climb from any other side (not realizing that
it is the same mountain), and similarly for the second man: their
readiness to undertake the climb in certain circumstances depends
upon the mode of presentation of the object at the time the belief
was formed. Their pattern of assent to sentences about the mountain will likewise vary according to their different modes of presentation. So it is evident that the same (type) thought can be had
under very different physical conditions of input and output. Now
ask yourself whether it is plausible to suppose that what transpires
physically *within* the person in the formation of the belief is itself
independent of the particular properties of the input and output
associated with it. It seems to me extremely implausible to hold that
the internal physical states that realize the belief miraculously coin-

cide in these different cases. Rather, the properties of the internal physical events occurring in the same-believers, from the afferent tracts to the central locus of realization in the brain and thence to the efferent pathways, will perforce reflect the particular modes of presentation and manifestation surrounding the formation of the belief.[34] It follows that the same belief can be realized by quite different physical states in the human brain. This conclusion has been arrived at, not by any method of direct inspection of the person's cerebral states, but by armchair reflection on our ordinary practice of belief attribution. (The same point carries over to other propositional attitudes inasmuch as they incorporate a belief component.)

Two observations may now be made. First, we have the consequence that states of belief are so loosely associated with physical properties of the brain as not to be correlated with them in any way that deserves the name of lawlike; and the symptom of this is that knowledge of the realizing physical state of a certain belief in a given creature will not dispose us to project the same physical realization onto other creatures judged to have the same belief, on pain of denying that people can acquire the same belief in different ways. Second, accepting this radical anomalism of belief with respect to the physical seems to make Davidson's argument for token identity go through no matter how relaxed one's notion of law is. For, singular causal statements relating thoughts and physical events have no chance of being backed by a law containing that sort of mental description if what I have just been saying is right; so the thought event will be constrained to satisfy some other description, and token physicalism results. But now if *some* mental particulars are thus demonstrably physical, we seem compelled to conclude that *all* are no matter what degree of nomologicality their mental descriptions exhibit, for surely it is intolerable to allow that some mental events are physical while some are not. (An analogous observation applies to the corollary thesis that thoughts have no physical or other real essence.) I conclude that Davidson's basic

---

[34] In 'Physicalism', *op. cit.*, Nagel remarks that the variation in the causes and effects of 'intensional mental states' renders their lawlike relation to physical states extremely improbable. It is worth noting that my own argument in the text relies upon a *special* feature of the causes (and effects) of propositional attitudes, namely that their representative content is mediated by causally operative modes of presentation of the objects the attitude is about.

position on psychophysical laws and anomalous monism can be vindicated, and by a number of different strategies depending on the concessions volunteered.

It is instructive to compare psychological reality with the realm of the semantical apropos of their relation to the physical world. We find on the one hand an analogy, and on the other a possible connexion. Consider semantical discourse, informal and formal, relating words and sentences to the world. Construing such discourse as a first-order theory we will discern a stock of semantical predicates – notably 'refers', 'satisfies', 'true' – and an ontology of entities over which these predicates are defined: these entities will include various object-language expressions, utterances of such, and extra-linguistic objects comprising the subject matter of the object-language expressions and utterances thereof. Set over against this semantical discourse we have a portion of physical theory describing and explaining the physical facts somehow involved in language use: neurophysiological descriptions of the brain states of speakers as they utter and understand, and physical relations between speakers (or expression tokens) and the extra-linguistic objects spoken of. Given these two areas of discourse we can, as with mental and physical discourse, raise the question of their relation, and the various options present themselves with respect to the objects and properties assigned to the terms and predicates of the theories. I want to claim that my earlier discussion of the mental (specifically of propositional attitudes) can be recapitulated, *mutatis mutandis*, in respect of the semantical. To avoid tedium, let me just summarize how this would go. The doctrine to be favoured is anomalous monism about semantical facts: thus the objects to which semantical properties and relations are attributed are physical objects, while the semantical properties themselves are anomalously related to physical properties. Arguments for the claim of token identity will parallel my earlier arguments about mental particulars: every semantical particular is of some natural or nomological kind, but semantical properties are neither natural nor nomological, so semantical particulars are constrained to satisfy other nonsemantical descriptions. If these objects have mental descriptions, then the earlier arguments plus transitivity of identity will entail token physicalism with respect to semantical particulars. Of course, philosophers have not typically been so extravagant as to suppose that there is a distinct ontology of semantical particulars – they have assumed them to be either clearly physical or psychological – so the above argument for token identity has an unsurprising conclusion.[35] It is therefore of more interest to address the question of properties, over which there has been greater dispute. How then do semantical properties relate to physical?

It is plain straight off that no physicalist type identity theory of semantical properties can be correct: creatures of diverse physical make-up should be describable in semantical terms, and so the semantical properties cannot possess any physical real essence. (This would explain the absence from semantical terms of the syndrome of features (i)–(ix) that we saw to be characteristic of natural kinds.) Nor do semantico-physical laws seem in prospect. Semantical concepts conform to their own distinctive principles (interlocking with the psychological), and there seems no chance of reducing these to physical concepts: knowledge of physics could not plausibly *constitute* knowledge of semantics.[36] Connectedly, semantical and physical concepts seem incongruous in such a way as to preclude intelligibly *explaining* any putative necessitations as between the two sorts of fact: and this again seems owed to the nominal character of semantical predicates. Neither does relaxing our conditions on lawhood qualify semantico-physical generalizations as (weakly) nomological. For we can repeat the observations made toward the end of the last section concerning the kind and amount of physical variation implicitly tolerated in our ordinary practice of semantical attribution: we are prepared to ascribe the same semantic property to speakers' utterances under quite heterogeneous physical circumstances, as when the same object is referred to from different perspectives. Such physical variation is evident also under the standard theories of reference: the causal-historical theory (or

---

[35] Note that I am here discussing an ontology of semantic *particulars* – utterances, inscriptions and the like. I am putting on one side the question of *abstract* entities possibly introduced by semantical discourse – expression types, intensions and so on. One would need to adjoin nominalism about semantics to make *all* semantical entities physical; I am engaged on the more limited enterprise.

[36] This conclusion is at odds with Hartry Field's project of reducing semantics to physics: see his 'Tarski's Theory of Truth', *Journal of Philosophy* 69 (1972). Putnam glosses Field as proposing a theoretical reduction of the reference relation analogous to that proper to natural kinds, e.g. 'water is H_2O': see Putnam's *Meaning and the Moral Sciences* (Routledge and Kegan Paul, 1978), p. 17. If I am right, this has to be the wrong model. (I must, however, defer a fuller discussion of the matter to another occasion.)

picture),[37] and the description theory.[38] Thus causal-historical theories allow that the reference relation may hold between pairs of objects related by quite diverse causal chains, of varying length, source and mechanism. This is also clear for one-place semantical predicates formed from the two-place 'refers' by closing up the second place, as in 'x refers to Everest': this predicate can be satisfied by speakers (or expression tokens) whose relation to the object of reference is, because of differences in the relevant causal-historical chains, physically heterogeneous. And if one characterizes the causal chain in psychological vocabulary, using the concept of intention say, then the heterogeneity of the chains that sustain the given semantical property will ramify with the physical variation in the states that realize that propositional attitude at successive links in the chain. Parallel remarks apply to description theories. One dimension of physical diversity in reference, say in respect of a proper name, is generated by the fact that different speakers, or the same speaker at different times, may bring off reference by means of different descriptive beliefs satisfied by the object of reference, and these beliefs will have distinct physical correlates. But further, compounding the diversity, variable physical realization of the same belief will cause the heterogeneity to ramify *within* a given descriptive belief. So on both sorts of theory of reference the underlying physical properties and relations will lie athwart the semantical properties they realize; and, as with belief, this consideration against semantico-physical laws is already embedded in our ordinary practice of semantical description.

That was the analogy; now the possible connexion. Hartry Field has suggested, motivated by the idea that belief is a relation to a sentence (or sentence analogue) in a system of internal representation, that we construe the belief relation as a composite of two other relations, thus:

x believes that p iff there is a sentence S such that x believes* S and S means that p.[39]

---

[37] See Kripke, *op. cit.*, pp. 298ff., for a sketch of this sort of 'theory'.
[38] See Michael Dummett, *Frege: Philosophy of Language* (Duckworth, 1973), *passim.*, for a systematic defence of such a theory.
[39] See Field's 'Mental Representation', *Erkenntnis* 13 (1978). I say 'possible' connexion because I am not convinced that the language of thought hypothesis is right (nor that it is wrong); neither do I wish to subscribe to Field's version of physicalism.

This analysis is subjected to much refinement, but Field's basic proposal is that we give, first, a materialistic account of the believes* relation and, second, materialistically explain the semantical relations implicated in the second conjunct. This latter, according to Field, is to take the shape (in part) of a Tarskian theory of truth for the inner language of which S is a sentence; thus giving the content of a belief a materialist account becomes a matter of materialistically characterizing the semantic relations such a theory introduces. This implies that the physical basis of a specific belief state, canonically specified by closing up the second term of the belief relation with a 'that'–clause, will be a function (*inter alia*) of the physical bases of the semantic relations in which the inner sentence S stands to extralinguistic reality. This implies, in turn, that the question as to the physical basis of propositional attitudes reduces to the same question about semantics (plus, of course, the relation expressed by 'believes*'). Granting this connexion, conclusions about the nomologicality or otherwise of semantics go over to the case of belief. So if you are inclined to agree with Field's analysis of belief, and if you reject semantico-physical laws, then you are committed to denying psychophysical laws for beliefs. I suspect that many people are antecedently more prepared to accept the anomalism of the semantical than that of the psychological; if so, Field's connexion advances my cause. In both areas I should say that it is the property of representative content that is operative in fixing our view of how mental and semantical facts relate to physical. For this reason alone it is good to have a theory that integrates propositional attitude psychology and semantics.

I have spoken above of physical properties (or state types) *realizing* mental properties (or state types). In this final section I want to address three issues bearing on this relation. They concern (i) realism about mental facts, (ii) realization, supervenience and conditional psychophysical laws, and (iii) the impact upon anomalous monism of the thesis that mental content is (in part) fixed by the environment.

(i) Anyone who calls himself a physicalist is apt to hold that there is a sense in which the physical facts about the world *determine* all the other facts. In consequence, the physicalist will be reluctant to recognize the reality of alleged facts for which no physical basis can be found. That is, physicalism imposes the following condition on a realist view of a given class of statements: the truths they express must not be *independent* of the truths of physics. I have denied that mental facts are physicalistically reducible. This denial may prompt the physical realist to suspect commitment to some sort of anti-realist or instrumentalist conception of the mental; and this he may regard (rightly) as unacceptable. The question we need to answer is then this: how is it possible to combine the irreducibility thesis and the physicalist condition on realism with acceptance of a realist view of the mental? I think the suspicion can be assuaged by distinguishing two senses in which a property can be said to have a physical 'basis': the word is ambiguous as between physical *reduction* and physical *realization*.[40] We can deny that mental properties have a physical basis in the first sense, but that denial is consistent with affirming the physicalist's nonindependence condition as formulated in terms of the second sense: the requirement that all genuine properties have a physical realization is, I suggest, enough to satisfy the demand for complete physical determination, since a property supervenes on what realizes it (see below). In particular, the causal-explanatory role of mental facts is, by virtue of physical realization, predicated upon the existence of *some* underlying system of physical facts appropriately related to the causal explanation formulable in mental vocabulary; and the *truth* of mental attributions (as against their mere instrumental usefulness) will imply the truth of some corresponding physical attribution.[41] Requiring a physical 'basis' for these features of mental concepts does not then imply physical reducibility; so realism about the psychological is compatible with what has gone before.

(ii) Davidson formulates the thesis of supervenience in these words: 'it is impossible for two events (objects, states) to agree in all

[40] A famous remark of Quine's encourages blindness to the intermediate position afforded by realization: 'One may accept the Brentano thesis [the irreducibility of intentional idioms] either as showing the indispensability of intentional idioms and the importance of an autonomous science of intention, or as showing the baselessness of intentional idioms and the emptiness of a science of intention.' *Word and Object* (Cambridge, Mass., 1960), p. 221. (Physical) baselessness is *not* entailed by irreducibility. In 'Physicalism: Ontology, Determination, and Reduction', *Journal of Philosophy* 72 (1975), G. P. Hellman and F. W. Thompson offer a rigorous model-theoretic account of the notion of physical determination, showing it compatible with the denial of physical reduction.

[41] One might, indeed, construct an *argument* of sorts to physical realization from the following premises: mental states must be construed realistically in view of their causal-explanatory role; no state can be realistically construed unless it has a physical basis.

their physical characteristics ... and to differ in their psychological characteristics'; he speaks also of the mental as 'strongly dependent' on the physical and of the latter as 'determining' the former.[42] His formulation seems best captured by means of a condition containing two occurrences of a necessity operator, thus: necessarily, for any mental property instantiated by a creature at a time, there is a physical property the creature instantiates such that, necessarily, if any creature instantiates that physical property, then it instantiates that mental property. That is to say, every mental property must be physically realized, and there are necessarily true supervenience conditionals whose antecedents express such realizing properties and whose consequents express the supervening mental property. It is natural now to ask whether the kind of determination affirmed by such supervenience conditionals is lawlike. One might be tempted to think so by the following line of reasoning: 'There are no *bicon*ditional psychophysical laws because variable physical realization of mental properties is incompatible with the necessity we expect of a law: but the converse conditional – from physical to mental – is explicitly formulated using a necessity operator (the second one in our formulation above), and so any reason for denying the lawlikeness of supervenience conditionals lapses'. I shall make three comments on this reasoning. The first is that we are accustomed to laws providing some sort of *general* answer to the question why a certain property is instantiated by an object at a time, an answer applicable to other circumstances in which the property is exemplified, but supervenience alone and as such is compatible with there being no such general explanation of why the supervening property is instantiated when it is. A second (and related) point is that, as insisted earlier, the mental and physical properties expressed in a supervenience conditional are categorially different in a way that precludes genuine explanation of the former by the latter. And third the necessity intended in the formulation of supervenience is not nomological in purport. This is evident from reflection on other areas in which supervenience theses have been maintained: the moral on the descriptive, the aesthetic on the physical, the modal on the actual, the semantic on the psychological, and so forth. The notion of determination intended here is clearly not nomological; and this is

---

[42] See 'The Material Mind', *op. cit.*, p. 717.

connected with the point that the necessitations here claimed do not have the intelligible transparency we demand of a genuine law of nature. One sees too that the sort of physical determination envisaged here is a far cry from conceptual or nomological reduction.

(iii) Methodological solipsism is defined by Putnam as the thesis that 'no mental state, properly so called, presupposes the existence of any individual other than the subject to whom that state is ascribed'.[43] Putnam is himself opposed to an analogous thesis about meaning: that no meaning has its existence and identity conditions fixed by the (actual) extension of that meaning (a Fregean thesis). But he apparently holds that intentional mental states, like belief, do fulfil the thesis of methodological solipsism: their content is independent of the existence of the objects we should normally say the belief is about.[44] So Putnam seems committed to the claim that (for example) the sense of a demonstrative *utterance* is fixed (in part) by the object(s) demonstrated, but that the content of a demonstrative *belief* is not similarly fixed by the identity of the object(s) the belief is demonstratively about. The environment contributes to the semantic content of sentences but not to the intentional content of thoughts. This divided account of representative content has seemed unacceptable to many; and they have preferred to extend Putnam's observations on meaning to mental content.[45] Under the extended account seeming sameness of belief is not sufficient for real sameness, as can be appreciated by constructing a Twin earth example in which the external objects of belief are distinct. (Our intuitions here depend upon our taking beliefs as essentially bearers of truth-value, as well as internal states explanatory of behaviour.) The slogan suggested by the extension is then that mental states are not (wholly) in the head: the external environment does its bit in fixing the content of a thought.

This conception of the nature of thoughts raises two questions for us: first, what are the implications for our view of the relation between mental and physical properties?; second, what are the implications for a token identity theory? About the first question, we seem compelled to acknowledge (what Brentano long ago urged)

---

[43] 'The Meaning of "Meaning"', *op. cit.*, p. 220.
[44] *Ibid.*, pp. 223ff.
[45] See my 'Charity, Interpretation, and Belief', *Journal of Philosophy* 74 (1977), where the extension is proposed.

that the representative character of mental properties makes them to be fundamentally different from physical properties, thus underlining the categorial difference insisted upon earlier (note the connexion between the rationality constraint on mental states and their being truth-bearers). But, more germane to present concerns, the contribution of the environment calls for a widening in our account of realization and supervenience: for we now see that co-satisfaction of nonrelational intrinsic physical properties does not entail co-satisfaction of (intentional) mental properties, as will be evident from reflection on a Twin earth example. We shall have to go outside of the individual and incorporate physical relations to external objects in our description of what realizes a given belief for a person at a time. Conversely, what the belief supervenes on now includes extra-individual factors.[46] This pretty much alters the traditional picture of what a psychophysical correlation would look like, and introduces further heterogeneity into the physical correlates of belief, given that sameness of belief content is compatible with variation in physical relations to the objects of belief – variable realization is now, so to speak, out in the open. Nomological connexions look even *less* feasible than before on this conception of propositional content.[47]

The second question is whether a nonsolipsistic view of token thoughts permits their identification with physical particulars. I shall suggest, though tentatively, that it does not, but that another relation between mental and physical particulars can serve the ends of materialism equally well. Suppose, to set the stage, that a particular thought about a certain object is prompted in a person by the impingement of energy emanating from that object, this causing a sequence of physical events in the person's body leading from sensory periphery to cerebral interior. Call the external object 'o', the internal brain event correlated with the onset of the thought 'e', and the physical relation between o and e 'R'. Now the token identity theorist proposes that the prompted thought is identical

---

[46] My assertion in 'Mental States, Natural Kinds, and Psychophysical Laws', ch. 5 of this book, that the ascription of mental facts is supervenient on behaviour was therefore strictly inaccurate; it applies only to mental states subsisting wholly in the head, such as sensations. For nonsolipsistic mental states one has to reckon the external objects in with the behaviour.
[47] Multiplying this source of anomalism by that identified at pp. 173–5 cuts belief properties yet further loose from physical properties.

with cerebral event *e*. It is then objected that there is a prima facie difficulty about this identification, in the shape of a violation of the indiscernibility of identicals with respect to modal properties. For, it appears that the particular thought is essentially about *o* but that *e* is only contingently *R* to *o*; the existence of the thought thus depends upon the existence of *o*, but the existence of *e* seems independent of the existence of *o*. If these appearances are correct, then Leibniz's law tells us that the thought cannot be *identical* with the internal brain event. Here are some ways an identity theorist might respond to these intuitive claims.

He might (a) accept the contingency of *R* and try to face up to the consequence that the thought is not essentially about *o*: both the aboutness relation and its physical realization in *R* are contingent (or nonrigid) relations. This response seems to me pretty implausible: it seems evident to me that thoughts can no more vary in their content than lecterns can vary in their composition. How could a particular thought that that table is dirty have been a thought that that chair is dirty (where the table and the chair are distinct objects)? Yet we appear to have to take that consequence if we allow that *e* could have been in some relation *R'* to the chair though actually it is related by *R* to the table, for in that circumstance the thought would have had the chair in its content. Those with unwarped intuitions will want to avoid this consequence. Response (b) tries to respect the necessity of thought content by asserting the *non*contingency of *R*: just as the thought is necessarily about *o*, so *e* is necessarily caused by *o* – hence the thought and *e* will exist in the same possible worlds. This claim about the existence conditions of *e* may be motivated by the rather plausible doctrine that (token) events have their causes essentially. In not denying that thoughts have their content essentially this response certainly seems preferable to (a), but it is still unsatisfying. For it does not I think speak to the real objection to the physicalist identification, namely that there is a sense in which the external object *enters into* or *constitutes* the content of the thought, whereas it is extrinsic to the identity of the brain event, despite their being (perhaps) rigidly related. Intuitively speaking, the object is *built into* the thought; so the original objection from Leibniz's law recurs with respect to *that* relation. Response (c) aims to accommodate this intuition: if the thought itself is partly out in the world, then why not make the physical object with which it is identical itself partly outside of the person's body? More exactly, let the thought be identical with something like the *aggregate* consisting of *e* and *o* (and possibly the intermediate physical events).[48] The merit of this proposal is that, plausibly, the existence of the physical aggregate does depend upon the existence of its member components, just as the thought depends for *its* existence upon its actual objects – and there is a clear sense in which the components of the aggregate are built into it. However, the proposal is flawed: for the aggregate has a property the thought appears to lack, namely it is divisible into extrinsically related parts, *e* and *o*, whereas one does not want to divide up the thought in this way. The point is that there is no conceptually prior and autonomous internal mental event which combines with the external object to yield a thought possessed of a specific content, yet the brain event *is* thus separable from its causes. So thought and aggregate seem discernible with respect to their mereological properties.

Nevertheless, the aggregate idea seemed promising. A way of preserving it and evading the objections from Leibniz's law would be to forego identity and introduce in its stead some other suitably physicalist relation: a natural suggestion, following this lead, is that the thought and its associated physical aggregate stand in a relation closer to that of *composition*.[49] That relation deserves to be called physicalist because it is reasonable to characterize an entity (wholly) composed of physical entities as itself a physical entity, and the composition relation is an indiscernibility relation with respect to many kinds of property (position, causality, mass, chemical make-up, etc.). But since composition is not an *unrestricted* indiscernibility relation we are relieved of the obligation to find all properties of thought and aggregate in common. Though this suggestion may not remove all puzzlement about how thought content and the associated physical facts fit together, I think it stands a better chance of

---

[48] The kind of notion I want is explicated in Tyler Burge, 'A Theory of Aggregates', *Nous* 11 (1977), though I need to let events and states be components of aggregates the other components of which may be continuant particulars. Invoking aggregates instead of sets or sequences of physical particulars has (at least) two advantages: first, we do not introduce physicalistically problematic *abstract* entities into the ontology of mental discourse; second, we naturally preserve the locutions in which we speak of various events as *caused* by beliefs.

[49] There is reason to apply this idea to actions too. An intentional action seems to involve essentially *both* an internal mental event (a 'willing') and an external physical event (a bodily movement); it cannot be identified with either event alone. A natural suggestion, then, is that the action is a *composite* of both events taken together.

7

Functionalism and Phenomenalism: A Critical Note*

Functionalism in the philosophy of mind is perhaps best understood as a response to a problem that is widely agreed to have interred classical reductive behaviourism. The problem stems from a certain feature of the mental that obstructs the behaviourist programme; functionalism claims to overcome the problem by registering this troublesome feature in its account of mental states. Behaviourism required, in effect, that there exists – and to specify the reduction we must construct – a one-one function from mental predicates to (dispositional) behavioural predicates such that, for any creature, satisfaction of the mental predicate entails satisfaction of the behavioural predicate, and vice versa. Such a function would warrant the thesis that mental states *consist in* behavioural dispositions. The problem with this claim is obvious when once noticed: a given mental state does not, in point of fact, determine a unique behavioural disposition on the part of its possessor, for the simple reason that mental states typically cause behaviour by way of interaction with *other* mental states. Because of this holism in the way mental states mediate sensory input and behavioural output, the behavioural correlate of a mental state will vary according to its relations to other elements of a creature's psychology. The central case of this, and the most commonly cited, is the joint determination by desire and belief of intentional action. A given desire does not dispose the agent to a kind of action independently of how it stands with the agent's beliefs, and symmetrically for belief *vis-à-vis* desire. More generally, the way an agent behaves in response to sensory

*   Previously published in *Australasian Journal of Philosophy*, Vol. 58, No. 1; March 1980, pp. 35–46. Appears here with permission.

input will depend, not on mental states of the agent singly considered, but on his total psychological condition. It follows that the only way to associate a behavioural correlate with a given mental state as its reduction would be to incorporate a specification of the collateral mental states with which the given one combines — but of course this makes for circularity. So reductive behaviourism seems precluded.

Functionalism promises an account of mental states that does justice to their interrelations while retaining the emphasis on behaviour. Instead of construing mental states as straightforward categorical dispositions to behaviour, it takes them to be conditional dispositions of a certain sort: they cause behaviour conditionally upon their (causal) interaction with other mental states (where these are to be specified otherwise than through mental predicates). What went wrong with behaviourism, then, was its attempt to characterize mental states on too exiguous a basis, purely in terms of behavioural dispositions; the remedy is to contrive a more holistic characterization of the causal role of a mental state, in terms of sensory input, intra-mental interactions, and behavioural output. This intuitive conception of the nature of mental states — that they are individuated by holistic causal role — requires, if it is to be made good, some method of definition that captures the mental interrelations in a noncircular manner. To this end, functionalists have advocated a method of implicit functional definition alternative to ordinary explicit definition. If this mode of definition worked, then it would seem that functionalists have an account of mental states that preserves an element of truth in behaviourism and thus conforms with a certain physicalism, since the definitions would contain only terms for (physical) input and output, along with topic-neutral vocabulary.[1]

The last remark demands a clarification. Functionalists commonly insist that their doctrine does not, contrary to classical behaviour-

---

[1] This general perspective on functionalism can be found in Gilbert Harman, *Thought* (Princeton University Press, 1973), pp. 40–6; N. J. Block and J. A. Fodor, 'What Psychological States Are Not', *Philosophical Review* (April 1972), esp. p. 167; N. J. Block, 'Troubles with Functionalism' in Wade Savage (ed.), *Minnesota Studies in the Philosophy of Science*, vol. 9, 1978; George Bealer, 'An Inconsistency in Functionalism', *Synthese* (July 1978). It is less clear that Hilary Putnam's machine state version of functionalism conforms to this description, but I think that it accurately reflects at least some of his remarks; see his 'The Nature of Mental States', in *Mind, Language and Reality* (Cambridge University Press, 1975).

ism, involve the ontological thesis that commitment to mental entities must be eschewed.[2] Quite the opposite: mental states are taken to be real internal states of an organism, causally responsible for its behaviour. Indeed, the standard account of functional definition (rehearsed below) involves precisely quantification over mental states. Here we need the distinction between what Quine calls the ontology of a theory and its ideology: i.e. between the domain of entities quantified over, and the stock of predicates (conceptual resources) in the language of the theory.[3] Classical behaviourism wished an ontological reduction, i.e. an elimination of mental entities, as well as a conceptual reduction of mental ideology. Modern functionalism should be understood as accepting a mental ontology, but as claiming that a physical ideology suffices for saying all that needs to be said in a finished theory of reality: it offers a conceptual, not an ontological, reduction of the mental. Mental states are not, as we might say, logical constructions out of behaviour; they are causes of behaviour. But they can be identified purely in terms of their extrinsic causal role with respect to input, output and one another. The import and importance of this will emerge in what follows.

The promissory thesis that mental states can be fully characterized by way of their holistic causal role receives a somewhat precise formulation in a technique of definition exploiting Ramsey sentences, advanced by a number of authors.[4] I shall focus on the account of this given by David Lewis.[5] (Lewis's treatment has the

[2] See, e.g., Hartry Field, 'Mental Representation', *Erkenntnis* 13 (1978), p. 26, and David Armstrong, *A Materialist Theory of Mind* (Routledge and Kegan Paul, 1968), esp. ch. 6, sec. VI.

[3] See, for the distinction, W. V. Quine, 'Ontological Reduction and the World of Numbers', in *The Ways of Paradox* (Random House, 1966), p. 202, and elsewhere.

[4] Accounts of this occur in David Lewis, 'Psychophysical and Theoretical Identifications', *Australasian Journal of Philosophy*, vol. 50 (1972), Harman, *op. cit.*, Field, *op. cit.*, and Bealer, *op. cit.* The invention of this technique is, I think, largely responsible for the confidence of many functionalists; as I shall argue, the confidence is misplaced.

[5] This is derived mainly from Lewis. *op. cit.*, but see also his 'How to Define Theoretical Terms', *Journal of Philosophy*, 67 (1970) and 'An Argument for the Identity Theory', *Journal of Philosophy*, 63 (1966). Though Lewis's explication of functional definition is widely applauded by functionalists, it is worth noting that there are three features of his overall account which many functionalists reject. These are, briefly: (i) he holds functional definitions of mental terms to be meaning specifying, whereas others take them as empirical in character; (ii) he combines functionalism with acceptance of an identity theory for mental state types, whereas others are motivated precisely by rejection of such an identity theory; (iii) the statements he invokes to define mental states belong to commonsense psychology,

great merit of rendering the functionalist thesis precise enough to permit a fairly sharp discussion of the issue. Too often, I think, functionalism has sheltered behind vague slogans and programmatic pronouncements, invulnerable to critical assessment.) Lewis's version of functionalism results from the conjunction of two claims: (a) a certain view (set out below) about the semantics and proper definition of theoretically introduced terms, and (b) the claim that mental terms are semantically like theoretically introduced terms. In the light of these two claims, Lewis invites us to proceed as follows. Begin by assembling all the platitudes of commonsense psychology that there are; let this be our everyday psychological theory T. Turn these sentences into a long conjunction; this is the *postulate* of T. Think of T as containing a batch of theoretical terms (T-terms) t_1 ... t_n (these are to be the psychological terms), and of the remainder as nontheoretical, the O-terms. T will, *inter alia*, ascribe to the denotations of the T-terms (namely mental states) certain kinds of causal role with respect to sensory stimuli, each other and behaviour: mental states are thus precisely (identical with) the occupants of those roles. Now replace each constant mental term with an appropriate free variable x_1 ... x_n. Say that any n-tuple of entities that satisfies the resulting open formula is a *realization* of the initial theory T. We can then get the effect of the original theory containing t_1 ... t_n by forming its Ramsey sentence – i.e. the existential closure of the derived open formula, or, according to Lewis, its modified Ramsey sentence – i.e. by demanding that the theory have a unique realization. With these materials to hand we can define the T-terms of the theory by means of its O-terms: a given mental term stands for the entity, whatever it is, which has the causal role ascribed by the O-terms of T. Since the O-terms comprise only topic-neutral and input-output vocabulary, we have, it is claimed, succeeded in defining mental terms, or individuating mental states, in functional vocabulary. (Notice that, as anticipated above, we reduce mental ideology to functional precisely *by* quantifying over mental entities.) The implication is that, in accordance with the intuitive motivation, we have entirely captured the content

---

whereas others wish to include the results of present and future scientific psychology, possibly discarding some of the 'platitudes' of psychological commonsense. I shall not comment on these differences in what follow: it should be evident that if my criticisms apply against Lewis, they apply also against these variant views.

of mental concepts in the net of physical (and topic-neutral) concepts: we have specified the *nature* of mental states. As Lewis remarks, quoting Armstrong, acceptance of theses (a) and (b) warrants the gloss: 'The concept of a mental state is primarily the concept of a state of a person apt for bringing about a certain sort of behaviour [and secondarily also, in some cases] apt for being brought about by a certain sort of stimulus'.[6] In other words, the availability of this functional definition enables us to define the intrinsic predicates of a mental state by way of its extrinsic causal relations. Armstrong again: 'We see the mind as an inner arena identified by its causal relations to outward act'.[7]

The foregoing is, I take it, a fair reconstruction of the sequence of thought that encourages the functionalist. My aim now is to question whether the considerations so far adduced in the statement and defence of functionalism sustain the intuitive gloss put upon them. I shall contend that these considerations do not have the interest and significance commonly attached to them. I do this by comparing the functionalist claim with a parallel series of moves apparently available to a certain kind of neo-phenomenalist about physical objects and their properties.

It is not a novel observation that the programme of classical phenomenalism bears certain structural parallels to that of behaviourism.[8] Both sought explicit definitions in the shape of straightforward reductive biconditionals, and both encountered obstacles of a similar sort. Just as a mental state does not determine a piece of behaviour independently of the conspiracy of other mental states, so a physical object does not determine a perceptual experience independently of other causally relevant physical conditions. An object's being red, for example, is not associated with a percipient's having an experience as of a red object unless various other physical facts obtain and interact appropriately with the red object: the percipient's body and sense-organs must be suitably positioned and oriented, his sensory receptors must be functioning normally, his brain be in certain physical states, and so forth. Without the conspiracy of these factors no experiential condition is entailed by a

---

[6] From Armstrong, *op. cit*, p. 82.
[7] Armstrong, *ibid.* p. 129.
[8] See Harman, *op. cit.* p. 11, and Christopher Peacocke, *Holistic Explanation* (Oxford University Press, 1970), *passim*.

physical object fact. To provide conditions sufficient for the experience one would have to include reference to these further physical facts; so again there is a circularity. The point is just that a perceptual experience results jointly from the external physical facts and physical conditions of the observer; there is no simple experiential disposition associated with a given physical object fact. As Chisholm put it once, the reductive phenomenalist is like an economist trying to define both supply and demand in terms of possible prices, whereas what we have is a kind of simultaneous determination by independent factors.[9] (The simile is even apter in the case of desire and belief.) There is a sense in which the causal role of a physical state with respect to experience is holistic.

This familiar parallel suggests the following thought. Might not a phenomenalistically inclined philosopher, acknowledging the difficulty that the above point makes for his reductive programme, respond as functionalists did to the analogous difficulty for behaviourism? We can imagine this philosopher proposing that physical objects and properties be individuated by their role in the causal manifold: what makes a physical property the property it is is its typical pattern of causes and effects, its propensity to enter into causal transactions with other physical properties and with experiences. We are to construe a physical object as what causes, together with other physical objects (to be specified abstractly), experiences in percipients. Of course this theory of the nature of the physical world departs from classical phenomenalism in not extruding, but rather invoking, a physical ontology in its account of physical concepts, just as functionalism differs from classical behaviourism in the parallel respect. But the modified phenomenalist will still claim to reduce our physical *ideology* to phenomenal and topic-neutral concepts by means of a causal role definition. Though not exactly an outright vindication of old phenomenalism, this would clearly be a substantive claim – just as substantive, at any rate, as the functionalist claim. With this general picture in mind, our phenomenalist will try to make good his thesis by supplying a formally adequate functional definition, employing Lewis's technique. We begin by assembling all our commonsense platitudes about

[9] Roderick Chisholm, 'The Problem of Empiricism', *Journal of Philosophy*, 45 (1948), and the Appendix to his *Perceiving: a Philosophical Study* (Cornel University Press, 1957).

physical objects. Some of these will specify the causal role of physical objects in the production of experiences; others will speak of the inter-relations and interactions between physical objects, properties and states themselves; yet others will tell of the changes in the physical world caused by various kinds of mental event (the analogue of input in the case of functionalism). Form the conjunctive postulate of this theory T'. Now replace the constant physical T'-terms $t'_1 \ldots t'_n$ by appropriate free variables $x'_1 \ldots x'_n$. Then say that any n-tuple of entities that satisfies the resulting open formula is a realization of T'. Again we could take the Ramsey sentence, or modified Ramsey sentence, to derive a theory with the same force as the original; and then go on to define $t'_1 \ldots t'_n$ by means of definite descriptions containing only causal and experiential vocabulary. Thus we definitionally eliminate physical object vocabulary (though not physical objects) in favour of terms acceptable to an ideological phenomenalist. In so doing we noncircularly capture the feature of joint or holistic determination that frustrated the classical phenomenalist programme. On the strength of such a functional definition our neophenomenalist will claim that physical objects have no irreducibly physical intrinsic properties; all physical concepts can be exhaustively accounted for in terms of extrinsic causal relations, notably to experiences.

I expect it to be agreed that this functionalistic phenomenalism does not give a satisfactory reductive account of physical concepts. It does not seem plausible to maintain that the applicability of the Lewis-type definition to physical terms preserves an insight of phenomenalism, nor that our ultimate theory can be basically idealist in its ideology. What I am insisting is that nothing so far said shows that functionalism proper is not in the same case. As I see it, the two definitions do serve to pick out, using their preferred ideology, mental states and physical objects, respectively, but I do not think that this warrants the reductive intuitive gloss put upon this fact. If we are reluctant to agree that physical concepts are primarily concepts of dispositions to cause experiences, to parody Armstrong, then we should be suspicious of the corresponding claim for mental states. To entitle ourselves to that claim we need to find some feature of the mental that distinguishes it from the physical in some relevant respect. And here I think the functionalist is compelled to fall back on nebulous slogans, as that a person is to be conceived of as a 'functional system' or something of the sort. What I have argued so far, in effect, is that the usual techniques of functional definition do not themselves confer a clear sense of this phrase, on pain of applying it equally to the world of physical objects. That is what I meant when I said that the considerations commonly adduced in support of functionalism do not have the significance popularly attached to them.

Someone may object that I have overlooked a key part of Lewis's case. As remarked, Lewis's account of mental terms results from two claims – a view about how to define theoretically introduced terms, and the claim that mental terms are semantically akin to such terms. What I overlooked, according to this objection, is the second of these: and it is the truth of that thesis which makes the functional definition appropriate, and on which the burden of Lewis' functionalism therefore falls.[10] However, it seems that the reasons Lewis offers for the claim in respect of mental terms have clear counterparts in application to terms for physical objects. Of course, as Lewis acknowledges, it is a myth that mental terms were, as a matter of history, theoretically introduced; but, he thinks, the myth can nevertheless be a good one if our mental words mean just what they would mean were the myth true. For the myth to be good it must be that the causal role of a mental state is definitive of the state, in the sense that its specification constitutes the corresponding term's meaning. Lewis cites two (related) pieces of evidence to support the claim that the myth is good in this sense: it explains why many philosophers have found behaviourism attractive and plausible, and it accounts for the odour of analyticity which (as he supposes) surrounds our psychological platitudes. I wish to question neither of these contentions, but I think they go over with equal plausibility to our physical object platitudes. The truth of functionalistic phenomenalism would explain why many philosophers have found phenomenalism proper attractive and plausible, and (connectedly) it would account for the analytic character of our physical object platitudes. For it is plausible enough that statements relating physical objects to perceptual experiences have the status of more than empirically established truths; and it was precisely the analytic

[10] This retort is not available to those, e.g. Field, who view the functionally definitive truths as synthetic and scientific; they must find something else with which to justify an asymmetrical attitude.

character of the conceptual links in both areas that encouraged philosophers to seek behaviourist and phenomenalist definitions of mental and physical vocabulary. In both cases it seems a priori that *either* mental states or physical objects do not exist *or* most of our platitudes about them are true. So we cannot find a principle of distinction in this observation.[11]

Perhaps some people will find themselves persuaded by the parallel but react, not by rejecting functionalism, but by accepting both it and functionalistic phenomenalism. A moment's reflection shows, however, that this way is blocked, at least if such definitions are to have the metaphysical significance usually accorded them. For the two doctrines are mutually incompatible. This is because, taken as programmes of definitional elimination, the definiens concepts of the one are the definiendum concepts of the other: they propose competing reductions, since behaviour is physical and experiences are mental.[12] Nor is it feasible to eliminate both sets of vocabulary simultaneously. Suppose you form the conjunction of our (commonsense) theories of the mental and physical realms. Now consider how you would carry out Lewis's Ramsification technique on this combined theory. You might start by eliminating the mental terms, in the prescribed way, from the conjunct expressing your psychological theory; you then eliminate the physical terms, in parallel fashion, from the conjunct expressing your physical theory. But then, of course, the resulting open sentence still contains terms – behavioural and experiential – to whose definition and elimination you are, as a global functionalist, committed. To implement both

[11] Nor does it help to appeal to a more full-blooded (and standard) notion of 'theoretical' term than Lewis, as relating to 'inferred entities.' For there have been those who have wished to see physical objects as theoretical posits, designed to explain the course of experience, just as some have interpreted mental states as theoretical constructs postulated as the best explanation of observed behavior. So the analogy holds up under that notion of theoretical term also. Not that any of these things is actually *denied* by Lewis.

[12] The argument here is essentially that of my 'An A Priori Argument for Realism,' *Journal of Philosophy*, 76 (March 1979), sec. II. Lewis's attitude on this point is discernible from fn. 15 of 'Psychophysical and Theoretical Identifications', *op. cit.*, p. 257. There he appears willing to define colour sensations in terms of the colours that cause them *as well as* defining colours in terms of the colour sensations they cause. Generalizing, he would find no inconsistency such as I allege between functionalism and wholesale phenomenalism. The reason is that he does not attach the metaphysical significance to such definitions as do other philosophers; he envisages no absolute hierarchy of conceptual priority. I shall not here contest this conception of philosophical definition, but remark only that functionalists at large have clearly wished their reductions to have more metaphysical bite and have interpreted Lewis's definitions accordingly.

doctrines you need to eliminate these terms too. But if you take the elimination to its conclusion, then the resulting Ramsified theory will contain *only* topic-neutral vocabulary. There seems little to be said for the suggestion that this colourless ideology suffices to confer the intended content upon the original mental and physical terms – to capture what the concepts essentially involve. Besides, what would have become of the original motivation to vindicate a basically physicalist or phenomenalist (ideological) metaphysics, as the case may be? So there seems no hope of accepting both doctrines.

To reinforce the symmetry claim I have been urging I now want to explore some further parallels between functionalism and phenomenalism. I shall suggest that some standard worries about functionalism have counterparts in the case of phenomenalism, and that setting these beside each other will help put both in perspective. This will also serve to back up my basic thesis that functionalism is in no better shape that neo-phenomenalism. In fact, I think that the implausibilities of both have a common source.[13]

A persistent focus of worry over functionalist definitions of mental terms has revolved around the so-called qualitative or phenomenological properties of mental states, around what have come to be called 'qualia'. It has seemed to many that these resist definition (analytical or empirical) in terms of causal dispositions: they are just not the *sort* of property to permit exhaustive functional characterization.[14] This intuition of categorial difference has, naturally enough, expressed itself as a contingency claim: namely that it is not a necessary truth that specific qualia should be associated with the causal roles with which they are actually associated. Thus

---

[13] I note, in passing, that there is one potential ground of objection to causal role analyses which threatens neo-phenomenalism with incoherence but to which a certain kind of functionalist can reply. This is that, if all of the intrinsic properties of physical objects get reduced to extrinsic causal dispositions, it is hard to see how facts about the physical world could *explain* (inter alia) the causation of experience. By contrast, a functionalist can appeal to the physical states that *realize* a mental state to explain its capacity to cause behaviour. Indeed, functionalism plus causal explanation by mental states might be used as an *argument* for physical realization. (An alternative, of course, is that unreduced mental terms *already* serve to specify the intrinsic properties that explain the causation of behavior.) However, this possible asymmetry does not seem to affect the points I am after.

[14] This intuition is endorsed by Thomas Nagel in 'What is it Like to be a Bat?', *Philosophical Review* (October 1974), pp. 436–7, and sympathetically discussed in Block and Fodor, *op. cit.*, pp. 172f., and Sidney Shoemaker, 'Functionalism and Qualia', *Philosophical Studies*, 27 (1975).

it has been suggested that the following possibilities are at least prima facie conceivable: that two creatures might agree in their functional description yet be such that their qualia are reversed in some systematic way; and that two creatures might be functionally isomorphic yet one enjoy no qualia at all.[15] What both intuitions come to is that a creature's functional description can be invariant under changes in its qualitative description. Since these qualitative features are essential to certain mental states, functionalism fails to capture all there is to being in such a state. This contingency claim can be formulated succinctly using a distinction of Kripke's.[16] The definite description recording causal role that we arrive at following Lewis's procedure is not a *rigid* designator of the mental state it actually designates; at best it serves merely to fix the reference of a mental term in the actual world. (If the contingency claim is correct, one might diagnose the functionalist's error as that of moving illicitly from a true point about reference fixing to a false conclusion about rigid designation.)

Examples of qualia reversal typically involve inversions of sensation with respect to behaviour *within* a given sense modality, as in the case of the inverted spectrum.[17] Let me now give a (putative) example that involves *inter*-modal qualia reversal. I choose this not because it is less controversial but because it is vivid, novel (to my knowledge) and a neat way of leading into my main point. My primary aim in what follows is not confidently to endorse and defend such possibilities – the issue seems to me complicated and hard to resolve – but rather to draw attention to what looks like an instructive analogy. Suppose (what is probably not true) that the human brain were equipollent in the visual and auditory cortices, in the sense that their information processing capacity was equivalent. Suppose also that the visual and auditory afferent nerves were somehow switched over so that now they fed into the auditory and

---

[15] Although the claim that subjective aspects of experience cannot be captured in terms of causal role has been expressed by this pair of contingency theses, it is not clear, I think, that it *requires* their truth. For it seems to me conceivable that subjective and functional properties should be necessarily correlated but that the latter be nonetheless incapable of capturing what the former *consist in*. (A parallel remark could be made about the relation between physical properties and their causal role with respect to experiences.) If so, the reductive inadequacy of functionalism would not *depend* upon possible cases of inverted and absent qualia.

[16] See Saul Kripke, 'Naming and Necessity', in Donald Davidson and Gilbert Harman (eds), *Semantics of Natural Language* (D. Reidel, 1972), *passim*.

[17] See Block and Fodor, *op. cit.*, and Shoemaker, *op. cit.*

visual cortices, respectively. (We can think of this as a surgical re-routing in a single individual or, to minimize irrelevant complications, of some individuals as constructed one way and some the other.) Then when the eyes and ears of the switched individual were stimulated with light and sound he would experience, respecively, auditory and visual qualia. Now it appears that transducing information borne by light and sound by way of such inverted qualia would not necessarily alter an individual's functional description, since what determine a creature's dispositions are apparently more abstract properties of its experiences, specifically the information it bears (think here of simple organisms). What makes this conceivable is that it seems merely contingent that we have just those qualitative experiences we do have in response to the external phenomena of light and sound: other creatures might be differently constructed. Now if it is true that visual and auditory qualia could be functionally equivalent – and this seems to be at least a prima facie possibility – then that presents a problem for functionalism, since such qualia are plainly distinct mental states. The possibility in question thus suggests that identity of causal role is neither necessary not sufficient to fix mental state.

This example may remind one of some remarks of Kripke, intended to make a quite different point.[18] He says that we use our sensations to fix the reference of certain terms for external phenomena; the reference of 'light', for example, may be fixed by the description 'the cause of this sensation', where the demonstrative picks out the sensation phenomenologically. But, since light and that sensation are (as he thinks) only contingently correlated, the definite description does not rigidly designate the external phenomenon. That sensation might, for example, have been caused by sound. Equally, the sensation actually caused by sound might have been caused by light. This implies, in effect, that there can be cases of reversal of external physical conditions with respect to qualitative experience, which is in fact part of what I imagined above. Now this Kripkean possibility contains the seeds of an objection to phenomenalism about such external phenomena. We cannot hope to define light (say) in terms of the experiences we actually have in response to it, because that association is only contingent. In other

---

[18] See Kripke, *op. cit.*, pp. 324f.

words, two physical phenomena could be experientially indistinguishable for different creatures and yet be really two. So identity of causal role with respect to experiences is neither necessary nor sufficient to fix identity of physical phenomenon. The contingency of the association between the external physical thing and the internal experience of it thus appears to preclude a phenomenalist reduction.

So we see that, on the one hand, the objection to functionalism from qualia reversal trades upon the seeming contingency of the relation between mental and behavioural, while, on the other, the objection to phenomenalism just given rests upon a contingency thesis concerning the physical world and the subjective mode in which we experience it. If that is a correct diagnosis, then both functionalism and phenomenalism are vulnerable to the same underlying intuition: that the (causal) relations between mental and physical types have an element of contingency. Just as the physical phenomena of light and sound are contingently (causally) associated with particular types of qualitative experience, so those experiences in turn are contingently associated (causally) with particular types of behaviour. And this contingency stands in the way of analysing one set of concepts, or reducing one set of properties, to the other. Physical objects do indeed have causal roles with respect to experience, as mental states have causal roles with respect to behaviour; but, if what has been said is right, those roles are possessed contingently: they may fix the reference of the terms but they neither give their meaning nor constitute the nature of the denoted entities. If this is correct, then we can say that functionalism and phenomenalism go wrong for the same basic reason: they are committed to denying the contingency of the relation between mental and physical types.[19]

A similar lesson seems indicated by the following parallel. Just as it is held that the truth of a functional description of an organism does not logically entail the existence of internal qualitative states, so it has often been claimed that no description of the course of

---

[19] Their mistake, then, turns out to be essentially the same as that diagnosed by Kripke in identity theories of the mind–brain relation. I should add that, pace Kripke, I do not take this point about mental and physical *types* to compromise physicalism very seriously. I discuss the matter in 'Mental States, Natural Kinds and Psychophysical Laws', *Proceedings of the Aristotelian Society*, supp. vol. 1978; ch. 5 of this book.

experience, be it ever so protracted and counterfactual, ever logically entails the existence of external physical objects. These claims may not be unquestionable, but they have considerable initial plausibility; and again they point to the contingency whose significance I have been pressing.

The second kind of parallel I want to mention concerns an objection to functionalism that has recently come to the fore.[20] The objection takes the form of a dilemma. Functionalism is out to define mental states by way of their sensory causes, interrelations and behavioural effects. This prompts the question of what sort of vocabulary is to figure in the descriptions of input and output. A dilemma is presented in the shape of two unsatisfactory but seemingly exhaustive replies to this question. Either inputs and outputs are characterized in (covertly) mental terms, or they are characterized in purely physical (physiological) terms. If we describe the input in terms of the kind of mental state caused and the output in intentional terms – as (say) seeing and acting – then the theory is circular. On the other hand, if we rigorously exclude psychologically tainted vocabulary and limit ourselves to strictly physical descriptions – retinal stimulation, muscle contractions, and the like – then we fail to provide a definition that has the requisite generality, for the familiar (and ironic[21]) reason that creatures can enjoy the same psychological states while differing radically in their composition and structure. The trouble here is that it appears hard to find a vocabulary somehow intermediate between these, and so functionalism seems impaled on one or other horn of the dilemma. What I want to point out is that a structurally analogous problem arises for phenomenalism. Suppose we try to devise an experiential condition definitionally equivalent to, and necessarily coextensive with, some given physical condition. What sort of vocabulary shall we use to characterize the experiences? If we identify the experiences in terms of their physical causes – e.g. 'the sensation of (caused by) *light*' – then our definition is circular. But if we restrict ourselves to purely phenomenal descriptions (possibly irreducibly

---

[20] The objection comes from Block, *op. cit.*, where it is stated more fully.

[21] Ironic, because a central motivation for functionalism was the recognition that the physical basis of mental states could vary from creature to creature; see Field, *op. cit.*, p. 28. Of course, the falsity of type-physicalism in no way entails functionalism; one needs (at least) a prior commitment to the reducibility of mental properties, and this is not, in my view, compulsory.

ostensive), then we shall fail to secure the required generality, since the same physical conditions could be (causally) associated with different phenomenological kinds, given that creatures can differ in their modes of experiential receptivity. The difficulty in both cases is that the proposed definitions will be adequately general to capture the concepts in question only if the vocabulary they employ adverts to the causes, mental and physical, of the events the properties of which are allegedly sufficient (along with topic-neutral terms) to yield definitions; but then the definitions are circular. And this seems a serious objection to both reductive theses. What is responsible for the problem is, I think, the same fact that generates the inversion problems discussed earlier, namely that mental and physical types are contingently related. For it is this which leads to the unsatisfactory heterogeneity and probable incompleteability of the purported definiens in the two cases, thus producing one horn of the dilemma.

I have argued in this chapter that some influential considerations thought to favour functionalism can be paralleled to yield a case for a certain kind of phenomenalism. The minimal conclusion to be drawn is that the functionalist has not yet formulated his thesis sharply enough to distinguish it from that intuitively unacceptable phenomenalism. The more ambitious conclusion is that functionalism, insofar as it is intelligible, is no more plausible than the analogous phenomenalism, and moreover these are incompatible. Why then have people so readily tacitly adopted an asymmetrical attitude toward the mental and the physical in this regard? I strongly suspect that it is because of a widespread and undefended anti-realism about the mental taken over from an officially repudiated behaviourism. My own conviction is that neither functionalism nor the analogous phenomenalism afford an exhaustive account of our mental and physical concepts, and that these inadequacies are reflected in and related by the contingency thesis. The content of *both* sets of concepts transcends the facts about causal role that have been supposed to constitute reductions.[22] But with that remark I must leave the topic.[23]

---

[22] Cf. my 'An A Priori Argument for Realism', *op. cit.*, in which essentially this conclusion is reached by a different route.

[23] I am grateful to David Lewis for helpful comments made in correspondence.

8

Could A Machine Be Conscious?*

I want to make some sobering remarks about an intoxicating question – the question that forms my title. It seems to me that, on reflection, this question does not have the interest it is popularly thought to have. Its power to excite stems largely from unclarity about what is being asked. In particular, we need to be clear what we mean by 'machine'.

I have formulated the question in terms of the notion of *consciousness*, but this too needs to be clarified. I could equally have asked whether a machine could have a mind. These formulations have a generality which disguises the diversity of the phenomena. For the question must be whether a machine could think or feel or perceive or will or create or imagine – or do whatever else we customarily dub 'mental'. And it is not obvious that each of these attributes will be equally accessible to a machine; they raise different issues and make different requirements. It is not even clear that consciousness belongs essentially to all of them – we are familiar with the idea of unconscious beliefs and desires, for example. In order to keep my question within manageable proportions I shall focus on a specific attribute of mind, namely subjectivity; and by this I shall mean what Thomas Nagel has meant in saying that for an entity to have subjectivity is for there to be something it is *like* to be that entity.[1] I do not pretend that this notion is particularly explanatory or even very clear (that is part of the problem we face

---

* Previously published in Colin Blakemore, *Mindwaves* (Basil Blackwell: Oxford, 1987). Reproduced here with permission.
[1] See his 'What is it like to be a bat?', in *Mortal Questions* (Cambridge University Press: Cambridge, 1979).

in this area), but I think it will serve to identify the kind of question I mean to be asking. Could a machine enjoy a distinctive 'phenomenology'? Could things *seem* a certain way to a machine – as the world seems a certain way to us and to bats? Could a machine be a subject of experience?

We can interpret the word 'machine' in a narrow sense and a wide sense. In the narrow sense we mean the kinds of device that have actually been constructed by human beings: motor cars, typewriters, aeroplanes, nuclear weapons, pocket calculators, office computers. Could any *such* device be conscious? Well, *is* any such device conscious? Surely not, as even the most ardent enthusiast of the word processor would agree. If not, then *extensions* of such devices, built by the same principles, will not be conscious either. Some people believe that consciousness is a *computational* property, but they do not believe that present-day computers and extensions thereof are conscious; the technology needed for implementing the computational properties in which con-ciousness consists lies (they would say) in the distant future. I shall return to this question; for now I am saying merely that consciousness is not to be found in the *current* extension of the word 'machine'. Nobody today knows how to design a machine that is conscious.

In the wide sense of 'machine' we mean anything, actual or possible, that is an *artefact*, that is, the intentional product of some kind of intelligence. Artefacts thus contrast with naturally occurring objects. The question then is whether an artefact could be conscious. This question can be considered in two parts: (a) could a *human* artefact be conscious? and (b) could an artefact of *any* conceivable intelligence be conscious? On the first question I should say that the matter is entirely an empirical one: it concerns whether human beings ever in fact achieve enough in the way of scientific and technological knowledge. It is like asking whether we shall ever travel to another galaxy. The second question is the one that raises the issue of principle, for it asks whether the *concept* of an artefact is such as to exclude the possession of consciousness. And here I think a quite definite answer is possible: certainly an artefact could be conscious. All that is required is an intelligence of sufficient ingenuity by and know-how. Suppose there were an intelligence clever enough to create beings physically just like us (or bats). Then I think this intelligence would have created conscious beings. Or consider the doctrine of creationism: false as it undoubtedly is, it is surely not self-contradictory. If we are the artefacts of God, this is not a reason to suppose ourselves unconscious. After all, there is a sense in which we *are* artefacts: for we are the products of natural selection operating upon inorganic materials to generate brains capable of subserving consciousness. It is, if anything, *harder* to see how consciousness could result naturally than to see how it could have been wrought by intelligence, as proponents of the argument from design have always maintained. At any rate, all intelligence needs to do to create conscious beings is to recapitulate what natural selection did mindlessly. There is thus no problem of principle about an artefact being conscious.

Why is the distinction between artefact and natural object irrelevant to the question whether an entity is conscious? Because of the following principle: the intrinsic nature of an object is logically independent of the manner of its genesis. Conjoin this with the claim that whether an entity is conscious is solely a matter of its intrinsic nature and you get the result that an artefact could be conscious. In other words, if we know that an entity a has the same intrinsic physical nature as a conscious being b, then we know that a is conscious in the same way as b, quite independently of whether a and b came into existence in the same way. This principle is an application of what has come to be called the *supervenience* of the mental on the physical: if x and y have the same physical constitution, and x has mental property P, then y must also have P.[2] How x and y came to have that physical constitution is irrelevant to whether they both have P. Hence whether something is an artefact is irrelevant to the question whether it is conscious.

It is important to note that my reason for holding that an artefact could be conscious is *not* that I take myself to have any theory or explanation of what it is about the brain that makes it the basis of consciousness. It is not that I can see what feature makes the brain conscious and can therefore see how to build a machine which incorporates this feature. On the contrary, as I shall explain later, I do not believe that we do possess such knowledge of the brain. All I am saying is that supervenience assures us that the brain has *some*

[2] See Donald Davidson, 'Mental Events', *Essays on Actions and Events* (Clarendon Press: Oxford, 1980), p. 214.

property which confers consciousness upon it; I do not say that I know *which*. Granted this degree of materialism (quite a modest amount, actually), there is no obstacle to artefactual consciousness. If you duplicate the brain you duplicate whatever it is about it that confers consciousness, and there is no reason to think the duplication must occur *naturally* if the duplicate brain is to have this unknown feature.

Any residual misgivings about this claim must, I think, devolve upon the assumed degree of materialism. How *can* consciousness depend on the brain in this way? This is a good question, in the sense that it is a very hard question to answer. But it is not a question about machines and consciousness; rather, it is an expression of that old set of anxieties known as the mind–body problem. It would be a mistake to convert these (legitimate) anxieties into a denial that artefacts could be conscious. The question about machine consciousness does indeed sharpen and vivify the mind–body problem, but the problem was there anyway and independently. It is just as hard to see how an entity constructed naturally from mere matter can be conscious as it is to see how an intentionally created material object can be. But we know that the former is possible, because we have seen it done. *How*, we do not know.

There is a different question that might be being asked by the sentence 'Could a machine be conscious?' It might be the question whether only *living* things can be conscious. Must a conscious being be animate, organic, alive? This is not the same as our last question, since we were allowing then that an artefact could be alive, that is, be a biological entity. The present question is whether, however an entity came into existence, it could be conscious only if living. Certainly this is one way in which the word 'machine' is used, conjuring up as it does images of cogs and pulleys, microchips and computer screens. Wittgenstein makes some suggestive remarks about this question in his *Philosophical Investigations*:

> . . . only of a living human being and what resembles (behaves like) a living human being can one say: it has sensations; it sees; is blind; hears; is deaf; is conscious or unconscious.

> We do indeed say of an inanimate thing that it is in pain: when playing with dolls for example. But this use of the concept of pain is a secondary one. Imagine a case in which people ascribed pain *only* to inanimate things; pitied *only* dolls!

Look at a stone and imagine it having sensations. One says to oneself: How could one so much as get the idea of ascribing a sensation to a thing? One might as well ascribe it to a number! – And now look at a wriggling fly and at once these difficulties vanish and pain seems able to get a foothold here, where before everything was, so to speak, too smooth for it.[3]

Clearly Wittgenstein is here making a conceptual link between being conscious and being alive. Let us examine this idea.

What, to begin with, is meant by 'living'? This question belongs to the philosophy of biology, and it is not altogether easy, but I think the following is along the right lines: an entity counts as a living thing just if it is made up of a system of interacting parts which control the growth and repair of the entity by means of some process of part duplication (cell reproduction), these parts deriving their substance from exogenous materials (food). No doubt this definition could be improved and refined, but for our purposes it will do as it stands. For the question is whether any *such* conditions could be necessary for the possession of consciousness (these conditions are obviously not *sufficient* for consciousness because plants and micro-organisms, which surely are not conscious, do satisfy such conditions). Now is there a *conceptual* connection between life, as so defined, and consciousness?

Here I think we feel pulled in two directions. On the one hand, it is hard to see how there *could* be a conceptual connection between something's being conscious and its being alive in the defined sense. For what have growth and repair and cellular structure got to do with the possession of subjectivity? Why should things seeming a certain way to a creature conceptually require that the body of the creature be structured in the way defined? On the other hand, Wittgenstein does appear to have hold of a sound intuition: how can what is dead and inert be a subject of conscious states? Surely the reason we ascribe consciousness as we do – to human beings and other animals but not to stones and pocket calculators – has something essential to do with being alive or not. I think we can resolve this tension by adopting an intermediate view, the view indeed which a careful reading of Wittgenstein's words suggests. This intermediate view says that a conscious being must either be

---

[3] L. Wittgenstein, *Philosophical Investigations.* (Basil Blackwell: Oxford, 1953), 281–4.

alive or must resemble what is alive, where the resemblance is between the *behaviour* of the things in question. In other words, only of what behaves *like* a living thing can we say that it is conscious. This claim connects consciousness with life, but not with what constitutes life; rather, with what manifests or expresses it. A non-living thing might therefore in principle qualify for the ascription of consciousness, so long as it behaved like a living conscious thing, for example ourselves. Only such an entity could *invite* the ascription of consciousness. It is presumably because of a tacit acceptance of this idea that we are so prone to count the robots of science-fiction films as conscious beings: they do not live, but they act as if they do.

But if we accept this idea, *why* do we? Why does the ascription of consciousness depend upon sufficiently lifelike behaviour? The reason, I think – and here again I follow Wittgenstein – is that our concept of a conscious state is the concept of a state with a certain sort of behavioural *expression*. We cannot really make sense of a conscious stone because the stone does not behave in ways we can recognize as expressive of its supposed consciousness. Think here of facial expressions: these are so integral to our notion of an emotion that we just do not know what to make of the suggestion that an IBM 100 might be angry or depressed or undergoing an adolescent crisis. The problem is not that the IBM is inanimate, not made of flesh and blood; the problem is that it is not embodied in such a way that it can express itself (and merely putting it inside a lifelike body will not provide for the right sort of expressive link-up). But I think that if we *could* make a non-living thing that behaved exactly like a fly, then we should have as much reason to attribute conscious states to it as we do to a living fly: whether its body could repair itself by cellular replacement is neither here nor there.

I conclude, then, that being biologically alive is not a necessary condition of consciousness, but that it is necessary that a conscious being should behave like a living thing (of a certain sophistication).

WHAT MAKES THE BRAIN CONSCIOUS?

Earlier I confessed ignorance about what properties of the brain make it the 'seat of consciousness'. I now want to criticize some attempts to be more positive on this question, in particular the thesis that consciousness is a computational property of the brain.

Let me first flog a dead horse – dead horses can still teach sound lessons. The most naive view of what makes the brain conscious is that it contains some special *substance* that makes it so. Thus it might be supposed that chemical analysis of the brain will turn up some especially subtle and ethereal substance, ectoplasmic in nature, which explains consciousness. This idea is both empirically false and conceptually misconceived. It is empirically false because the brain does not contain any such radically special kind of substance – generally speaking it has the same kind of chemical composition as other organs of the body. It is conceptually misconceived because even if there were such a unique substance in the brain, this would not be the *kind* of thing to explain consciousness: for how could *any* chemical substance *be* consciousness? So plainly it cannot be the chemical properties of the brain – which chemical substances compose it – that explain consciousness. The materials of the brain are of the same kind as those found in non-conscious nature, so how could they explain why consciousness is found in the brain but not elsewhere (for example, the kidneys)? It follows that, no matter how well we come to understand the chemistry of the brain, this will not enable us to understand consciousness.

Reflections such as these have led philosophers (and others) to seek a different kind of brain property which might explain conscious phenomena. Thus there developed the doctrine known as *functionalism*.[4] Instead of identifying consciousness with the material composition of the brain, we should identify it with certain higher-order properties of the brain, namely the (supposedly) more abstract *causal* properties possessed by physico-chemical states of the brain. The first-order physico-chemical properties are admittedly of the wrong kind to constitute consciousness, but their causal roles will do better: they will, among other things, have the desired specificity. Pain, for example, is a higher-order property of physical states which consists in having a certain pattern of causes and effects, as it might be mediating bodily injury and avoidance behaviour. To build a machine that feels pain it will then suffice to

[4] For a survey and criticism, see Ned Block, 'Troubles with Functionalism', in Ned Block (ed.), *Readings in Philosophy of Psychology*, vol. 1. (Harvard University Press: Cambridge, Mass., 1980).

install mechanisms that mediate input and output in this way.

Functionalism has been subjected to a good deal of critical discussion, and I do not have space here to recapitulate the usual criticisms. I will just make one central point: it does not seem plausible to claim that possession of functional properties is *sufficient* for the possession of consciousness. For is it not entirely conceivable that something should have the functional properties of chemical structures in the brain and yet not be conscious? Nor is it surprising that this should seem possible, since the functionalist's causes and effects are themselves just physico-chemical events. True, states of the brain have different causal roles from states of the kidneys, but the causal roles of *both* are defined in terms of physical causes and effects; so how can the former 'give rise' to consciousness while the latter do not? The kidneys have a characteristic pattern of inputs and outputs, and hence higher-order functional properties; so why are the kidneys not a second centre of consciousness? The problem again is that the suggested properties are not specific enough to the brain, and anyway turn out upon examination to be the wrong *kind* of properties to determine consciousness.

COMPUTATIONALISM

What *other* sort of property might the brain have which makes it uniquely the organ of consciousness? This property will have to be specific to the brain, and it will have to be of the right 'kind'. The idea that has been gaining adherents is that the brain has (in addition to material and functional properties) computational properties; and it is these that 'underlie' the presence and operations of consciousness.[5] In particular, it is held that *thinking* is a computational process. This thesis has a direct bearing on the question of machine consciousness, because if we can design computing machines and consciousness is computation, then we know, at least in general outline, how to *design* a conscious machine: we simply (!) build in the computational structure of the brain. In order to evaluate this thesis we need to get more exact about what a computational property is.

---

[5] See P.N. Johnson-Laird, *Mental Models* (Cambridge University Press: Cambridge, 1983), esp. ch. 16.

To say that the brain carries out computations is, presumably, to say that certain physical processes may be described as (literally) performing mathematically describable operations: the brain does sums. Thus the optical system calculates (say) the distance of an object from information about the magnitudes of certain variables to which the retina is sensitive, for example, size in the retinal image. So we can say of a physical process or structure in the brain: 'It just calculated that the distance of x was d on the basis of the light having intensity i.' Such ascriptions attribute propositional content, signified by the clause following 'calculated that', to physical processes and structures in the brain. It is natural to suppose that such propositional contents are represented in a system of internal symbols, so that the brain's computations (like the kind we do externally on paper) involve the manipulation of these symbols. It further appears that the brain is performing a great many such computations at any given time, and that their results are typically integrated into higher-level computations; there is, in the jargon, much 'parallel processing'. A computer likewise, it is said, performs computations (that's why it is called a *computer*), and so the brain is rightly described as a computer. The claim then is that mental attributes, in particular consciousness, can be identified with such computational processes: to have a mind is to instantiate a computer program. Is this view plausible?

Let me first warn against a potential *non sequitur*. From the fact that the brain is a computer and the fact that the brain has mental attributes it does not follow that those attributes are computational in nature. For it may be that the brain's computational properties, like its material composition, do not constitute mentality – they simply coexist with it. Nor do we get an identification from the fact (if it is one) that computations are part of the causal background of conscious mental phenomena. We need more than this for a genuine identification (such as is exemplified by the identification of water with H_2O or heat with molecular motion). But now *could* consciousness be identifiable with cerebral computations? I think not, but before I say why let me dissociate myself from two other critical responses that are sometimes made to the computational theory of mind.

I do not, firstly, wish to question the literal and non-derivative truth of ascriptions of computations to subconscious physical processes in the brain. I think that the brain really does carry out subconscious computations, quite independently of our so describing it – it is not merely *as if* it does. Content is thus not the prerogative of the properly mental (as *information* is not in the mathematical theory of 'communication'). And so far as I can see, these computations need a medium, that is a system of internal symbols, for example symbols standing for light intensities at the retina.

Secondly, I do not object to the computational theory for the same reason John Searle does in his 'Chinese room' argument.[6] His argument is that a computer program is a set of rules for performing *syntactic* operations on symbols, and therefore instantiating a computer program can never add up to the possession of *semantic* properties; hence intentionality cannot be explained in terms of computations. With one part of this argument I completely agree: you cannot get semantics out of syntax alone; so *if* a computer program deals only in syntax it cannot confer semantic features such as our conscious intentional states have. However, it does not follow that the symbols manipulated by a computer program cannot have semantic properties – all that is shown is that they cannot have these in virtue of the rules of the program. The clear-headed computational theorist will agree with Searle about the non-semantic character of program rules but point out that the symbols manipulated can have other sorts of property too, and these might be what give the symbols semantic features. Thus a symbol in the visual system might get to stand for light intensity at the distal source in virtue of the extrinsic causal links between that symbol and circumambient objects. Internal manipulations do not determine reference, but causal relations to the environment might. There is no reason why such an account of semantic properties should be unavailable in respect of computing machines. On this way of looking at the matter, computing machines might have intentionality – that is, world-directedness – but not simply because of the program they instantiate. To put it differently, when the visual system computes that p (where p stands for a proposition) this is a matter not just of syntactic features of its internal code but

---

[6] See J. Searle, *Minds, Brains and Science* (BBC Publications: London, 1984); also his second Reith Lecture, 'Beer cans and meat machines', reprinted in *The Listener*, 14 November 1984.

also of how the symbols of the code are related to the subject matter of *p*. Since I believe that the brain does compute, I think that it must have semantic properties, and so there must be something about it that *confers* these properties. Accordingly, my objection to the computational theory of mind cannot be that it cannot provide for semantic intentionality.

My objection is in a way simpler than this. The problem I see is how such computational processes as those in the retina and central visual system could ever explain the existence of conscious subjectivity. Since such computations go on without subjectivity – they are subconscious – how could their presence be sufficient to explain subjectivity? How can consciousness be got from something that does not essentially involve consciousness? A pocket calculator computes but is not conscious, so how could consciousness be a matter of computations? If computations can go on without consciousness, they cannot be *sufficient* for consciousness. Such computations may indeed be possessed of semantic features, but this falls short of there being something it is like for that which performs these computations.

To this objection it will be replied that not just *any* kind of computation is sufficient for consciousness – consciousness requires a special *sort* of computational complexity or structure. Thus it has been claimed that integrated parallel processing is what makes for consciousness, or again the existence of a self-scanning unit which monitors what is going on in the brain's various computational departments.[7] But it seems to me that these sophistications do not evade the fundamental problem, namely that such properties could be instantiated in the absence of consciousness. And the reason for this is simply that they are of the wrong *kind* to explain the phenomenon of subjectivity. You cannot get the 'qualitative content' of conscious experience – seeing red, feeling a pain, etc. – out of computations in the nervous system. No matter how many pocket calculators you put together, and however you link them up, you will not get a conscious experience out of them – how could you? The difficulty here is one of principle: we have no understanding of how consciousness *could* emerge from an aggregation of non-conscious elements such as computational devices; so the prop-

---

[7] This would appear to be Johnson-Laird's position, *Mental Models*.

erties of these devices cannot *explain* how consciousness comes about or what it is. It may indeed be true that, as a matter of fact, organisms get to be conscious just when their brains reach a certain level of computational complexity, as it is true that consciousness seems to require a certain degree of physiological complexity; but this observation does nothing to *explain* how consciousness depends upon computational complexity, as a like observation about physiological complexity does not. A proper theory of consciousness in terms of properties of the brain should make it *intelligible* that the brain is the basis of consciousness, but the computational properties of the brain do not furnish such a theory: it remains a mystery how cerebral computations could give rise to consciousness, as much a mystery as how mere matter could form itself into the organ of consciousness.[8]

It follows from what has just been said that knowing how to build a computing machine is not knowing how to build a conscious machine. So we do not know the design of a conscious machine. We do not know this because we do not know what makes the brain conscious. If we knew what properties of the brain made *it* conscious, then we should know the design of a machine that would be conscious – where the machine in question might precisely duplicate the physical nature of the brain. The two questions go together. Still, the brain is a physical entity and it is conscious, so it must have *some* design feature, presumably 'physical' in nature (whatever that might mean), that *makes* it conscious. My point has been that we do not at present know what that feature is, and so we do not at present know how to build a machine which matches this achievement of the brain's. But this is not to say that a machine could not be conscious. It needs merely to be the same kind of machine as the brain is, whatever that kind may be.

---

[8] The argument of this paragraph owes much to Thomas Nagel's 'Panpsychism', in *Mortal Questions*.

INDEX